THE FUTURE OF COPYRIGHT IN A DIGITAL ENVIRONMENT

INFORMATION LAW SERIES - 4

THE FUTURE OF COPYRIGHT IN A DIGITAL ENVIRONMENT

Proceedings of the Royal Academy Colloquium

organized by the Royal Netherlands Academy of Sciences (KNAW) and the Institute for Information Law

(Amsterdam, 6-7 July 1995)

Editor

P. Bernt Hugenholtz

Contributors
Egbert J. Dommering
Ejan Mackaay
Paul Edward Geller
Dirk J.G. Visser
Thomas Dreier
Jaap H. Spoor
P. Bernt Hugenholtz
Bruce Lehman
Mihály Ficsor
Charles Clark
Ferdinand Melichar
Paul Vandoren
John Perry Barlow
Jane C. Ginsburg
Madeleinde de Cock Buning
Jaap Haeck
Paul Goldstein

1996
KLUWER LAW INTERNATIONAL
The Hague • London • Boston

Published by Kluwer Law International
P.O. Box 85889
2508 CN The Hague, The Netherlands

Sold and distributed in the USA and Canady by
Kluwer Law International
675 Massachusetts Avenue
Cambridge, MA 02139, USA

Sold and distributed in all other countries by
Kluwer Law International
P.O. Box 85889
2508 CN The Hague, The Netherlands

Coverdesign: Studio DUMBAR
Printed on acid-free paper

ISBN 90 411 02671

Kluwer Law International incorporates the publishing programmes of Graham & Trotman Ltd, Kluwer Law and Taxation Publishers and Martinus Nijhoff Publishers.

Preface

The emerging digital environment is having a profound, and sometimes disturbing, impact on the scope, nature and structure of copyright law. As the Internet experience clearly demonstrates, the new environment raises difficult, but important questions - both from a theoretical and a practical perspective. What is to be the nature and scope of protected rights on the information superhighway? Can existing 'old media' rights survive in the new environment? What copyright exemptions will apply? How to solve conflicts of law in an environment that makes territoriality all but obsolete? What role, if any, will collecting societies play in the electronic future? Will copyright be replaced by technical protection measures and/or direct contractual relationships? Is there a future for copyright in the digital environment?

These were the themes of the Royal Academy Colloquium on The Future of Copyright in a Digital Environment that took place in Amsterdam on July 6-7, 1995. The colloquium was organized by the Royal Netherlands Academy of Sciences (KNAW) and the Institute for Information Law, University of Amsterdam. A group of renowned experts on copyright law and practice was invited to discuss, over a two-day period, the most important copyright problems of the emerging information superhighway. This volume comprises the edited proceedings of the colloquium: fourteen contributions of outstanding quality, an account of the lengthy and lively discussions, and a brilliant summary by Prof. Goldstein.

We wish to express our sincere gratitude to the Royal Netherlands Academy of Sciences (KNAW) for co-organizing and sponsoring the colloquium in the most excellent and generous manner, and for serving as host to the colloquium participants in the wonderful Trippenhuis. Special thanks are due to Manita Kooy and Susi Nap for making it all happen, and to Madeleine de Cock Buning and Jaap Haeck for writing and editing the colloquium minutes. We also wish to thank our other sponsors: the European Commission (DG XIII), Wolters Kluwer Publishers, SDU Publishers, BUMA/STEMRA, and the University of Amsterdam. Last, not least, we are most grateful to the contributors to this volume, and to the other colloquium participants.

The articles in this book appear in the order of the original colloquium programme. Prof. Ginsburg's article, originally published in the Columbia Law Review, was added in a later stage.

The editor wishes to thank Samantha Janssen and Leslie Hugenholtz for their kind assistance in the editing process.

Egbert J. Dommering
P. Bernt Hugenholtz

Institute for Information Law

Table of Contents

Copyright Being Washed Away through the Electronic Sieve. Some Thoughts on the Impending Copyright Crisis

*Egbert J. Dommering**

The economic foundation of copyright has been a subject of much discussion for economists of law. In their treatises, the *raison d'être* of rights is sought in the economic efficiency of subjective rights. These subjective rights are counterproductive at certain times, efficient at others.[1] Other treatises are written in a more sociological vein, describing the slow but steady growth of the family of intellectual property rights as an autonomous process transpiring in the interaction between interested parties and legislative bodies.[2]

In this historical-futuristic treatise I will attempt to take a more macro-economic approach, combined with the role played by technology. At this point in time, it cannot but be an overview of a number of hypotheses, which is why I will not include an extensive list of literature references.

1. The Players: Emergence, Allocation and Exploitation of Rights

In the paper society that did not manifest the characteristics of an information economy, copyright involved a well-delineated group of players and acts of exploitation. I would like to distinguish between works that exist in themselves (books, paintings) and works that only exist when they are performed (music, drama, dance).

1.1 Works that Exist in Themselves

To establish a copyright in the former category, the author creating the work only had to record it onto an irreplaceable information carrier (a manuscript) and take it

---

* Professor of Information Law, University of Amsterdam; Director, the Institute for Information Law; advocate, Stibbe Simont Monahan Duhot, Amsterdam. This article was previously published in *Computerrecht* 1994, 109-113. Part 3 comprises an account of discussions with Bernt Hugenholtz. The author does, however, take full responsibility for the contents.

1. R. Teijl and R.W. Holzhauer, *De toenemende complexiteit van het intellectuele eigendomsrecht* (The increasing complexity of intellectual property), Arnhem, 1991.

2. *J.H. Spoor, De gestage groei van merk, werk, en uitvinding* (The steady growth of brand, work and invention), Zwolle, 1990.

to a publisher, who would 'wrap' the original, reproduce it as a consumable product (a book) and market it. The market was clear-cut, and the product was priced in relation to a quantifiable turnover with which both parties would obtain a profit margin based on the exploitation rights transferred by the author. Since the publisher played an important role in the distribution of the work, he immediately acquired a position of power over the author. Consequently, publisher's right emerged before author's right.

In painting, this was different. The 'maker' produced a finished, unique, non-reproducible, wrapped (the framing of the picture) product for a wealthy group of insiders with whom he had a direct customer-commission relation, especially in the 15th-19th centuries. He brought the product onto the market himself (shop, customer). Although the publisher function hardly developed here, the art trade started taking on publishing and shop functions at a later stage.

This constellation yielded two properties characteristic of copyright. The owner of the copy of the work was free to do with it what he wanted, as long as this left the author's moral rights intact, i.e., as long as he respected the integrity of the work. Copyright was subservient to the unrestricted individual transfer of knowledge about the work to the work's owner. A second characteristic was that, economically speaking, the price of the copyright in the copy of the work was paid for the moment the copy of the work itself was paid for. This 'exhausted' the copyright and further selling or use of the copy of the work could not be limited pursuant to copyright. Further selling and distribution became the responsibility of printers and booksellers, who, historically, often acted as publishers; later they became independent intermediaries on the buyer's market, as distinct from the publisher.

We will see how these two properties of copyright (exhaustion and unrestricted use by the lawful possessor of the copy of the work) gradually eroded. This development started with the distribution of knowledge that led to the division of the reading market into a buyer's and a lender's market; intermediaries in the latter market included public libraries. In painting, this secondary market did not emerge until the invention of reproduction technology; this resulted in the merger of pictures and text that gave the market for reproduction books its characteristics as a book market. Lending markets for original works appeared as late as the second half of the 20th century, in the form of art lending libraries as part of the government's stimulation policy (the market for originals had proved too inaccessible). A similar merger of pictures and text appeared later for book and film. Books are turned into films, and best-sellers are written with a view to being adapted for the screen. This will start a convergence process of printed and electronic media.

Despite certain differences between the various legal traditions, the relationship between publisher and author had always been one in which the author possessed all rights, which he would partially or wholly transfer to the publisher. This changed with the emergence of the information society, in which business and universities became important organizers of knowledge and creativity. This resulted in the employer's copyright (cf. article 7 of the Dutch Copyright Act), a good example of an economic solution. As explained in Coase's classic 1937 article *The Nature of the Firm*, the company assumes the transaction risk from the individual (who must sell his work on the free market in which the shares of goods and services are determined by price mechanisms) by employing him for wages (i.e. by internalizing the transaction into the company, as it were) and by integrating, at a permanent, periodical remuneration, the individual performance into a product the company attempts to sell to the market at its own risk.[3]

This solution was more efficient than the individual transaction. It was, of course, also influenced by the development of the technology for the manufacture of complex products that requires individuals with different kinds of expertise. In that respect, employer's copyright ran parallel to the industrial revolution. Universities did not succeed in internalizing the transaction risk, because of past and present objections of principle to employer's copyright[4], which was presumably the upshot of the fact that universities had become lodged between the individual literary copyright tradition and the more business-like exploitation of knowledge.

Universities continued to trade in the intellectual prestige of individuals, which stirred up antagonism between publishers and universities. Universities found out that the authors they employed sold the rights to their works to publishers, which meant that, within the scientific cycle, universities had to pay once again for the (re)use of information that had been generated at their expense in the first place (e.g., royalties for reprographic reproduction, educational uses, lending rights etc.). As a result, universities attempted to commandeer part of the publishing function, a phenomenon clearly manifest in the United States, where each university has its own publishing firm (which subsequently became independent enterprises, but that is a different story).

A great deal more could be said about this development, but I will move on to the second category.

1.2 WORKS THAT EXIST ONLY WHEN PERFORMED

From the outset, the works that only exist when they are performed were distinctive in that they involved a different market mechanism and a different form of exploitation. The producer of the work was an essential link in the exploitation chain. Exploitation required a theatre, a theatre company or orchestra, business managers and artistic leaders, etc. This gave the producers-intermediaries a strong legal position, with their own rights, or rights derived from the author, to exploit the performances. There is a direct line from the position of the theatres to the film rights of film 'makers', who eventually amassed all exploitation rights. Here, too, we see the development toward internalizing the individual authors' transactions within a larger organization, and the transfer of the collective exploitation risk of the work to the producer. Since these works are one-off, the employment relations are only partly suited to realize this transfer, thus requiring transfers linked to specific performances by means of legal assignment (e.g., a film score).

3. R.H. Coase, 'The Nature of the Firm', in: *The Firm, the market and the law*, Chicago/London, 1988, 33.

4. J.H. Spoor and D.W.F. Verkade, *Auteursrecht* (Copyright), 2d ed., Deventer, 1993, 38-40.

The exhaustion principle has never applied in the area of performance, as the first *Coditel* decision by the European Court of Justice so clearly demonstrated: a performance (*in casu* a film broadcast on television) is not put into circulation to be 'exhausted', but is 'made available to the public by way of the unlimited repeatability of performances.'[5] This has major consequences for the exploitation of works in this branch. If the exploitation proceeds for a single-copy work are obtained by adding up a finite number of copies sold, for a work consisting of an unlimited number of repeatable performances it is necessary to regularly measure and pay for the number of performances.

This has led to the emergence of a different kind of intermediary, the collecting society, which has its own, legally established authority to settle the performances with the performing parties every year. This introduces a different kind of collective efficiency to copyright than the employer's and film author's right. Collective sums of money are settled collectively through contracts with major performers, which sums are transferred to the entitled parties in conformity with certain rough criteria. Because copyright was confronted with the problem of potential massive infringement relatively early in the industrialization process (a large number of illegal performances), the need for a collective form of action arose much earlier than for, e.g., product liability (a different kind of massive injustice generated by industrialized society).

Incidentally, this only holds true for music; theatre performances are apparently sufficiently easy to trace to make individual licensing by rightholders possible. This seems to be true for film as well. It was not until the appearance of the small-scale VCR that the need for collective action arose. Conversely, artists and music producers have become powerful market parties only at a later stage, wanting to keep exploitation away from the musical rights societies. Thus, a process of decollectivization is occurring.

The individual, unrestricted use of works is subject to the same conditions as that of paper information carriers. Only performances in private circles are allowed. In this case, the criteria for permitted use are found in the private nature of the performance.

In the paper society, we thus see that there are various forms of exploitation, various collective legal relations, and various intermediaries for various types of work. We discern reproduction markets and performance markets with corresponding reproduction and performance rights. However, the electronic era will dramatically change this structure.

2. The Electronic Sieve

Users began to reproduce works in which the copyright was expired or which were freely available, by means of a combination of old technology, with which information is recorded onto material information carriers, and new chemical and electromagnetic reproduction techniques. Photocopying machines produced paper

5. European Court of Justice, Judgement of 18 March 1980, Case 62/79, *Coditel v. Ciné-Vog I*, (1980) ECR 881, recital 12.

copies of paper information carriers. Sounds and images that were communicated to the public by playing video or audio tapes in studios, and subsequently broadcast by means of (ether or cable) radio and/or television links, were recorded with video or audio recorders and copied onto magnetic tape. The spoken words, images and sound of the copyrighted work started to 'drain away' through the copying equipment of users and intermediaries. Thus, the *electronic sieve* was born, even though the drops that fell through the sieve still condensed into material information carriers.

This development has put pressure on free private use. A legal decision illustrating this development is the *Betamax* case in the United States on 'home taping' of television programmes.[6] Applying the American fair use principle, the final decision favoured the consumer. The private use of paper information carriers was put under pressure as well. Photocopying a paper information carrier was limited to making a few copies for study purposes and private use (cf. article 16b of the Dutch Copyright Act), but that was not all. As it became possible to produce photocopies of paper information carriers on a large scale, it became necessary to establish an intermediary, similar to collecting societies for musical performances. In the Netherlands, this intermediary became the 'Stichting Reprorecht', the Dutch reprographic rights organization, which was given the task of tracing all individual acts of photocopying not covered by allowed private use, that occurred within a certain time period, collecting fees from users and distributing the proceeds to the rightholders. This was, of course, an impossible task: counting the drops.

It is now time to bring up some questions concerning the reprographic right. Isn't it strange that a collection agency is established to collect fees for the use of copies in which the copyright is exhausted? Does the exhaustion principle still apply in that case, or rather: is there really any difference between a work that exists in itself and a work that exists through performance only? Isn't it strange that private copying is restricted, while the private use of a copy of the work is still allowed? Have we become confused by the fact that the performance of the paper work yielded just as many paper 'reproductions', because we have learnt to think along the lines of that concept in copyright terms? Couldn't a photocopy simply be a performance of the work? But let's leave these questions for a while and concentrate on the development of the sieve for now.

The emergence of the computer marks the beginning of the end for the paper information carrier, or rather the emergence of a new, electronic information carrier that will eventually take over most of the function of the paper information carrier. Thus, copyright is faced with the question of how this information processor is to be incorporated into the law. From the point of view of exploitation, the question is whether the processing of information in a machine (which is, in point of fact, a process of constant electronic copying) is to be considered reproduction. Under the European Software Directive[7] merely 'technical' acts of reproduction are considered restricted acts of exploitation.[8] With respect to phono

6. *Sony Corp. of America v. Universal Studios Inc.*, 464 US 417 (1984).

7. Council Directive 91/250, O.J.EC L 122/42 of 14 May 1991.

8. *Cf.* E.J. Dommering, 'Reverse Engineering: a software puzzle', in: H.W.K. Kaspersen and A. Oskamp (eds.), *Amongst Friends in Computers and Law*, Deventer/Boston, 1990, 32; Spoor-Verkade, *supra* note 4, 102.

records or CDs this is a new development; as far as I know, the mechanical copying acts taking place when these are played have never resulted in a debate on principles. Thus we have basically abandoned the principle of free private use.

Paper is no longer required to record information in or outside a computer. The computer contains a hard disk internally; a floppy disk externally. The information can be retrieved on screen an unlimited number of times. A hard copy is only one of the many different ways the stored information can be made visible. The difference between original and copy becomes blurred, because the information (in the form of bits) can be manipulated without restrictions. The drops entering the sieve have fallen from a large cloud, condense briefly and immediately evaporate into a new cloud.

A second phase in this development (which we are in the middle of) is the connection of computers to a network through which information can be transmitted over long distances (world-wide, e.g. the Internet). Thus the information made available in a publicly accessible computer can be consulted and copied from anywhere in the world. This is sometimes referred to as *electronic document delivery*. Is this in any way related to the old-fashioned method of copying? This question was thoroughly discussed during the (failed) amendment of the reprography provisions of the Dutch Copyright Act.[9] Urged on by publishers, the 'electronic copy' was to be excluded from the reprographic right. Interestingly, the advocates of this measure continued to think in terms of paper information carriers:

> 'It presents new and serious threats for printed publication as a source, threats that are difficult to keep track of. The regular exploitation of written documents, as protected under article 9 of the Berne Convention could suffer from this development.'[10]

With the virtual disappearance of paper information carriers (which have become by-products), we have to repeat the previous question in a rhetorical sense. Hasn't the distinction between work that exist in themselves (and can be copied) and works that exist only in their being performed (and can be performed for an unlimited number of times) become obsolete? Doesn't the merger of images, words and sounds on a digital level (all zeroes and ones – with images containing more zeroes and ones than text) have ramifications for our concept of exploitation?

My answer this question is *yes* – but that was already implicit in the rhetoric. What is the difference between the 'playability' of music on a CD and the 'retrievability' on screen of a text on a diskette? Even for the proponents of other solutions for the electronic copy in copyright law, the paper spectre continues to play a role: they continue to speak in terms of pages of originals, and electrocopies

---

9. Copyright Amendment Bill, Kamerstukken 22600; the bill was eventually rejected by the First Chamber of Parliament.

10. N. van Lingen, 'Reprorecht in revisie' (Reprographic right under revision), *Informatierecht/AMI* 1993, 132-133; *see also* M.J. Frequin, 'De ontwikkelingen van de informatietechnologie en het reprorecht' (Developments in information technology and reprographic right), *Computerrecht* 1993, 97.

and electronic copying.[11] Has the thought ever occurred to us to consider the projection of a film on our television screen as an electrocopy of a film image of a rotating film reel that is being broadcast at that same moment? Or: has the thought ever occurred to us to find the basis for compensation for the airing of a film in the number of 'electrocopied' images?

In my opinion, multimedia thinking means that, for copyright, we must abandon the distinction between *performance* and *reproduction* as principally distinct categories. As far as computer networks are concerned, we must start to think in terms of the performance of stored information: in image, sound or text. This primarily means that we must abandon 'repro-thinking' as outdated paper-thinking.[12] I will try to explain some of the consequences of this process in the final part of this paper.

3. The Electronic Sieve: New Relations

3.1 Exploitation concepts for networks

Approaching the network not from the perspective of the paper information carrier ('repro-thinking'), but in terms of '(electronic) performance', it is only logical to explore the legal development of radio and television. After all, this is an electronic network with which copyright has long-standing experience, and which copyright law and doctrine have considered in terms of performance from the very beginning.

There are a number of phases in that development. The first phase concerns the performance of works transmitted by radio or television. Under article 11bis of the Berne Convention these are considered as new communications to the public by the original broadcaster and everything that is considered to be part of it (the *organisme d'origine*). Copyright fees are settled with the original transmitting parties (the broadcasting organizations). Because of the 'lighthouse effect' that occurs when distribution is diffuse (the beam of light from the lighthouse that, in classical treatises on law and economics, is presented as the collective good that cannot be exclusively exploited), broadcasting corporations cannot pass on the copyright costs to individuals. As often occurs with payment of collective goods, we have therefore opted for a *fiscal* solution: a levy for the individual user, the radio and television licence fee.

As regards the user, the question of whether the audio or video presentation of a programme using a private receiving station yielded a new copyright-relevant

11. D.J.G. Visser, 'De elektronische kopie en het reprorecht' (The electronic copy and the reprographic right), *Computerrecht* 1993, 7; Thomas K. Dreier, 'Copyright in the age of electrocopying', *Informatierecht/AMI* 1994, 3.

12. Cf. the 'diffusion right' for point-to-(multi)point transmissions mentioned by Nicholas Higham, 'The new challenges of digitisation', 10 *EIPR* 1993, 356; see also Paul Geller, 'The Universal Electronic Archive: Issues in International Copyright', 25 *IIC* 54, 58.

performance was answered on the basis of the criterion of whether that performance took place *in private*.[13]

Subsequently, new networks appeared on the horizon: *cable systems*. These networks were linked to the wireless broadcasting network. With regard to a cable network retransmitting broadcast programmes, the question was raised whether the network belonged to the *organisme d'origine*. Like many other courts in Europe, the Dutch Supreme Court ('Hoge Raad') answered this question in the negative.[14] This decision led to a system of collective licenses for secondary exploitation acts. This was made possible by the fact that two opposing parties could be identified: the broadcasters and music collecting societies on the one side, organized cable operators on the other side, who could charge the costs to their subscribers. Here, too, the question of the private circle was raised. Did this rule also apply to small cable networks, having less than 100 subscribers? In the opinion of the Dutch Supreme Court, the existing legal framework (article 12 of the Dutch Copyright Act) was insufficient. The Court referred the case to the legislator for a regulatory solution, if necessary by means of a *compulsory licence* to be based on article 17a of the Dutch Copyright Act.[15]

The next step was that technology enabled the settlement of fees for services with users individually: subscription television. This *technological* solution still has a *collective* character, because subscribers subscribe to an entire package of programmes, which they receive in the form of coded signals that are decoded in the home. Subscribers pay a fixed monthly sum to purchase the encoded package. New technical measures in the network will eventually allow *pay per view* in the near future.

The final phase in this development is the installation of a world-wide super-network in the form of satellite systems superimposed on the ether and cable networks. For this the European Union has opted for a so-called *injection right*: the injection of the programmes into the satellite system is considered to be the only relevant act of communication.[16]

As may be clear from the above, the electronic broadcasting network employs a combined approach towards exploitation rights. Settlement based on secondary exploitation rights by means of collective or individual licences is but one of the solutions, that will only be opted for when there are well-defined exploitation moments and identifiable parties. This demonstrates how one-sidedly the problem of information network exploitation is approached. Thinking in terms of putting books into computers, people persist in the notion of secondary exploitation acts related to (pages of) books, rendering the exploitation of a network more and more difficult and expensive. This repro-thinking should make way for network-thinking.

---

13. Hoge Raad (Supreme Court of the Netherlands), Judgement of 6 May 1938, *NJ* 1938, 635.

14. Hoge Raad (Supreme Court of the Netherlands), Judgement of 30 October 1981, *NJ* 1982, 435.

15. Hoge Raad (Supreme Court of the Netherlands), Judgement of 24 December 1993, *Informatierecht/AMI* 1994, 66.

16. Cf. P.B. Hugenholtz, 'De Europese richtlijn inzake satellietomroep en kabeldoorgifte' (The European Directive on satellite broadcasting and cable transmission), *Informatierecht/AMI* 1994, 87-90.

In this shift to network-thinking, we should not forget that an information network is different from a broadcasting network. The exploitation of a broadcasting network is a form of centralized editing and dissemination of information to homogenous audiences. The exploitation of a multimedia network is much more complex because heterogenous users purchase different amounts and different kinds of information at different times. A wide variety of networks (variety in terms of technology, target groups and information services) is linked together. The borderline between private and public use within the network is even more difficult to determine than for broadcasting.

This only goes to show how important it is that we search for a mix of exploitation modalities, depending on social and technical possibilities. Licensing electrocopies is not the most appropriate solution, because drops of water cannot be counted, and evaporate. A technological solution that allows individualized usage by means of encryption techniques (applied in the stored information, in accessing to data bases, in transmitting) could become of paramount importance. Copyright might become part of a complicated telecommunications accounting system. Some envisage a future in which the consumer will pay for all his multimedia services (i.e. for the transmission and use of the information) through a monthly account, much as we do now for gas and electricity.

This new and more complex situation will result in different alliances and actors, and new ways of allocating of rights and pricing.

3.2 New alliances, new ways of allocating rights

In the previous paragraphs I have briefly discussed how the different forms of exploitation of the different categories of works result in differing players in the field. The multimedia development of public networks stimulates the formation of combinations of telecommunications, media and cable companies in an attempt to gain control of the entire package to supply *video on demand* services to users. Similar developments are involved where the formation of information networks is concerned. Publishers will also start organizing themselves on a multimedia level in order to control multimedia exploitation rights: in traditional books, CD-ROMs, electronic data banks, paper and electronic magazines, etc.

The question remains whether other players on the market will agree to this. After all, the new intermediaries are data banks who, in giving access to information on the network, will carry out as important a 'performance' task as the theatre and film producers of the past. And will the universities that have the information produced take a passive stance in the new situation? I don't think so: they will continue to wonder what price they themselves have paid for the production of information, and what price the publishers are paying for it. And we should not forget that governments are also producing more and more exploitable information. Governments are starting to take an entrepreneurial viewpoint towards their own products; they want to be paid for them.

It is conceivable, therefore, that we will see a new power struggle over the allocation of rights, in which the producers of knowledge try to obtain rights, either by way of employers' copyrights or otherwise. The same holds true for intermediaries like libraries. The more added value their intermediary function generates, and the more they are bogged down by all the secondary exploitation rights publishers throw at them, the more consideration they will give to their position of power in the process of information provision.

It is also high time that authors start thinking about whom they will assign which electronic performance rights and at what price, and in what constellation they will have the best negotiating position. Publishers will reconsider their past and present position. As usually happens when a revolution in market relations occurs as a result of economic and technological transformation, vertical integration cannot be ruled out. This is illustrated by the purchase of cinema chains in the film industry, or in the book trade. This development is sometimes followed by separation spurred on by the need for independent intermediaries. The separation of the printed press and publishers has been partly completed; once this new product cycle is started, will information producers or publishers and telecommunications and information companies become involved in the same integration process as is currently developing in the film industry?

And what will be the position of the collecting societies? Should pay per use and individual repartition become a reality, will we still need collecting societies with exclusive rights? Wouldn't it be more efficient when agencies on a competitive basis or right owners would take over the role of these intermediaries?

3.3 PRICE AND FREE USE

Multimedia exploitation rights involve a different pricing system than rights to works exploited through a single medium. Just like the legal regulations of the old medium can, ultimately, not be transformed to the electronic network simply because the information is entered into the network as text, image or sound, it is important that the pricing rules for the old media be abandoned. Broadcasting companies take the size of the public to which the network is accessible as a criterion (cable operators, for instance, pay in accordance with the number of subscribers). A similar system could be used for text, possibly in combination with collective subscription and *pay per use* systems.

I have no cut-and-dried answers at this stage. All I want to do is point out that the entire pricing system must be reviewed and that electrocopying is a notion that must be abandoned. The multimedia network requires a different approach and the development of new criteria for free use. After all, the object of copyright is not only to protect the author's intellectual efforts, but also the distribution of knowledge. One of the serious threats of the new technology is that it could give to the right owners a dominant position to control the flow of information from the input in the databases, through the network to the site of the end users.

4. Conclusion: the Electronic Tower of Babel

The electronic network not only confronts us with problems concerning copyright and the economy of this new medium, it is also linked with questions concerning privacy and freedom of expression. Paul Geller distinguishes between three different legal levels of protection in that network:[17] privacy rights at the basic level, contract rights at the second level, and copyright at the third level. In my view these are conflicting claims: copyright would benefit from *pay per use* systems, but this may conflict with the privacy claims aimed at anonymity of the individual user. Centralized control over reproduction and performance also conflicts with the right of freedom of expression. This might mean level upon level of protection, so that encryption codes will not reveal the identity of individuals. And too much encryption, in turn, conflicts with the government's wish to monitor a suspected offence. The multimedia network calls for an integral approach so that problems of copyright, privacy and freedom of expression are addressed at the same time. The electronic highway should be governed by *information law*.[18]

It is not just that the electronic network will consist of a labyrinth of secret languages for reasons of legal protection, it also is a melting pot of nationalities. What national law will apply to these information relations? The law of the electronic highway has to be international. In short, it is a grand and extremely complicated construction. Will the electronic highway end up as the tower of Babel, which could not be completed; not due to a lack of technical ingenuity, but due to a confusion of tongues? And what is more: will cyberspace be as enlightened a society as the Republic of Letters of the 18th century that invented copyright and freedom of expression?[19]

---

17. Geller, *supra* note 12, 60.
18. See Egbert Dommering, 'An Introduction to Information Law', in: Egbert J. Dommering and P. Bernt Hugenholtz (eds.), *Protecting Works of Fact*, Deventer/Boston, 1991, 10.
19. *See* Paul Geller, 'Copyright between Market Place and Authorship', in Brad Sherman and Alain Strowel (eds.), *Of Authors and Origins*, Oxford, 1994, 161, 164.

The Economics of Emergent Property Rights on the Internet

*Ejan Mackaay**

1. Introduction

'Everything you know about intellectual property is wrong.' John Perry Barlow wrote this in the March 1994 issue of *Wired.* [1] Intellectual property rights on the Internet were, in his eyes, a return to the 'Bad Old Days of property,' being 'the divine right of thugs'.[2] In the same breath, Barlow invited everyone to come and dance 'on the grave of copyright and patent'. To which, not quite a year later, Lance Rose replied, '(..) copyright is dead. Long live copyright'.[3]

Barlow's message is reminiscent of that propounded by economists who see intellectual property rights, patents in particular, as arbitrary privileges or monopolies granted by government.[4] On that view, such privileges distort incentives to innovate rather than correct supposed deficiencies of the unaided market process. Intellectual property rights amount to taxi permits.

---

* Professor of Law, Faculty of Law and CRDP, Université de Montréal.

1. Barlow, John Perry, 'The Economy of Ideas – A framework for rethinking patents and copyrights in the Digital Age (Everything you know about intellectual property is wrong)', (1994) 2.03 *Wired* 84-90, 126-129, reprinted elsewhere in this book, 169-187. The message has been echoed recently in Dyson, Esther, 'Intellectual Value', (1995) 3.07 *Wired* 136-141, 182-184.

2. *See supra* note 1.

3. Rose, Lance, 'The Emperor's Clothes Still Fit Just Fine – Or, copyright is dead. Long live copyright', (1995) 3.02 *Wired* 103-106.

4. Plant, Arnold, 'The economic theory concerning patents for inventing', 1934 *Economica*, repr. in Plant, Arnold (ed.), *Selected Economic Essays and Addresses*, London, 1974, 35-56; Rothbard, Murray N., *Power and Market – Government and the Economy*, Kansas City, 1977, (2d ed.), 71-75; Rothbard, Murray N., *Man, Economy and State – A Treatise on Economic Principles*, Auburn, 1993, (2d ed.), 652-660; Palmer, Tom G., 'Intellectual Property: A Non-Posnerian Law and Economics Approach', (1989) 12 *Hamline Law Review* 261-304; Palmer, Tom G., 'Are Patents and Copyrights Morally Justified? The Philosophy of Property Rights and Ideal Objects', (1990) 13 *Harvard Journal of Law and Public Policy* 817-865; Lepage, Henri, 'Les brevets dans la stratégie des entreprises: le cas français', (1989) 1 *Journal des économistes et des études humaines* 153-177; Lepage, Henri, 'Propriété industrielle, propriété intellectuelle et théorie de propriété', in: *La 'nouvelle économie' industrielle,* Henri Lepage (ed.), Paris, 1989, 153-177; Bouckaert, Boudewijn, 'What is Property?', (1990) 13 *Harvard Journal of Law and Public Policy* 775-816 and Bouckaert, Boudewijn, 'Repliek op Mackaay', in: *De sociaal economische rol van intellectuele rechten,* M. Van Hoecke (ed.), Brussels 1991, 31-37, at 33-35, a reply to Mackaay, Ejan, 'Economisch-filosofische aspecten van de intellectuele rechten', in: *De sociaal economische rol van intellectuele rechten,* in same, 1-30.

Barlow's point, I take it, is that one cannot realistically hope to control information flows on the net, as copyright would require. Attempts to control it go against the grain of the phenomenon: information works best hopping from mind to mind, being adapted in the process; the Internet provides such free flow in spades; attempts to reward information creators by controlling the information flow in traditional ways (intellectual property rights) will make havoc of the creative processes and ordinary freedoms of the creators.

Full scale enforcement of intellectual property rights will trespass on people's fundamental rights in their person and material goods. To prevent illegal copying, for instance, one would have to exercise wide surveillance powers and regularly burst into people's homes and other private spaces. To realise just how far this might go, consider the entirely judicial creation of the *Anton Piller order*: wide ranging search powers granted on the basis of *ex parte* proceedings.[5] And was not the *Electronic Frontier Foundation* created to defend people against such practices, spiced up with a touch of nationality security concerns?

The end of property? Scarcely. To see why not, one must look at the essential features of property rights and not remain fixated on the specific forms in which they have been cast at particular times in history, as in the Napoleonic codification of 1804 or the first copyright acts. Property rights come in many forms. New forms are continually being developed. What we are really interested in is at whose initiative new rights emerge, what is required for such a development, what we are likely to observe while the process is going on, and finally, how this translates into written law. A dynamic view of the economics of property rights.[6]

2. Property Rights: the Statics

2.1 PROPERTY RIGHTS AND LAW

Property rights have existed during all of recorded history of mankind. Bentham was surely right in observing that '[p]roperty and law were born together, and would die together'.[7] Game theory allows one to understand how these rights could

5. *Anton Piller K.G.* v. *Manufacturing Processes Ltd.*, [1976] 1 All E. R. 779 (C.A.); *Rank Film Distributors Ltd and others* v. *Videa Information Centre*, [1981] 2 All. E. R. 76 (H. L.).

6. A dynamic perspective on property rights is explicitly adopted in Libecap, Gary D., *Contracting for Property Rights*, Cambridge, 1989; Ellickson, Robert C., *Order without Law – How Neighbors Settle Disputes*, Boston, 1991; Knight, Jack, *Institutions and Social Conflict*, Cambridge, 1992; Merges, Robert P., 'Of Property Rules, Coase, and Intellectual Property', (1994) 94 *Columbia Law Review* 2655-2673; Riker, William H. and David L. Weimer, The Economic and Political Liberalization of Socialism: The Fundamental Problem of Property Rights, in: *Liberalism and the Economic Order*, Ellen Frankel Paul, Fred D. Miller Jr and Jeffrey Paul (eds), Cambridge, 1993, 79-102, in particular 90-99 and in some of my earlier work: 'Problématique' and 'La propriété est-elle en voie d'extinction?' in: *Nouvelles technologies et propriété*, textes présentés par Ejan Mackaay, Montréal, 1991, 1-4 and 217-247. The classic piece on the subject is Demsetz, Harold, 'Towards a Theory of Property Rights', (1967) 57 *American Economic Review* 347-373.

7. Frankel Paul, Ellen, *Property Rights and Eminent Domain*, New Brunswick, 1987, 212, quoting Bentham, *Theory of Legislation*, Oxford, 1914, 146-147.

be discovered in all regions around the globe, in very different cultures and very early in history.[8]

Property rights are the institution normally chosen by default for managing resources that have become scarce. Scarcity arises where, for resources that hitherto could be used without restriction and were in that sense abundant, new uses are invented and one must decide which use should prevail. Such competing uses may give rise to conflict. The conflict signals emerging scarcity of the resource in question. It may be solved, or altogether avoided, by defining property rights over that resource. Property rights attribute the decision about the use of a resource to a particular person or group of persons.[9]

Property rights are an essential element in a legal system supporting a market economy.[10] Economic historians have amply shown the deleterious effects of incompletely defining property rights or tinkering with them.[11] Property rights, according to economic theory, provide the incentives to husband scarce resources wisely and to develop new and better uses for them. When transferable, as they are in most instances, property rights drive the price mechanism, from which market participants draw clues to discover opportunities for exchange and profit.[12]

The legal structures securing these advantages do not necessarily go by the name of property rights in the sense of the Civil Code. Indeed, wherever someone has the more or less exclusive control over some resource, allowing him or her to decide what to do with it and to collect the gains or suffer the losses resulting therefrom, he or she has, to all intents, a property right in the broad sense

---

8. Axelrod, Robert, *The evolution of cooperation*, New York 1984; Hargreaves Heap, Shaun P. and Yanis Varoufakis, *Game Theory – A Critical Introduction*, London, 1995; Mackaay, Ejan, 'L'ordre spontané comme fondement du droit – un survol des modèles de l'émergence des règles dans la société civile', (1988) 22 *Revue juridique Thémis* 347-383, and (1989) 3 *Revue internationale de droit économique* 247-287; Mackaay, Ejan, 'Le droit saisi par le jeu', (1991) *Droit et Société* 57-81, and in: *Le jeu: un paradigme pour le droit,* François Ost and Michel van de Kerhove (eds), Paris, 1992, 81-110; Sugden, Robert, *The economics of rights, co-operation & welfare*, Oxford, 1986; Taylor, Michael, *Community, anarchy & liberty,* Cambridge, 1982; Taylor, Michael, *The possibility of co-operation*, Cambridge, 1987.

9. Plentiful resources are usually held in common and are open to all. As scarcity sets in, rules about usage of the common good may be adopted. As scarcity becomes more severe, one may move to individual ownership or to stick with common ownership but strictly regulate its use. On the stages of this development in the case of water rights, *see* Rose, Carol M., 'Energy and Efficiency in the Realignment of Common Law Water Rights', (1990) 19 *Journal of Legal Studies* 261-296, at 294-96; also Rose, Carol M., *Property and Persuasion – Essays on the History, Theory and Rhetoric of Ownership*, Boulder, 1995.

10. Epstein, Richard A., *Simple Rules for a Complex World*, Cambridge, Mass., 1995, ch. 3. Property rights are one of the six basic principles underlying a mature legal system.

11. *See* e.g. North, Douglas C. and Robert Paul Thomas, *The Rise of the Western World – A New Economic History*, Cambridge, 1973; North, Douglas C., *Structure and Change in Economic History*, New York, 1981; Rosenberg, Nathan and L.E. Birdzell Jr, *How the West Grew Rich – The Economic Transformation of the Industrial World*, New York, 1986; Baechler, Jean, *Le capitalisme – 1. Les origines*, and *2. L'économie capitaliste*, Paris, 1995.

12. *See* for instance Barzel, Yoram, *Economic Analysis of Property Rights*, Cambridge, 1989; Mackaay, Ejan, 'An economic view of information law,' in: Korthals Altes, Willem F., Egbert J. Dommering, P. Bernt Hugenholtz and Jan J.C. Kabel (eds), *Information Law towards the 21st Century*, Deventer, 1992, 43-65, 48-54.

economists give to the term, whatever its legal name.[13] Transferability enhances the economic functions of such rights.

The prerequisite for property rights is a reasonable measure of exclusive control. Where this condition cannot be met and the resource is nonetheless scarce – given to multiple competing uses – we frequently see problems. Witness the difficulties in managing environmental resources or fish stock, to mention two current examples.[14] In such cases, other institutions are pressed into service for managing the conflict that signals scarcity: violence, authority, queuing, lotteries, nepotism. Or the resource may continue to be held in common property, with strict rules about how and how much each interested person may use it.[15]

2.2 Fences

On the nature and role of fences

In the case of land, exclusive control is typically secured by means of a fence. Fences of some sort – they may be ditches – are a necessary and normally also sufficient condition for creating property rights. New fencing techniques make new property rights viable or old ones more viable. They may give rise to striking improvements in the use of scarce resources. Consider, by way of example, the spectacular success of the invention of barbed wire for cattle breeding in the American West.[16]

Fences may be physical stops. In the world of software, copy protection and encryption are such fences. But fences need not be physical stops. A contractual

---

13. A different term, that could not be confounded with the legal concept, would have been better. But there appears to be no going back. *See* Barzel, *supra* note 12, at xi.

14. *See* for instance Block, Walter E. (ed.), *Economics and the Environment – A reconciliation*, Vancouver, 1990; Anderson, Terry L. and Donald R. Leal, *Free Market Environmentalism*, San Francisco, 1991.

15. Epstein studies such common property regimes for water rights: Epstein, Richard A., 'On the optimal mix of private and common property', in: *Property Rights,* Ellen Frankel Paul, Fred D. Miller Jr and Jeffrey Paul (eds), Cambridge, 1994, 17-41. On water rights, *see* also Rose, Carol M., 'Energy and Efficiency in the Realignment of Common Law Water Rights', (1990) 19 *Journal of Legal Studies* 261-296, at 294-96; Anderson, Terry L. (ed.), *Water Rights: Scarce Resource Allocation, Bureaucracy, and the Environment*, San Francisco, 1983. Other work, with a wealth of case studies and historical material, include Dahlman, Carl J., *The open field system and beyond*, Cambridge, 1980; Libecap, Gary D., *Contracting for Property Rights*, Cambridge, 1989; Ostrom, Elinor, *Governing the Commons – The evolution of institutions for collective action*, Cambridge,1990; Ellickson, *infra* note 16; Schmidtz, David, The institution of property, in: *Property Rights,* Ellen Frankel Paul, Fred D. Miller Jr and Jeffrey Paul (eds), Cambridge,1994, 42-62. These studies look into the question of comparing different institutions, attempting to explain in particular under what circumstances common property will be adopted as the most advantageous institution.

16. Ellickson, Robert C., *Order without Law – How Neighbors Settle Disputes*, Boston, 1991, 25. Ellickson, Robert C., 'Property in Land', (1993) 102 *Yale Law Journal* 1315-1400. At 1330, Ellickson relates how the invention of barbed wire changed the economics of land use for cattle breeding, making smaller lots viable. Historical observation confirmed what economic theory predicted here. *See* also Anderson, Terry L. and Donald R. Leal, *Free Market Environmentalism*, San Francisco, 1991, at 29.

arrangement by which one party gives the other access, under strict conditions, to a trade secret in his possession acts as a fence. Associations may be the depositaries of protected knowledge which they make available to members under strict rules. The association rules act as fences.[17] Generally '(..) institutions are enforcement technologies too, and they are often generated intentionally to reduce transaction costs and thus increase the value of assets'.[18] In the software world, updating policies restricted to registered users of legitimately acquired copies of the product act, to an extent and in conjunction with other measures, as a fence for it.[19] Legal sanctions, be they civil action to protect trade secrets or to halt 'parasitic activities', or criminal prosecution of 'pirates', or the threat of such actions, act as partial fences as well.

It will be helpful in what follows to use the term 'fences' for a wide range of devices and techniques and arrangements invented and used to secure some measure of exclusive control over a scarce resource. Fences seem to behave like other economic goods. Bringing new ones to the market is an entrepreneurial gamble. Existing fences may become obsolete when newer ones are put into service. To illustrate obsolescence, consider how the physical fence provided by the printing process in earlier days is cracking under the impact of photostatting and other copying techniques. To say that a property right is 'technologically dated' may mean merely that the fencing technique on which it relies is no longer as good as it once was.

How good is 'good enough' in fencing? We like to think that a fence shuts out hermetically. But this need not be so. A property right may be viable even where the fence is not fool proof.[20] The risk of burglary does not stop people from buying homes, although the risk of recurrent looting probably would. The 'holes in the fence', as well as the expense of activities (e.g. patrolling) designed to reduce losses due to what slips through those holes (pilferage), are simply costs to the owner. Property rights are worthwhile so long as they offer a net return over cost comparable to other possible investments. Closing a hole in the fence may be costlier than the losses it prevents.

---

17. Marie-Angèle Hermitte relates how such an arrangement worked for plant breeding knowledge in France before the enactment, in 1970, of an intellectual property right on such knowledge. Marie-Angèle Hermitte, 'Histoires juridiques extravagantes – La reproduction végétale', in : *L'homme, la nature et le droit*, B. Edelman and M.-A. Hermitte (eds), Paris, 1988, 40-82. *See* also my 'Problématique,' in: *Nouvelles technologies et propriété*, Ejan Mackaay (ed.), Montréal, 1991, 1-4, 2, and 'Economic incentives in markets for information and innovation', (1990) 13 *Harvard Journal of Law and Public Policy* 867-909, 902.

18. Robert P. Merges, 'Of Property Rules, Coase, and Intellectual Property', (1994) 94 *Columbia Law Review* 2655-2673, 2679. He mentions several associations in the United States acting to define and protect informal rights of their members.

19. Lance Rose, *supra* note 3. Among the more obvious measures are surveillance and prosecutions organised by the Software Publishers Association, the Business Software Alliance and other similar groups.

20. [E]xclusivity is frequently a matter of degree.' Steven N.S. Cheung, 'The Structure of a Contract and the Theory of a Non-Exclusive Resource', (1970) 13 *J. Law Econ.* 49-70, repr. in: Eirik G. Furubotn and Svetozar Pejovich (eds), *The Economics of Property Rights*, Ballinger, 1974, 11-30, 27. Or as Lance Rose, *supra note 3*, puts it: 'Cops have plenty of experience in sweeping the public markets clean enough for business.'

A similar reasoning determines whether a new fencing technique is worthwhile. It is if the increased revenue the fence allows one to draw from the property more than offsets the additional cost of the new fence, net of savings due to the abandonment of earlier fences.[21]

Fences and the Internet

The Internet changes the fences used for intellectual property rights. Traditionally, the copyright laws distinguish amongst several kinds of object of intellectual property rights. Section 5 of the Canadian Copyright Act, for instance, recognises four kinds: literary, dramatic, musical and artistic works. The distinction corresponds in part to differences in the fences used. By controlling the most obvious ways in which each kind of fence can be jumped, the creator effectively obtains a property right.

The Internet, and more broadly information technology, transforms all these kinds of information into a single, digital form. The digital form can be copied and transmitted with an ease that appears to put paid (or rather not paid) to the delicate legal machinery engineered to reign in misuse under older fencing technologies. One can only agree with Lance Rose, that '[t]he Net did not introduce low-cost, anonymous infringement to the world. Anyone can buy a photocopier, tape deck, or computer and become a small-time infringer who's almost impossible to detect'.[22] But the Internet amplifies the corrosion of the older fences and creates the appearance of an open field in which all take whatever they can click their mouse on.

Does the Internet spell the end of property rights? The old fences may not work so well any more. Yet information, while apparently abundant once in existence, still needs to be created and the creator needs to be encouraged. Information is scarce in that sense and calls for property rights or other institutions to cope with scarcity. The software industry, in spite of a flourishing shareware market and allegedly rampant piracy, does not appear to be moribund. Apparently a solution exists in practice.

Fences and the law

If the old fences no longer work so well, one reaction is to cry to heaven that pirates are upon us and that the very foundations of civilisation which are property rights are being undermined. And to call the police (or the secret service).

---

21. This principle may be also found in De Jasay, Anthony, 'The Cart before the Horse. On Emergent and Constructed Orders, and their Wherewithal', in: *Contending with Hayek – On Liberalism, Spontaneous Order and the Post-Communist Societies in Transition,* Christoph Frei and Robert Nef (eds), Berne, 1994, 49-64, 57. De Jasay moves on to consider how property rights owners can externalise part of the exclusion cost to the community at large, through an agency of the state in charge of looking after property rights. This last consideration appears to have been the driving force behind the emergence of intellectual property rights through royal or princely privileges, from the 16th till the 18th century, as Seignette tells the story: Seignette, Jacqueline M.B., *Challenges to the Creator Doctrine – Authorship, copyright ownership and the exploitation of creative work in the Netherlands, Germany and the United States*, Deventer, 1994, 7-24.

22. Lance Rose, *supra* note 3.

But should the police – and by extension, the law – be on call to shore up property rights based on crumpling fences? My reading of the history is that law does not generally do this. As a matter of principle, I believe it should not. If laws and law enforcement power are available to shore up rights whose owners cannot fence for themselves, we are overstepping the boundary separating legitimate property rights from illegitimate rent-seeking.[23] Rights secured as a result of rent-seeking could not subsist in the market. Competition would weed them out. They subsist merely by the grace of the coercive power of the authorities and procure artificial advantages or revenue.

But, one may ask, is not the role of government in Western societies to protect property rights? The answer must surely be affirmative. The point is that these services are supplemental to the more basic efforts of rights holders to defend their property rights themselves.[24] Law enforcement is available for gross violations of property rights through violence or fraud; the basic fence is to be set up and patrolled by the owner and backed by civil action against violators.

Elsewhere I have termed this the 'realism' of the law.[25] Law enforces solutions that basically work, not those that have broken down. 'Copyright was never meant to stop people from repairing or reselling or reading or using material in customary ways'.[26] Law is realistic in other ways as well. It has to rely on rules that can be understood and applied by people of varying ability in different contexts. Such rules must be kept simple.[27] The law is also realistic in that it does not concern itself with trifles: *De minimis non curat praetor*. Law specifies the boundaries between neighbouring property rights only to the extent that conflicts have actually arisen between neighbours.

---

23. The term 'rent-seeking' was first used in Krueger, Anne O., 'The Political Economy of the Rent-Seeking Society', (1974) 64 *American Economic Review* 291-303. It designates a variety of activities through which special interest coalitions succeed in using the political process to obtain wealth transfers for their members which they could not gain in the market. Various forms of protectionism, price ceilings or floors, legal barriers to entry into a market, as well as direct subsidies and benefits are examples of such transfers from citizens, tax payers or consumers in general to members of special interest groups. Good recent overviews of the subject are Tullock, Gordon, *Rent Seeking*, Aldershot, Hants, Edward Elgar Publishing Cy, 1993 (The Shaftesbury Papers, 2), and Rowley, Charles K., Robert D. Tollison and Gordon Tullock (eds), *The Political Economy of Rent-Seeking*, Boston, 1988. The study of rent-seeking is part of the theory of public choice, which is the analysis of political processes by means of economic concepts. On public choice generally, *see* Mitchell, William C. and Randy T. Simmons, *Beyond Politics – Markets, Welfare, and the Failure of Bureaucracy*, Boulder, 1994.
24. De Jasay, *supra* note 21, 49-64, 58.
25. *See* Mackaay, Ejan, 'Economic incentives in markets for information and innovation', (1990) 13 *Harvard Journal of Law and Public Policy* 867-909, 903.
26. Vaver, David, *Rejuvenating copyright, digitally*, Draft notes for a presentation at the Symposium on Digital Technology & Copyright, Wilson House, Meech Lake, Canada, 3 March 1995, 6. Lance Rose, *supra* note 3, argues that since home taping cannot be stopped, it is no longer considered a copyright violation.
27. Epstein, *supra* note 10, ch. 1.

3. Property Rights: the Dynamics

3.1 BUILD YOUR OWN FENCE

If the old fences no longer work very well and the law is not available to shore them up, there appears to be vacuum. This does not mean a breakdown of law and order. The Internet may not have a constituted central authority and hence be anarchic in the true sense, but it is by no means an order-less place. On the contrary, surfing on the Net, one is struck by the efforts within discussion groups – repeat players, to use the language of game theory[28] – to discover the proper norms that should govern their dealings. It is true that, at the outer edge of this process, there are penalising actions such as 'flaming' one who clearly oversteps the boundaries of what others find proper. The systems operator may even exclude a person from access to the server. But these severe sanctions are exceptional. The dominant impression is one of communities looking for the rules they should live by, creating their own order. For those willing to see it, spontaneous orders are being built here.[29]

With regard to property rights, the point of the story is that those who seek to make money with novel products for which no known rights and fences exist, can nonetheless create 'experimental rights'.[30] Given that they control their product at the outset, they can design new fences, using whatever devices and techniques are available to them and making contractual arrangements. These fences must secure them sufficient control to bring the product to market and make a profit from it. The realm of property rights can thus be gradually extended by directly interested persons themselves. They can use freedom of contract and existing property rights in anything that can be used as a fence to secure these 'experimental rights'.

Understandably, interested persons will try to collect revenue only in places where they have a realistic hope of creating effective fences. New fencing techniques may lead to new divisions between what is product – to be paid for – and advertising – offered freely to induce sales of the product. John Perry Barlow submits that only live information is paid for: consultations of doctors and other professionals; live performances of artists. Dead information should be freely available. Could one not read this distinction more mundanely as a matter of where, with current knowledge, one can hope to create effective fences and collect revenue? At all events, where to collect your revenue and what to treat as

28. *See supra* note 8.

29. *See* Barry, Norman P., 'The Tradition of Spontaneous Order', (1982) 5 *Literature of Liberty* 1-58; Sugden, Robert, 'Spontaneous order', (1989) 3 *Journal of Economic Perspectives* 85-97; Vanberg, Viktor J., 'Unsichtbare-Hand Erklärung und soziale Normen', in: *Normengeleitetes Verhalten in der Sozialwissenschaften*, Berlin, 1984, 115-146; Ellickson, *supra* note 16, 168.

30. Ellickson makes this point more generally for land rights. Ellickson, Robert C., 'Property in Land', (1993) 102 *Yale Law Journal* 1315-1400, 1366. Riker and Weimer put it as follows: 'People may find creative ways to make de facto property rights more effective and credible': Riker, William H. and David L. Weimer, 'The Economic and Political Liberalization of Socialism: The Fundamental Problem of Property Rights', in: *Liberalism and the Economic Order,* Ellen Frankel Paul, Fred D. Miller Jr and Jeffrey Paul (eds), Cambridge, 1993, 79-102, at 100.

advertisement (given away free) is a matter of private entrepreneurial decision and enters into the calculation of whether a given creative effort is worthwhile.

In keeping with the innovative spirit reigning on the Internet generally, one must expect much experimentation with new fencing techniques. This is indeed happening. Witness the appearance of demo or 'light' versions of software alongside with more fully equipped 'commercial' versions, as, for example, are proposed for Eudora and Netscape. Microsoft is said to have inserted in Windows 95 a small worm program to interrogate computers on a network and report back on what programs are run on them (and, presumably, whether the copies are legal). Some databases are 'sponsored' by organisations that collect their money elsewhere: West sponsors the listing of American lawyers on the Internet; many databases are created by university people, for whom this fulfils part of their academic obligations. *Wired* sells its monthly publication with the colours and the graphics; the basic text is subsequently available without cost by FTP: community service, sharing philosophy or advertisement?

In the logic set out here, it falls to the interested persons to make the first moves towards the recognition of these new rights. They should build their own fence. Legislators, the authorities generally, should not step in at this stage. Their role is to recognise or acknowledge the new right once sufficient experience has built up allowing us to discover how the 'experimental right' works in practice. Legislation may then simplify the multitude of forms that practice comes up with or put a stop to a margin of fraud that new developments inevitably attract. The courts should similarly limit themselves to sanction only the grossest violations and resist drawing liberally on open-ended concepts such as 'parasitic activities'. This restraint is part of the 'realism' of the law. Once new rights have been recognised in law, they form part of the arsenal from which, at a later date, elements may be used to fashion fences for as yet unimagined new objects. The property rights logic is thus indefinitely extendible.

The logic of 'build/mind your own fence' is historically apparent, I submit, in property rights in land and other goods.[31] It also appears to be part of the traditional trade secret law. If you seek remedies against a violator of your trade secret, you will have to show that you took the proper steps to keep the knowledge in question confidential: warnings, restricted access, and so on. The law merely supplements

31. *See* Ellickson, *supra* note 16; Umbeck, John R., 'Might makes right: A theory of the foundation and initial distribution of property rights', (1981) 19 *Economic Inquiry* 38-59; Umbeck, John R., *A theory of property rights with application to the California gold rush*, Ames, 1981. De Jasay writes 'Systems of property and complex exchanges did not have to wait for states to lay their legal infrastructure; in many known instances, they laid their own as they went. (..) Enforcement, at all events, has no demonstrable temporal precedence over exchange'; de Jasay, *supra* note 21, 49-64, at 61. On the emergence of limited liability companies and other enterprise forms and their subsequent formal recognition in law, *see* e.g. Patault, Anne-Marie, *Introduction historique au droit des biens*, Paris, 1989, 196; Rosenberg, Nathan and L.E. Birdzell Jr, *How the West Grew Rich – The Economic Transformation of the Industrial World*, New York, 1986, ch. 7 (189-210); Braudel, Fernand, *Civilisation matérielle, économie et capitalisme, XVe-XVIIIe siècle*, Paris, 1979, Vol. II, 383-402. For a study of 'experimental rights' in intellectual products such as trade names, know-how or goodwill, see Van Engelen, Th.C.J.A., *Prestatiebescherming en ongeschreven intellectuele eigendomsrechten*, Zwolle, 1994. Consider also the recent phenomenon of franchising.

your efforts at creating your own fence. It is this restraint in the law that guards us from sliding into rent-seeking.

One may find it regrettable that no official rights appear to be available for apparently desirable creative activities. But this very vacuum constitutes the spur necessary to stimulate the creation of new types of fences. The reward available for the fence maker is part of the revenue that the creator or distributor hopes to draw from marketing the as yet unexploited creation. One must not pierce this vacuum by creating rights too soon, since that would kill the process by which to discover the proper scope of new rights.[32]

3.2 ON THE LIMITS OF PROPERTY RIGHTS AND THEIR DISCOVERY

If everything is 'up for grabs' by whoever can come up with a fence for it, will we not slide into 'undue information lock-up?'[33] The issue arises because of the cumulative nature of knowledge. Current inventions build on earlier ones, indeed may incorporate them. Too strict rights on inventions or other creations, while encouraging current creators, may hamper future creative efforts. The rights logic competes with the idea of free flow of information.[34] Property rights in information may also conflict with other kinds of property rights, for instance where personal information (privacy, reputation) is concerned.[35]

What concerns me here is the procedure by which we arbitrate between these competing values. If, as I submitted before, the new rights emerge at the initiative of interested persons, rather than by legislative or judicial decree, then surely it would essential to show that the boundaries, too, may be discovered through such a decentralised process and codified into law only later, on the basis of practical experience.

We might conduct surveys on questions such as whether interfaces ought to be protected by intellectual property rights. Surveys like that have been conducted and the results come rather as a surprising contrast to public discourse clamouring

32. This aspect of the dynamics of property rights has been studied in particular by the neo-Austrian economists, such as Kirzner and Rizzo. *See* Kirzner, Israel M., *Discovery and the Capitalist Process*, Chicago, 1985; Kirzner, Israel M., 'Discovery, private property and the theory of justice in capitalist society', (1990) 1 *Journal des économistes et des études humaines* 209-224; O'Driscoll Jr, Gerald P. and Mario J. Rizzo, *The Economics of Time and Ignorance*, Oxford, 1985; *see* also Baechler, Jean, *Le capitalisme – 2. L'économie capitaliste*, Paris, 1995, Pt IV, Ch. IV, 77, in particular 86.

33. Hammond, R. Grant, 'The Misappropriation of Commercial Information in the Computer Age', (1986) 64 *Canadian Bar Review* 342-373, at 373.

34. Nelson, Richard R., 'Intellectual Property Protection for Cumulative Systems Technology', (1994) 94 *Columbia Law Review* 2674-2677; as Epstein, *supra* note 27, at 330, puts it: 'With information the coordination problems can never be ignored: free exchange of information in scholarly endeavors is often worth more than any system of exclusive rights. (..) The difficult problem is not that of the conceptual framework, but that of the magnitude of the relevant trade-offs between open access (the coordination problem again) and the incentive to produce (sapped by external use).' *See* also Dam, Kenneth W., 'Some Economic Considerations in the Intellectual Property Protection of Software', (1995) 24 *Journal of Legal Studies* 321-377.

35. See Mackaay, *supra* note 12, 60.

ever greater piracy and need for clamping down on it, in law as well as by police measures.[36] This suggests that public discourse does not necessarily reflect the interests of people in the field. Public choice theory suggests that organised groups are more likely than individuals to make themselves heard in public discourse as well as before the legislature or its committees. This, in turn, must make us wary of the idea that the legislature necessarily balances all relevant interests fairly.[37]

Judicial decisions fare no better. How will judges come by the information required to balance, without arbitrariness, the as yet incompletely articulated interests of groups that may or not be parties to the trial? Not surprisingly, the judicial process operating under such constraints has been likened to central planning: navigating in the dark.[38]

How then should we arrive at the proper balance? We should like to find it in arrangements worked out amongst persons who can be creators as well as borrowers of new creations. The dual roles would tend to prevent rules skewed one way or the other. A proposal to this effect has been put forth by Jerome Reichman.[39] It provides for associations within each branch of innovative industry setting terms on which discoveries by members are available to others. Peter Merges has documented the existence of several such associations in recent American history.[40]

The risk with the associations is that they come to be dominated by the less innovative members and that the rules will be skewed towards the borrowers. This would lower the incentives to innovate, to the detriment of the general public. The history of the medieval guilds is there to show that this risk is not imaginary.[41]

---

36. *See* e.g. Samuels, Linda B. and Le Thi Cao, 'Survey of the Opinion of Software Development Companies Concerning Intellectual Property Protection', (1992) 32/4 *IDEA* 343-359; Samuelson, Pamela and Robert J. Glushko, 'Survey on the Look and Feel Lawsuits', (1990) 33/5 *Communications of the ACM* 483-487; Samuelson, Pamela and Robert J. Glushko, 'Comparing the Views of Lawyers and User Interface Designers on the Software Copyright Look and Feel Lawsuits', (1989) 30 *Jurimetrics Journal* 121-140; Samuelson, Pamela, Michel Denber and Robert J. Glushko, 'Development on the Intellectual Property Front', (1992) 35/5 *Communications of the ACM* 33-39; Samuelson, Pamela, 'Survey on the Patent/Copyright Interface for Computer Programs', (1989) 17 *AIPLA QJ* 256.

37. A small anecdote may illustrate this. A few years ago, the Canadian parliament decided to write into the Copyright Act a provision authorising back-up copies of software or adaptation for the purpose of compatibility as fair use (sect. 27(2) (l) and (m)). Initial proposals would have authorised several copies, as the state of the technology required. The provision ultimately adopted after heavy lobby by large software producers authorises a single copy for either purpose. How many legitimate owners of copies in fact respect this provision? On this later point, *see* Ellickson's analogous story on the lawlessness of academic photocopying: Ellickson, *supra* note 16, 258-264.

38. Aranson, Peter H., 'The Common Law as Central Economic Planning', (1992) 3 *Constitutional Political Economy* 289-319.

39. Reichman, J.H., 'Legal Hybrids between the Patent and Copyright Paradigms', (1994) 94 *Columbia Law Review* 2432-2558; Zentaro Kitagawa, Comment on *A Manifesto concerning the Legal Protection of Computer Programs*, (1994) 94 *Columbia Law Review* 2610-20 (relating the Copymart experience).

40. Merges, *supra* note 18, 2655-2673.

41. Black, Antony, *Guilds and Civil Society in European Political Thought from the Twelfth Century to the Present*, Ithaca, NY, 1984.

Competition law has been used as a weapon against such trade association 'conspiring against the public interest'. But the record of antitrust prosecutions in the United States in particular is not encouraging.[42] Antitrust law has been used by companies in a branch of industry to stifle a competitive advantage secured by a more innovative competitor, as was the case with IBM two decades ago and as appears to be happening once more in the case against Microsoft now. On this reading, competition law is used, as public choice theory would suggest, as yet another weapon in the competitive struggle for market share. It should not be.

To guard against the risk of associations stifling innovation, membership in them should not be mandatory. A member – in particular an innovative one – should be able to exit and to form a new, competing association.[43] Competition, here as elsewhere, is the proper way to discover what rules we want.

It might appear that the rights which associations or individuals exercise lead to 'undue information lock-up'. But one should resist the temptation to legislate in order to counter it. Robert Merges tells the story of compulsory licensing introduced in the United States for certain classes of musical works (the 'jukebox' licence) and television programmes.[44] The associations in charge of collecting royalties were judged to be insufficiently forthcoming with licences. But the difficulty leading to this legislative intervention was, in his view, a matter of developing institutions that would have reduced the transactions costs associated with collecting royalties. This problem is best left to the interested persons to solve. It may take some time and some may get impatient with what they see as an abuse of power or monopoly position. Yet the alternative has its own problems. Compulsory licences, once introduced, are difficult to root out. And the compulsory licence granted to one group may lead another, as public choice theory would predict, to seek the same form of salvation through the political process rather than the market.

4. Conclusion

The starting point of this article is the thesis that intellectual property rights don't work on the Internet. Some conclude from it that we should forget about them; others call for more police and more enforcement. Lawyers like to work by analogy. They extend known concepts to situations with novel features. It is a workable simple strategy, but it lands us into problems when we look at the Internet. To take but one example, should downloading files be likened to photostatting or to browsing in a book store? The legal conclusions drawn from these analogies are opposites.

---

42. Demsetz, Harold, *100 Years of Antitrust: Should We Celebrate? – Brent T. Upson Memorial Lecture*, Arlington, VA, 1991; McChesney, Fred S. and William F. Sughart II (eds), *The Causes and Consequences of Antitrust – The Public-Choice Perspective*, Chicago, 1995.

43. This point is further developed in Mackaay, Ejan, 'Legal hybrids: Beyond property and monopoly?', (1994) 94 *Columbia Law Review* 2630-2643, p. 2642-3.

44. Merges, *supra* note 18, 2668, referring to §§ 115, 116, 111(d) and 118 of the American Copyright Act (17 USC).

The problem is that 'fencing techniques' on which copyright relies for works in traditional form are not readily transposable to the Internet, where everything is in digital form, easily copied and transmitted and not easily tied to particular places. The relative failure of the older fencing techniques does not mean that we can do away with property rights. They are the basic institution in a market system, which, in turn, is still our best bet for producing things that do not come falling out of heaven.

What the economics of property rights tells us is that such rights may operate without being formally recognised as such in law. What is needed are devices or techniques allowing one effectively to fence off whatever one hopes to claim as one's property. A variety of fencing techniques are known, including such unexpected ones as marketing practices and elaborate contractual arrangements, and further ones may be discovered as entrepreneurial ventures. Existing property rights in known objects provide the building blocks with which to fashion fences for yet to be recognised property rights in novel objects. The ambit of property rights, in the economic sense, is essentially open-ended. The relevant social practices on the Internet to watch are those through which people attempt to create new fences.

Law, as Richard Epstein has recently reminded us, operates, in its core, with simple rules. For our topic here, two principles appear to govern the creation of new property rights. The first is 'Build your own fence'. The burden of fencing in property rests foremost on the primarily interested person, and in particular, not on the State. State enforcement should be supplemental and redress only the grossest violations.

The second principle concerns the proper boundaries for the new property rights. These can not be discovered through abstract reasoning. Preferably they should be drawn from arrangements worked out amongst interested persons or associations themselves, representing both sides of the fence. The downside of this procedure is that it is likely to take time and that such arrangements have, in the past, sometimes been turned to the detriment of the public. Against this latter risk competition law, as recent American history has shown, may not be as effective a remedy as some would have us believe. The better approach is to allow for the possibility of competing associations in which such arrangements are worked out.

The two principles recast law as in origin a largely spontaneous order. This is deliberate. Where legislatures tackle the problems of new technology, they navigate in the dark about what solutions will really work. Legislatures are likely to listen disproportionally to the voices speaking for large organised interests. The recent history of the 'jukebox' licence in America stands as an example of developments to avoid.

The conclusion of this article is that, even if fencing techniques crystallised in the existing copyright law do not work very well on the Internet, property is by no means dead and the net is buzzing with initiatives exploring alternative fencing techniques and new extensions of property rights.

Conflicts of Law in Cyberspace: International Copyright in a Digitally Networked World

*Paul Edward Geller**

Starting in the sixteenth century, the Netherlands published books unavailable in the rest of Europe. The so-called Republic of Letters then arose, in which the most advanced European minds networked with each other in writing across national borders.[1] It is only appropriate that the Royal Netherlands Academy of Arts and Sciences now host this conference devoted to communication through new digital media.

New media communicate works of the mind world-wide at the speed of light. What law or laws should govern how these works are protected when they cross borders?[2] Suppose that, without any right-holders' consent, I colorize Buster Keaton's classic film work *The General*. From my database in the United States, I make this version digitally accessible in a trans-Atlantic network. End-users in France and Germany can order it sent to themselves through the network, while I am paid through their credit-card accounts for providing this access. In the United States, copyright in this work has lapsed; in France, moral rights protect it, but not economic rights; in Germany, all rights in it still subsist.[3]

This hypothetical case might remind us of the conflict of laws already notorious in satellite broadcasting.[4] If the law of the United States applied to the

---

* Attorney, Los Angeles; Adjunct Professor, International Intellectual Property, University of Southern California Law Center. For their comments, I thank Lorin Brennan, Ivan Cherpillod, Thomas Dreier, Bernard Edelman, Mihály Ficsor, Ysolde Gendreau, I. Trotter Hardy, André Kerever, Henri-Jacques Lucas, Richard Solomon, and Alain Strowel.

1. *See* Elizabeth L. Eisenstein, *The Printing Press as an Agent of Change*, Cambridge, Mass., 1979, at 138.
2. *See generally* Paul Edward Geller, 'The Universal Electronic Archive: Issues in International Copyright', 25 *IIC* 54 (1994) (anticipatory analysis of implications of digitally generated networks for copyright).
3. *Compare* French *Keaton* decision, Cour d'appel Paris, 1re ch., 24 April 1974, *RIDA* 1975, no. 83, 106, English trans. in 7 *IIC* 130 (1976), affirmed Cass. civ. I, 15 December 1975, *RIDA* 1976, no. 88, 115 (lapse of U.S. copyright results in expiry of French right) with German *Keaton* decision, Bundesgerichtshof, 27 January 1975, *GRUR Int.* 1979, 50, English trans. in 10 *IIC* 358 (1979) (work still protected in Germany). *See also* French Code de la propriété intellectuelle, art. L.121-1 ('perpetuel' moral right).
4. *Compare* Mihály Ficsor, 'Direct Broadcasting by Satellite and the "Bogsch Theory"', *International Business Lawyer*, June 1990, 258 (favors applying laws of receiving countries) with Gunnar W.G. Karnell, 'A Refutation of the Bogsch Theory on Direct Satellite Broadcasting Rights', *id.* at 263 (favors applying law of transmitting country). *See also* Adolf Dietz, 'Copyright and Satellite Broadcasts', 20 *IIC* 135 (1989), at 144-150 (questioning whether law of receiving country is not more appropriate in cases such as those involving differing term or colorization of work); Jane C. Ginsburg, 'Global Use/Territorial Rights: Private International

entire case, I could transmit the work to France or Germany with impunity. If the law of each receiving country applied to reception in that country, I would have to obtain consent country by country.[5] But this case differs critically in its fact pattern from broadcasting which, like publishing, transmits works from active centers outward to passive receivers. Digital media allow transmitters and receivers to switch roles interactively, and to be linked among themselves in fluid and variegated patterns, potentially affecting both creation and dissemination at any and all points in increasingly global networks.[6]

We are caught here between geographical space and cyberspace. Copyright was born in the eighteenth century, into a world of print and live theatre, where courts could pinpoint the territories in which works originated and were disseminated. Even in the twentieth century, courts have continued to tie the choice of law to points fixed in geographical space, most often dealing with works published or broadcast from known centers to surrounding audiences. However, now, at the threshold of the twenty-first century, diverse authors located continents apart can collaborate in creating the same work, and global networks can make works simultaneously accessible world-wide at once. It is then no longer possible to localize works at any single point in transterritorial cyberspace, which William Gibson prophetically called the 'space that wasn't space'.[7]

This shift from geographical to cyberspace, I shall argue, requires a shift in choice-of-law analysis, initially in national courts and eventually in international copyright treaties. First, I shall ask how, in focusing analysis less on abstract rights than on concrete remedies, courts may more judiciously choose between copyright laws in cases of transborder infringement. Second, in this new framework of analysis, I shall consider how courts may resolve conflicts between copyright and other laws likely to arise in a digitally networked world. Third, I shall consider how, in the Berne Union, this shift may begin to be codified.

Law Questions of the Global Information Infrastructure', 42 *Journal of the Copyright Society of the USA* 1995, 318, at 322-323 and 337-338 (proposing 'combination' of law of forum and transmitting country, despite 'risk' of 'forum shopping' and transmission 'from the least protective country').

5. *Compare* Austrian *Directsatellitensendung* decision, Oberlandesgericht Vienna, 30 November 1989, *GRUR Int.* 1990, 537, especially at 539, *affirmed* Oberster Gerichtshof, 16 June 1992, *GRUR Int.* 1992, 933, English trans. in 24 *IIC* 665 (1993) (to discourage transmission from countries with lowest levels of protection, satellite broadcast localized in receiving country) with E.C. Council Directive 93/83/EEC of 27 September 1993 on the coordination of certain rules concerning copyright and rights related to copyright applicable to satellite broadcasting and cable retransmission, recitals 9-15 and art. 1.2, O.J.E.C. No. L. 248/15 of 6 October 1993 (to avoid need to obtain licenses for all E.C. countries, satellite broadcast localized in transmitting country).

6. *See* Ithiel de Sola Pool, *Technologies of Freedom*, Cambridge, Mass., 1983, at 213-217. *But cf.* Richard Lick, *La juste communication*, IDATE La Documentation Française, 1988, at 116-123; W. Russel Neuman, *The Future of the Mass Audience*, Cambridge, Mass., 1991, at 104-113, 158-163 (ambivalences toward media).

7. William Gibson, *Count Zero*, New York, 1986, at 38.

1. Shifting Choice-of-Law Analyses

As the media have extended their reach, private parties have increasingly extended their transactions across borders. For example, since the introduction of print into Europe, publishers in one country have distributed their books in other countries. At the same time, rising nation-states promulgated the doctrine of territoriality, namely that laws were effective only within their respective national territories.[8]

Courts have had to choose which law should govern border-crossing transactions: that on one side of this or that national border or another? I shall consider distinct frameworks of analysis in which to respond to this question: first, that of categorical analysis and, second, that of functional analysis. I shall then argue that, to respond to the challenges of the shift from geographical space to cyberspace, courts would do well to move from categorical to functional analysis.

1.1. CATEGORICAL ANALYSIS

In the nineteenth century Friedrich Karl von Savigny crystallized European choice-of-law analysis. He did this at a time when the formation of nation-states within the tight European geographical space was reaching completion. Hence, to quote Savigny, parties to border-crossing transactions were sure to encounter 'the possibility of (..) entrance into the territory of a rule of law alien to' their own home law.[9]

At the threshold of analysis, Savigny distinguished between laws of automatic application and laws subject to choice of law. On the one hand, Savigny recognized that the forum state, where the court sits, will have compelling public interests in having certain of its laws applied automatically, no matter what the foreign elements of a given case, because such laws are based on 'moral grounds' or 'on reasons of public interest (*publica utilitas*)'.[10] On the other hand, the court might serve as a neutral arbiter choosing laws in cases in which no such public interests come into play, but rather in which private individuals subject their relations to legal regimes such as property, contract, and tort.[11]

Savigny then focused on these cases involving private relations. As *desiderata*, he posited that courts should not discriminate against foreign parties and should choose the same law in the same categories of cases.[12] With these aims in mind, Savigny correlated the distinctions between legally governed relations between

8. *See* Paul Alliés, *L'invention du territoire*, Grenoble, 1980, pt. 2. *Cf.* Nicholas K. Bromley, *Law, Space and the Geographies of Power*, New York, 1994, ch. 3 (nation-states start mapping their territories with greater precision).

9. Friedrich Carl von Savigny, *A Treatise on the Conflict of Laws*, Wm. Guthrie (trans.), Edinburgh, 1880, 2nd ed., at 55 (§ 345).

10. *Id.*, at 78 (§ 349). *But cf.* Yvon Loussouarn and Pierre Bourel, *Droit international privé*, Paris, 3rd ed., 1988, at 177-183 (§ 129-131) (distinctions between *lois de police*, *d'ordre publique*, *politiques*, and *d'application immédiate* difficult to draw).

11. *See* Savigny, *supra* note 9, at 132-142 (§ 360-361).

12. *See* Savigny, *supra* note 9, at 69-70 (§ 348).

private parties, such as property and tort, with the territories in which these relations seemed by nature to be most appropriately connected. For example, a property claim would be best ruled by the law of the state on whose territory the property at issue was situated, and a tort claim would be so connected to the territory of the state where the tortious act took place. It would then become indispensable to characterize any claim raised in a case as falling into a given category before knowing to which jurisdiction to look for dispositive law.[13]

Professor Troller indicated why this framework of analysis does not easily fit over intellectual property.[14] In theory, the immaterial objects of intellectual property are ubiquitous, susceptible of appearing everywhere at once. In practice, however, the law, ultimately the police, only seem capable of controlling material objects on the territories of nation-states. Troller posited that the objects of intellectual property, notably works and inventions, could only be misappropriated in the form of material things, such as books or machines. These could then be localized in the territory on which such things are actually produced, marketed, or used.[15]

This territorial approach fails to take account of the possibility of misappropriating works as pure data.[16] Specifically, in a digital environment, we can move works of the mind back and forth between immaterial and material forms, as well as across geographical space at the speed of light, by giving our computers simple commands. Courts can then no longer play the game of localizing infringement under the shell of one national law or another.[17] To choose between such laws when they conflict in cyberspace, courts might consider a more flexible analysis.

---

13. *See* Savigny, *supra* note 9, at 70 (§ 348), 174-181 (§ 366), 221-233 *passim* (§ 372-373). *See also* Ernst Rabel, *The Conflict of Laws: A Comparative Study*, Ann Arbor, 2nd ed., 1958, vol. 1, at 54-55 (any conflicts rule connects facts of case to jurisdiction whose law governs specific claim arising out of facts, but that claim 'must be susceptible of interpretation' in terms of both forum and foreign laws).
14. Alois Troller, *Das internationale Privat- und Zivilprozeßrecht im gewerblichen Rechtsschutz und Urheberrecht*, Basel, 1952, at 39-67.
15. *See* Troller, *supra* note 14, at 44-45, 61-67. *See also* Jacques Raynard, *Droit d'auteur et conflits de loi: Essai sur la nature juridique du droit d'auteur*, Paris, 1990, at 406-411 (copyright protected work, while ubiquitous, is 'addressed to senses' in specific national territories).
16. *Cf.* Egbert Dommering, 'An Introduction to Information Law. Works of Fact at the Crossroads of Freedom and Protection', in: *Protecting Works of Fact: Copyright, Freedom of Expression and Information Law*, E.J. Dommering & P.B. Hugenholtz (eds.), Deventer, 1991, 1, at 13-15, 18 (works as original arrangements of signs subject to digital appropriation).
17. *See e.g.*, the Austrian *Tele-Uno II* decision, Oberster Gerichtshof, 28 May 1991, *GRUR Int.* 1991, 920, English trans. in: 23 *IIC* 703 (1992), at 707 (admitting that '*alongside* the law of the country of emission, in addition the copyright provisions of all those countries must be applied, which are situated at least to a considerable extent within the regular reception scope of such broadcasts').

1.2. FUNCTIONAL ANALYSIS

In the twentieth century, Brainerd Currie led the American revolution in choice-of-law analysis. He would have found it meaningless to ask whether copyright, 'by nature', should be governed by the law of the country of origin or by that of ultimate use. Currie dismissed any such categorical 'choice-of-law rule' as an 'empty and bloodless thing', to the extent that its application would turn on theoretical debates more than practical results.[18] He rather elaborated a framework of analysis for analyzing how choices between laws function relative to the interests motivating these laws.

Currie effectively collapsed Savigny's distinction between, on the one hand, forum laws that apply automatically because of compelling public interests and, on the other hand, other forum or foreign laws subject to choice because they protect only private interests. Currie instead wrote of 'economic and social policies', what he called 'governmental' interests, that would motivate all rules of law and, therefore, potentially affect the resolution of all conflicts of laws.[19] Such public interests would inevitably be at stake, in varying combinations and permutations, alongside private interests asserted in all cases where laws of different jurisdictions conflicted. A court dealing with any such case would then have to sort out the interests that its own forum state, as opposed to those of foreign states, had in the outcome of the case.[20]

According to Currie, where all such interests at stake in a case pointed to the same decision, there would be a 'false conflict' and the court could reach that decision without making any choice of law.[21] If, however, compelling interests of the forum state are implicated in the decision, the court must defer to them in choosing that state's law; otherwise, the court may accommodate the interests of foreign states in choosing their laws to reach the outcomes their interests tend to favour.[22] This method changes the focus of the threshold question of characterization that we encountered in our initial example of the transmission of the colourized classic film work from the United States to Europe: *inside* what country do acts subject to copyright in the work take place? Interest analysis, rather than limiting itself to the acts subject to the particular rights asserted in a case,

18. Brainerd Currie, 'On the Displacement of the Law of the Forum', in: *Selected Essays on the Conflict of Laws*, Durham, N.C., 1963, 3, at 52

19. *See* Currie, *supra* note 18, at 62-65. *But cf.* Thomas G. Guedj, 'The Theory of the Lois de Police, A Functional Trend in Continental Private International Law – A Comparative Analysis with the Modern American Theories', 39 *American Journal of Comparative Law*, 1991, 661 (critical of collapsing European distinctions in undifferentiated interest analysis).

20. *See* Currie, 'Notes on Methods and Objectives in the Conflict of Laws', *supra* note 18, 175, at 178-181.

21. *See id.*, at 180; Currie, 'Married Woman's Contracts: A Study in Conflict-of-Laws', *supra* note 18, 77, at 107-110.

22. *Compare* Currie, *supra* note 20, at 180-184 (only when forum has no interest in applying its own law should it apply foreign law) with David. F. Cavers, *The Choice-of-Law Process*, Ann Arbor, 1965, at 73-102 *passim* (looking to rules that help to accommodate purposes behind both forum and foreign laws).

tends to focus on the remedies sought to vindicate those rights, asking whether interests at stake in the case are served by such remedies.[23]

As Professor Vivant points out, in cases of intellectual property, the sense of territoriality varies depending on where courts may effectuate judicial remedies.[24] On the one hand, a court might limit itself to enjoining infringement inside the forum state to the extent it doubted its ability to police an injunction outside that state's territory. On the other hand, it might well award damages, especially against a party located inside the forum state, even for infringement that party committed outside that state's territory. Vivant acknowledges that, since they have been empowered by the Brussels Convention on jurisdiction, European courts in different countries adhering to this treaty may now cooperate to enforce injunctions in appropriate cases across borders.[25]

Of course, courts can best control the use of works by granting relief on the territory that their agents can police.[26] It nonetheless remains unclear how judicial relief, such as injunctions or damages, will have effect in a digitally networked world, where works can be made virtually present almost everywhere at once. In particular, injunctions may have effects on diversely localized computers that operate as crucial servers in networks either for disseminating the works, or for collecting monies for their delivery, across borders. It falls to the courts to explore such effects by asking: how might choosing this or that law impact on the interests at stake in granting specific remedies in the case at hand?[27]

1.3. RESOLVING OLD DILEMMAS

I do not contend that the shift from geographical space to cyberspace is decisive with regard to the ultimate validity of categorical or functional choice-of-law analysis. No doubt, categorical analysis generated relatively reliable rules for dealing with recurrent cases of conflicts in the tight European geographical space of the nineteenth century. If I now propose to shift to a more functional analysis, it is merely to open up new lines of judicial inquiry into the hard cases increasingly

---

23. *See* Currie, 'The Silver Oar and All That: A Study of the Romero Case', *supra* note 18, 360, at 364-373. *See also* Albert A. Ehrenzweig, 'Characterization in the Conflict of Laws: An Unwelcome Addition to American Doctrine', in: *XXth Century Comparative and Conflicts of Law: Legal Essays in Honor of Hessel E. Yntema*, K.H. Nadelmann, A.T. von Mehren, and J.N. Hazard (eds.), Leyden, 1961, 395 (characterization nothing but interpretation of legal rules, ultimately in terms of their purposes).

24. Michel Vivant, *Juge et loi du brevet*, Paris, 1977, at 201-202.

25. Michel Vivant and Jean Foyer, *Le droit des brevets*, Paris, 1991, 54-56. *But cf.* Heleen Bertrams, 'The Cross-Border Prohibitory Injunction in Dutch Patent Law', 26 *IIC* 618 (1995) (critical analysis of Dutch injunctions prohibiting patent infringement outside the Netherlands).

26. *But cf.* I. Trotter Hardy, 'The Proper Legal Regime for "Cyberspace"', 55 *University of Pittsburgh Law Review* 1993, at 1052-1053 (1994) (questioning sanctions on tortfeasors in global networks).

27. *Cf.* Dieter Stauder, *Patentverletzung im grenzüberschreitenden Wirtschaftsverkehr*, Cologne, 1975, at 182-197 *passim* (weighs interests of patent-granting and patent-free analysis of which border-crossing acts should be enjoined or subject to liability in the former).

arising in the digitally generated cyberspace of the twenty-first century. It is matter of adapting 'old rules to new border-line cases'.[28]

To test this more flexible analysis, turn back to our initial example. Recall that, hypothetically, I digitized and colourized Buster Keaton's classic film work *The General*, loaded it into a database, and put it on-line. Suppose that Keaton's successors in interest sue me in the United States, asking the court to enjoin me from making this work accessible from the United States. I object that copyright law in the United States justifies no such remedy because it no longer protects the work at issue. But end-users in France and Germany can only enjoy the work after interactively ordering it to be transmitted and paying by credit card. On the basis of their acts, it is argued that French and German laws, which still protect the work, should apply to the case.[29]

The court does not have to reinvent the wheel in resolving the conflicts of law in this case. It is true, of course, that European and American courts will take account of conflicts-relevant interests within very different frameworks of analysis.[30] Nonetheless, in adhering to the Berne Convention and the Agreement on Trade-Related Aspects of Intellectual Property Rights (TRIPs), most countries have reached a consensus on the interests that these treaties serve. To start, the Berne Convention, to quote the Preamble of its Paris Act, confirms the common interest in protecting authors' rights 'in as effective and uniform a manner as possible' throughout the Berne Union. The TRIPs Agreement, incorporating Berne provisions, also calls for border-control procedures in the interest of preventing pirates from raiding intellectual property on global markets.[31]

Furthermore, the Berne Convention, specifically article 5(1) in the Paris Act, imposes the principle of national treatment. This principle requires that courts govern copyright claims in Berne-protected works by choosing the law of the Berne country where copyright protection is sought.[32] The difficulty posed by our hypothetical case is that of localizing such protecting countries: it is not self-evident whether protection is sought in the United States, where the film work at issue is stored in a database, or in France or Germany where this work is received. To resolve this difficulty, it must be kept in mind that Berne national treatment

28. Moffatt Hancock, 'Three Approaches to the Choice-of-Law Problem: the Classificatory, the Functional and the Result-Selective', in: *XXth Century Comparative and Conflicts of Law: Legal Essays in Honor of Hessel E. Yntema*, *supra* note 23, 365, at 378.

29. *Cf.* Paul Katzenberger, 'Urheberrechtsfragen der elektronischen Textkommunication', *GRUR Int.* 1983, 895, at 914-917 (transborder broadcasting and network communication subject to distinct choice-of-law analyses, the latter with reference to acts triggering transmissions).

30. *Compare* Swiss *Loi fédérale sur le droit international privé du 18 décembre 1987*, arts. 13 (foreign public laws), 15 (law with 'closest tie' to case), 17 (*ordre public*), 18-19 (laws with mandatory application by virtue of purposes) *with* U.S. *Restatement (Second) of Conflict of Laws*, American Law Institute, 1971, sec. 6(2) ('needs of international systems' considered along with 'policies' of forum, those of 'other interested states', and those 'underlying the particular field of law').

31. *See* Paul Edward Geller, 'Intellectual Property in the Global Marketplace: Impact of TRIPS Dispute Settlements?', 29 *The International Lawyer* 99, at 104-105 (1995).

32. *See* Eugen Ulmer, *Intellectual Property and the Conflict of Laws*, English trans., Deventer, 1978, at 6-14; Sam Ricketson, *The Berne Convention for the protection of literary and artistic works: 1886-1986*, London, 1987, at 193-195.

secures authors' moral stakes in their works such as their reputations, as well as rightholders' economic stakes in media markets for these works, within each Berne country, respectively. At the same time, both Berne and TRIPs provisions that preclude other countries from serving as pirate havens imply the *desiderata* of catching infringing acts in as seamless and coherent a web of remedies and sanctions world-wide as possible.[33]

To localize protecting countries, we then have to ask: where might, most notably, authorial reputations or media markets be threatened by alleged infringing acts? In our hypothetical suit, there is no longer any protection in the United States, while moral claims are protected and threatened in France, as are both moral and economic claims in Germany. Even if suit is brought in the United States, where the film work at issue is stored in a database but not protected, a U.S. court with jurisdiction may apply the laws of France or Germany to protect the work in each of these other countries.[34] For example, the court could issue an order that allowed continuing transmission of the film work in the United States but compelled reprogramming the database so that it could not transmit the work in colourized form to France nor in any form to Germany. Of course, the law of the forum, here the law of the United States where suit is brought, would procedurally govern how such an order is granted and policed. Still, the laws of the protecting countries, in our case, France and Germany, would provide the substantive legal bases for the order.[35]

Suppose that the film work were, like the proverbial cat, let out of the bag, that is, already transmitted across the Atlantic to numerous end-users. The court could still award damages for reputation and markets lost in countries where copyright was still in effect, notably, in our hypothetical case, France and Germany. Other remedies are imaginable: for example, since my network business depends on payment through some transnational credit-card system, the court might make orders regarding my credits in that system attributable to unauthorized uses in each protecting country. Indeed, it could order me not to draw on my credits from Germany until infringement was fully adjudicated.[36]

---

33. *See* Paul Edward Geller, 'International Copyright: An Introduction', at § 3[1][b][ii] in: *International Copyright Law and Practice*, P.E. Geller & M.B. Nimmer (eds.), New York, 1991, vol. 1.

34. *See*, e.g., U.S. decision, *London Film Productions Ltd. v. Intercontinental Communications, Inc.*, 580 F. Supp. 47 (S.D.N.Y. 1984) (court rejects argument that it should not exercise jurisdiction over infringement claims subject to foreign laws because it could not properly apply these laws).

35. *See*, e.g., French decision, *Hersocovici c. Société Karla et Société Krizia*, Trib. gr. instance, Paris, 23 May 1990, *RIDA* 1990, no. 146, 325 (French court issues remedies against infringing use of Magritte picture on sweaters made in Italy under Italian law and sold in France under French law).

36. *Cf.* U.S. decision, *Reebok International, Ltd. v. Marnatech Enterprises, Inc.*, 970 F.2d 552 (9th Cir. 1992) (on basis of preliminary showing of transborder trademark infringement from Mexico to U.S., court freezes alleged infringer's bank account in U.S.).

2. Choosing Law in Cyberspace

This shift from categorical to functional analysis might seem to leave courts adrift in cyberspace, without any doctrinal guidance system. If only to provoke debate, I shall formulate some 'principles of preference' to guide courts in choosing laws in cases arising in the digital environment. Professor Cavers initially contemplated such principles, ostensibly to bring together the best of Savigny's conceptualist heaven and Currie's realist hell. They are to serve as 'guides for decision, leaving ample room for independent judgment to any courts that resorted to them'.[37]

Return to the distinction between geographical space and cyberspace. In geographical space, mass media trace lines of communication that tend to radiate out from active centers of publishing, broadcasting, or cablecasting to passive audiences. In cyberspace, digital media weave lines of communication together in multifarious combinations and permutations between possibly hundreds of millions of nodes. This process results in increasingly dense, interconnected, and far-reaching networks, in which human relationships overlap in novel patterns, thus increasing the chances of conflicts, not only between copyright laws themselves, but between copyright laws and other laws. I shall then consider principles of preference for resolving such conflicts on three levels of law in any global network: privacy, contract, and competition laws.[38]

2.1. PRIVACY RIGHTS VERSUS COPYRIGHT?

The most basic level of law in networks is that of privacy. Consider another variation on our hypothetical case of Keaton's classic film work. Suppose that end-users, as dilettante artists, digitally reprocess pieces of the film work into multimedia works that they exchange over the network. Should a court enjoin such possibly private reprocessing or exchanges of copyright materials?

Privacy rights entitle individuals to control how their expression is communicated and who may access it.[39] Like common-law copyright and the moral right of divulgation, they allow creators to test their experiments against feed-back from close colleagues, without fear of premature disclosure. That is, even after limited disclosure from the originator of a message to a controlled audience, privacy rights would preclude further release to the public at large without the originator's consent. In cases of conflict, privacy has priority over copyright, since it is a basic human right intimately bound up with freedom of expression. I therefore start with

37. Cavers, *supra* note 22, at 136.

38. Geller, *supra* note 2, at 60.

39. *See generally* Stefano Rodotà, 'Protecting Informational Privacy: Trends and Problems', in: *Information Law towards the 21st Century*, W.F. Korthals Altes, E.J. Dommering, P.B. Hugenholtz & J.J.C. Kabel (eds.), Deventer, 1992, 261, at 262-263 (privacy being redefined with 'new stress on the aspect of circulation and control').

a principle of preference for laws favouring privacy, and disfavouring its waiver, in global networks.[40]

To apply this principle, we have to distinguish between the private leakage and the public haemorrhaging of copyright materials.[41] Privacy tends to shield individuals who might leak the works of others by privately copying and retransmitting them to a small number of third parties. But a principle of preference favouring privacy would not protect pirates who haemorrhage works by making them accessible to the public at large on networks, usually but not necessarily for profit. Of course, authors and media enterprises can use technological fences, to use Professor Mackaay's suggestive term, to reduce both leakage and haemorrhaging on the public marketplace.[42] They can weave data-headers into digital copies, encrypt transmissions of works, or arm terminals with copy-control and use-monitoring systems. Such measures identify unauthorized copies, condition enjoyment of a work on crediting the right-holder's account, or otherwise control uses.[43]

Suppose that a media enterprise encrypts its works or valuable data. The principle favouring privacy would disfavour any waiver of this right to control communication. By the same token, this principle could provide a basis for relief against pirates marketing decoders that interfere with such control. An encrypted transmission would be treated like a sealed envelope in the post, even one containing a widely known publication. That is, our principle of preference supports the presumption that all communications within global networks are confidential.[44] It remains to be seen to what extent the privacy rights of individual authors can inure to the benefit of their contractual transferees, whose interests in confidentiality do not have the same personal character as that of the authors.

---

40. *See* Universal Declaration of Human Rights, art. 12; International Covenant on Civil and Political Rights, art. 17; European Convention on Human Rights and Fundamental Freedoms, art. 8. *Cf.* Ysolde Gendreau, *La protection des photographies en droit d'auteur français, américain, brittanique et canadian*, Paris, 1994, at 285-303 *passim* (comparative analysis of case laws largely subordinating copyright in photographs to privacy rights of persons photographed or of owners of things photographed).

41. *See* Pamela Samuelson, 'Copyright and Digital Libraries', *Communications of the ACM*, April 1995, vol. 38, no. 3, 15, at 21. Cf. U.S. decision. *United States v. LaMacchia*, 871 F. Supp. 535, 544-545 (D.Mass. 1994) (distinguishing single copying by 'home computer users' from 'willful, multiple infringements').

42. Ejan Mackaay, 'The Economics of Property Rights on the Internet', elsewhere in this book, 13-25 *passim*. *See also* Charles Clark, 'The Answer to the Machine is in the Machine', elsewhere in this book, 139-145 (computer-automated methods of collecting copyright revenues on subscription and per-use bases).

43. *See* Branko Gerovac and Richard J. Solomon, 'Protect revenues, not bits: identify your intellectual property', in: *Technological Strategies for Protecting Intellectual Property in the Networked Multimedia Environment* (Interactive Multimedia Association), 1994, vol. 1, 49; Ryoichi and Masaji Kawahara, 'Superdistribution: The Concept and Architecture', *The Transactions of the IEICE* (Special Issue on Cryptography and Information Security), 1990, vol. E73, no. 7, 1133.

44. *But cf.* U.K. decision, *BBC Enterprises Ltd. v. Hi-Tech Xtravision Ltd.* (Chancery Division), [1992] 9 R.P.C. 167, at 183, *reversed* (Court of Appeals), *id.*, at 183-193, *reversal affirmed* (House of Lords), *id.*, at 194-203 (privacy argument raised, considered skeptically by lower court in *obiter dictum*, but not ruled upon by higher courts).

2.2. CONTRACTS VERSUS COPYRIGHT?

Turn to the middle level of law in networks, where parties control the flow of messages by contract. Suppose that artists, from all over the world, collaborate over the global network to create their multimedia works and license them to a media enterprise for use in video games. What laws should apply to govern the contracts allocating copyrights among the authors or between them and the media enterprise?

Until now, authors have most often collaborated among themselves, or worked for media enterprises, in their home countries. Given a conflict of laws, a court would normally apply that home country's copyright-contract rules only to its own local authors and media enterprises in local endeavours.[45] Courts might then rightly hesitate to apply mandatory rules, specifically fashioned for copyright contracts in only one locality, to agreements stretched across any global network. In effect, national laws vary considerably in their rules governing, *inter alia*, the following issues. In whom does copyright initially vest? Should mandatory copyright-contract rules supersede the actual agreements of parties? What presumptions, if any, should apply to points on which agreements are silent? I shall propose related principles of preference to help resolve resulting conflicts of laws on these points.[46]

The issue of the first owner of copyright is by far the most difficult. The laws of different countries often initially vest copyright quite differently in natural persons or corporate enterprises. In addition, the rules governing who first owns copyright often turn on characterizing the work in question; for example, while multimedia works might resemble collective, audiovisual, or software-related works, they do not consistently fall into any one of these categories.[47] There are three possible solutions to the conflicts of law that might well arise on this point: first, apply the law of the country of origin of the work; second, apply the law of the country of ultimate use of the work, that is, where protection is sought; third, presume that rights vest in the natural persons who actually create the work, no matter where they do so.[48] The first and second solutions, being territorial in the strict geographic sense, may prove difficult to apply in many cases arising in any global network, leaving the third solution as the default position for a principle of preference in cyberspace.[49]

---

45. *See*, e.g. French decision, *Anna Bragance c. Michel de Grèce*, Cour d'appel Paris, 1e ch., 1 February 1989, *RIDA* 1989, no. 142, 301 (court declines to apply French copyright-contract law to agreement negotiated to ghostwrite book in United States, with a clause selecting U.S. law to govern its terms).

46. *See generally* Ulmer, *supra* note 32, at 36-54 (considering solutions of copyright-contract conflicts in anticipation of 1980 Rome Convention on the law applicable to contractual obligations).

47. *See* Bernard Edelman, 'L'oeuvre multimédia, un essai de qualification', *Recueil Dalloz Sirey*, 1995, 15e cahier, chronique, 109.

48. *See generally* Ginsburg, *supra* note 4, 328-329, 331-332 (review of positions); *see also* Geller, *supra* note 33, at §§ 4[2][a][i] and 6[3][a] (critical analysis).

49. *Cf.* Adolf Dietz, 'The Concept of Author under the Berne Convention', *RIDA* 1993, no. 152, 2 (position in favor of vesting rights in human creators is consistent with Berne principles). *But cf.*

The issues regarding contracts between authors and enterprises are somewhat easier. The interests that have motivated national rules concerning local author-enterprise relationships no longer coherently come into play for a double reason. Not only do the digital media make cultural production increasingly transnational, but, as Professor Goldstein has predicted, these media will transform author-enterprise relations, as well as those among creators themselves.[50] As a result, there will less frequently be reason to apply contract rules fashioned for purely local relationships, and courts will find themselves thrown back to the default principle of preference for choosing law to govern contracts in general: freedom of contract.[51] Freedom of contract would assure authors and media enterprises of the chance to elaborate consensual relations appropriate to networks. In our example, if the artists can collaborate over the net in creating works, they can make their deals there too.[52]

A rather straightforward presumption seems appropriate to copyright contracts in global networks. If a contract is silent on specific points, the parties have not exercised their freedom to make a deal on these points. In global networks, contracts will often be concluded between relative strangers, outside local customs and prior dealings. By the same token, in such networks, third parties will often rely only on the face of contracts, not knowing their original contexts or purposes. Another principle of preference could favour presumptions of restrictive construction: if the terms of a contract do not specify a right, that right is not transferred – in short, what you see of the contract on screen is what you get. Adapted to commerce on global networks, this principle of preference could well govern all transfers along the chain of title.[53]

2.3. COMPETITION LAW VERSUS COPYRIGHT?

At the top level, networks hopefully form an open but orderly marketplace. Copyright law maintains order inside the market for information by preventing

---

Jacqueline M.B. Seignette, *Challenges to the Creator Doctrine: Authorship, copyright ownership and the exploitation of creative works in the Netherlands, Germany and the United States*, Deventer, 1994, chs. 3-6 (policies and principles in favor of initial vesting of rights in possibly corporate producers).

50. *See* Paul Goldstein, *Copyright's Highway: The Law and Lore of Copyright from Gutenberg to the Celestial Jukebox*, New York, 1994, at 234-236. *See also* P.B. Hugenholtz, 'Adapting Copyright to the Information Superhighway', elsewhere in this book, at 84 (new roles for authors, other information producers, publishers, users, etc., in global networks).

51. *See* Albert A. Ehrenzweig and Erik Jayme, *Private International Law*, Leyden, 1977, vol. 3, 15-19. *But cf.* Loussouarn & Bourel, *supra* note 10, at 262-270 (§§ 176-178) (different approaches to freedom of contract).

52. *Cf.* Hardy, *supra* note 26, at 1028-1036 *passim* (ease of contractually resolving legal issues in networks).

53. *But cf.* André Lucas, *Traité de la propriété littéraire & artistique*, Paris, 1994, at 426-429; Paul Katzenberger, 'Anwendungsbereich', in: *Urheberrecht. Kommentar*, G. Schricker (ed.), Munich, 1987, at 1254-1255 (rules of restrictive construction developed to protect authors as weaker parties to copyright contracts).

creative works from being pirated. Copyright law avoids conflicts with law governing competition on the marketplace, especially antitrust law, when it excludes ideas and raw data from protection and exempts such uses as quotation, criticism, or parody. Professor Reichman has asked: could media enterprises in global networks impose contracts on end-users that override such copyright limitations to endanger competition in the marketplace?[54]

In the case of Keaton's classic film work, suppose that I contractually prohibit users from retransmitting even black-and-white pieces of my digitally colourized version. By contrast, consider as well a case in which an enterprise conditions access to its geophysical statistics on the contractual promise not to retransmit even small sets of data for research purposes.[55] In such cases, courts could face manifold conflicts of laws on a wide variety of issues: for example, what law of intellectual property draws the line between protected and public-domain materials? Ultimately, in cases where claimants are unique sources of the information at issue, courts would have to choose competition laws to determine whether contracts governing access to the information are invalid as adhesive or abusive of dominant market positions. Any principle of preference helpful in resolving such conflicts of laws should take account of interests common to copyright and competition laws. Both laws seek to enhance the variety of works accessible in the marketplace, that is, to optimize data flow there.[56]

It is unfortunately not clear how this principle might apply to concrete cases. In the spectrum of cases in question, enterprises might have invested heavily in organizing digitally exact versions of creative works or systematic bodies of scientific data. What results if, among the laws of many states that a global network covers, a court chooses law to invalidate contractual terms imposed by an enterprise which, from a dominant market position, sought to monopolize information?[57] Consistently with the principle of preference for law enhancing the variety of works made accessible, such a choice of law might suffice to liberate the flow of the particular works or data at issue in our examples. However, this precedent, weakening contractual leverage, might inhibit enterprises from releasing

54. *See* J.H. Reichman, 'Electronic Information Tools – The Outer Edge of World Intellectual Property Law', 24 *IIC* 446, at 461-467 (1993).

55. *Cf.* U.S. decision, *American Geophysical Union v. Texaco, Inc.*, 802 F. Supp. 1 (S.D.N.Y. 1992), *affirmed* 37 F. 3d 881 (2d Cir. 1994) (prohibiting commercial enterprise from copying learned journals for research use).

56. *Compare* Paul Edward Geller, 'Toward an Overriding Norm in Copyright: Sign Wealth', *RIDA* 1994, no. 159, 2, at 42-43 (copyright criteria of enhancing variety of, and access to, works) *with* Ejan Mackaay, 'An Economic View of Information Law', in: *Information Law towards the 21st Century, supra* note 39, 43, at 56-58 (competition criteria for intellectual property look to enhancing data flows).

57. *Compare* U.S. decision, *Vault Corporation v. Quaid Software Limited*, 847 F. 2d 255, 267-270 (5th Cir. 1988) (license precluding certain uses of works struck down as adhesive, and state law providing a basis for license clause preempted by federal law, leaving copyright law dispositive) *and* E.C. decision *RTE, ITP v. Magill TV Guide Ltd.*, E.C. Court of Justice, 6 April 1995, Joint Cases C-241/91P and C-242/91P, [1995] E.C.R. I-743 (refusal to license data found abusive of dominant market position, leaving duty to offer license of data on reasonable terms).

their information freely in global networks. It is therefore not clear that it would optimize data flow in the marketplace as a whole.[58]

Consider a rather different case: an enterprise owns a key system in a network, either hardware like cables and switches or software like that running popular electronic bulletin boards. There is a concern that such an enterprise might abuse its dominant market position by preventing third parties from making their own works available on the network, thereby limiting copyright content. In this context, the following issue arises: whose law governs whether such an enterprise is liable for torts, including copyright infringement, if its system conveys materials introduced by third parties?[59] Again, in line with the principle of preference for laws enhancing variety and access, it has been argued that rules exempting such enterprises from vicarious liability if they become common carriers could encourage them to open networks to third parties. This argument, however, does not fully take account of the possibility that such enterprises might choose, for a variety of reasons, to carry only materials that they have selected and license or own.[60]

In all these cases, the relevant market will tend to be world-wide. Thus choosing the law of any one state as the site of the relevant market will not be feasible. It would be even more arbitrary to choose the law of the jurisdiction where the enterprise in question is headquartered. It takes no gift of prophecy to anticipate that, even more than applying copyright law, the application of competition law, especially antitrust law, to global networks will generate hard, borderline cases. For that reason, cases in which both laws apply together will prove most frustrating for any attempt to confine them within the established categories of choice-of-law analysis. The courts may then best ask how their choices might function to serve the hopefully converging policies of copyright and competition laws.[61]

---

58. *Cf.* Egbert Dommering, 'Information Law and the Themes of this Book', in: *Information Law towards the 21st Century, supra* note 39, 3, at 4-5 (need to balance exclusivity and free flow); Mackaay, *supra* note 56, at 54-61 *passim* (need to make information a transferable commodity in order to facilitate data flow on market).

59. *Compare* U.S. decisions: *Cubby, Inc. v. Compuserve, Inc.*, 776 F. Supp. 135, 139-140, 142-143 (S.D.N.Y. 1991) (electronic bulletin board not liable for defamation if it posts messages without inspecting or editing them); *Playboy Enterprises, Inc. v. Frena*, 839 F. Supp. 1552, 1555-1559 (M.D. Fla. 1993); *Sega Enterprises v. Maphia*, 857 F. Supp. 679, 682-688 (N.D. Cal. 1994) (electronic bulletin boards infringe copyright in making works publicly accessible for downloading on subscribers' commands).

60. *Compare* Niva Elkin-Koren, 'Copyright and Social Dialogue on the Information Superhighway: The Case Against Copyright Liability of Bulletin Board Operators', 13 *Cardozo Arts & Entertainment Law Journal* 345, at 405-410 (1995) (arguing against liability because it might hamper information flow through such intermediaries as bulletin boards) *with* Hardy, *supra* note 26, at 1002-1008, 1041-1048 (difficult to decide on general liability rule for diverse carriers on network).

61. *But cf.* Hans Ullrich, 'TRIPS: Adequate Protection, Inadequate Trade, Adequate Competition Policy', 4 *Pacific Rim Law Journal and Policy Journal* 153, at 196 (1995) ('antitrust is by no means bound to take intellectual property-based territorial divisions as sacrosanct').

3. Berne Solutions

To this point I have considered only judicial options. At most, I have invoked the Berne Convention as a text implementing governmental interests that might guide the courts in resolving conflicts of laws. I can now almost hear the question asked *sotto voce*: how might this chief instrument of international copyright be formulated to assure the reliable choice of law in the digital environment?

It is crucial, in responding to this question, to distinguish between interim and definitive solutions. A Berne protocol could effectuate interim solutions by interpreting already existing Berne provisions, notably those of the Paris Act, to facilitate applying them in a digitally networked world. Only a full Berne revision could bring a definitive solution by establishing sufficiently uniform minimum rights, enforceable in all Berne countries, so that there would be no more true conflicts between the copyright laws of these countries. Here I shall largely stay within the horizon of a possible interim solution, but not without at moments trying to look over that horizon toward a more definitive solution.

3.1. OLD RIGHTS FOR NEW NETWORKS

Since the eighteenth century, rights have been distinguished according to media. The seminal copyright laws recognized reproduction rights with regard to book publishing and public-performance rights with regard to live theatre. During this century, we have responded to new media by adding minimum rights to the Berne Convention, for example, to control sound recording, broad- and cable-casting, and the cinema; now, at the threshold of a new century, digital technology is consolidating all prior media while globalizing them.[62] In response to this historical challenge, any solution would have to begin to consolidate already existing Berne rights hitherto recognized piece-meal in the Convention. In this it would follow the lead of article 9 of the Paris Act which explicated the reproduction right already implicit in prior Berne Acts.[63]

Dr. Ficsor points out that, if considered separately and out of context, each of the presently formulated Berne rights does not stretch across the full range of multimedia works that digitization makes possible.[64] In the Paris Act of the Berne Convention, for example, article 11 concerns dramatic and musical works and article 14 concerns cinematographic works, while article 2 lists categories of works but not multimedia works that fall into many categories at once. One solution would lie in extending any distinct Berne right to any multimedia work that displayed features of the categories for which the right was fashioned, say, article

62. *See* Paul Edward Geller, 'New Dynamics in International Copyright', 16 *Columbia-VLA Journal of Law & Arts* 461, at 464-470 (1993).

63. *See* Ricketson, *supra* note 32, at 369-370; Wilhelm Nordemann, Kai Vinck & Paul W. Hertin, *Internationales Urheberrecht und Leistungsschutzrecht. Kommentar*, Duesseldorf, 1977, at 79-80.

64. Mihály Ficsor, 'Towards a Global Solution: The Berne Protocol and the "New Instrument"', elsewhere in this book, 111-137.

11 to multimedia works including dramatic or musical materials even if these works did not fall exclusively into these categories. Another solution would be to assimilate multimedia works to cinematographic works, much as article 10(1) of the TRIPs Agreement codifies the consensus that computer programs are enough like literary works to warrant full Berne coverage. This interpretation would make multimedia works, even those largely composed of text, subject to the full range of Berne rights made available in article 14(1) of the Paris Act.[65]

Dr. Ficsor has proposed 'an umbrella-type provision' for a Berne protocol which would leave 'the legal qualification', that is, the characterization of rights covered in the provision, 'to legislation'.[66] Thus, while obligated to protect copyright in global networks, Berne countries would be free to determine whether such rights as reproduction, public performance, communication to the public, or distribution, or any combination of such rights, should come into play in specific cases. Necessarily, to formulate the umbrella provision, so that it encompassed any and all such rights, Berne drafters would have to resort to abstract, open-ended notions such as 'making works available to the public', whether in material of immaterial forms, or 'network dissemination'. Courts could, in turn, only give such notions concrete meaning by interpreting them to require adequate means of redress relative to unauthorized uses in global networks that a Berne protocol might, but need not, specify with more or less precision. This proposal has the advantage of side-stepping current and, to my mind, rather scholastic debates about the 'nature' or 'essence' of rights appropriate to enabling authors and their successors in interest to control such network dissemination. These debates nonetheless seem inevitable as long as diverse legal cultures conceptualize rights differently.[67]

Thus, following the conflicts perspective I proposed above, this 'umbrella' Berne provision should help us focus, not merely on abstract rights, but on concrete remedies.[68] It remains to be seen what might constitute adequate means of redress relative to acts of disseminating works within networks and how far they should be extended. Of course, such remedies would include civil damages and injunctions, but it may be necessary to make explicit that they may apply to both primary and secondary acts of infringement and include criminal sanctions as well. For example, the right to control public communication, most notably under article 11*bis* of the Paris Act of the Berne Convention, and *a fortiori* under any more-inclusive right to control network dissemination, should allow the rightholder to control the act of communication or dissemination from beginning to end. In particular, there should be no doubt that remedies are required, not only against

65. *See* Nordemann, Vinck and Hertin, *supra* note 63, at 109-110.

66. Mihály Ficsor, 'International Harmonization of Copyright and Neighboring Rights', in: *WIPO Worldwide Symposium on Copyright in the Global Information Infrastructure*, Mexico City, 22-24 May 1995, Geneva, 1995, 369, at 376-377.

67. *Compare* Hugenholtz, *supra* note 50, at 86-87, 89-90, 101 (proposing, from a European perspective, a variant of the public-communication right for such networks); Elkin-Koren, *supra* note 60, at 380-390 (critique, from U.S. perspective, of distinctions between rights to apply to such networks).

68. *See supra* §1.

primary acts of commencing network delivery of a work without authorization, but also against secondary acts intended to circumvent the right-holders' intervening control of such delivery, such as acts of selling unauthorized devices to interfere with encryption or use-monitoring systems.[69]

3.2. THE PROBLEM OF LIMITING NETWORK RIGHTS

Even if existing minimum Berne rights, once appropriately consolidated, might respond to the digital environment, existing Berne exceptions and limitations pose special difficulties. For example, the exceptions to the Berne right of reproduction are vague and open-ended, while the Berne right of public communication by broadcasting or cable transmission may be made subject to variable conditions, including legal licenses in appropriate cases.[70] In national and European Community laws, the right of distribution is variably subject to the first-sale doctrine or exhaustion, and it is not clear whether or at what point in network dissemination this right or limitation should come into play.[71]

As long as Berne countries are free to characterize rights at different phases of network dissemination, their respective legal systems and cultures will push their law-makers to limit these rights, or provide exceptions to them, differently.[72] There seems to be little choice, at this juncture in Berne harmonization, but to let law-makers follow their respective methodologies of characterizing rights and, accordingly, of conditioning the scope of these rights. For example, while legislators in Europe might limit some rights definitionally by applying them only to 'public' communication or access, judges in the United States might experiment with the exception of 'fair use' for all rights on the network.[73] That said, overriding interests specific to international copyright, as well as principles of preference

69. *See*, e.g., North American Free Trade Agreement, art. 1707 (providing for civil and criminal measures against commerce in pirate decoders of satellite-relayed telecasts). Such a provision would clarify an issue that the courts have not fully understood. *See*, e.g. Swiss decision, *Canal Plus c. GE*, Order of 18 December 1986, Trib. cantonal, Vaud, *Rev. Suisse de la prop. industrielle et du droit d'auteur*, 1987, 257, at 262 (refusing to enjoin sales of pirate decoders for failure to characterize such sales as acts of 'public communication').

70. *See generally* Nordemann, Vinck & Hertin, *supra* note 63, at 80-81 (comments to Berne, art. 9: exceptions to reproduction right at best provisional), 95-97 (comments to Berne, art. 11*bis*: legal license limiting broadcast right may not usurp market operation), 110 (comments to Berne, art. 14: rights in cinematographic works, including distribution right, limited like corresponding minimum rights that Berne sets out elsewhere).

71. *See generally* Hugenholtz, *supra* note 50, 95-98 (also pointing out occasional application of exhaustion doctrine to the rights of public communication).

72. *See generally* Alain Strowel, *Droit d'auteur et copyright: Divergences et convergences*, Brussels and Paris, 1993, at 144-149, 290-291 (differences in legislative and judicial techniques, as between Anglo-American and Continental European legal systems, for determining the scope of copyright).

73. *Compare* Hugenholtz, *supra* note 50, at 101 (more elegant to delimit the scope of network rights definitionally to avoid interference with legitimate end-users' rights than to carve out miscellaneous exceptions) *with* Elkin-Korin, *supra* note 60, at 369-371 (critical analysis of exception of fair use as applied to uploading and downloading works by end-users on network).

relating copyright to other general fields of law, may be invoked to guide such developing limitations and exceptions into convergent paths.

Consider, on the one hand, the distinction between public and private. Lawmakers need only define the 'public' to the point necessary to establish the media acts over which copyright law itself gives rightholders exclusive control. For example, in the case of a hotel operator who routes work-carrying transmissions to clients in hotel rooms, the act of routing may be subject to copyright because the clients constitute a public, but that characterization in no way renders their enjoyment in their rooms less private.[74] If there is any need for copyright legislators to consider what lies on the other side of the threshold of the public marketplace, it is only to avoid intrusions into the privacy of either the author creating works or the ultimate end-user enjoying works. Most notably, in contemplating criminal sanctions, it is necessary to focus on commerce intended to circumvent technological self-help measures, thus attacking electronic piracy in the public marketplace rather than at the level of private end-users. Thus the principle of preference favouring privacy in global networks will be respected.[75]

Consider, on the other hand, distinctions between protected expression and unprotected ideas or facts, as well as doctrines of fair dealing or use and of free utilization. This family of limitations and exceptions allows prior works to be used in new works, for example, to critique prior works, to treat them historically, or to transform them, as in parodies. Judges have developed these conditions on the scope of prior authors' copyrights to avoid imposing copyright remedies that would restrict new authors' freedom of expression by preventing the latter authors from elaborating materials from prior works while creating new ones.[76] In effect, judges best balance the claims of prior and new authors to copyright and freedom of expression, respectively, by considering the creative options singularly at stake in the works at issue on a case-by-case basis. Such cases will become more frequent with the advent of digital media that facilitate the retrieval of prior works across global networks and their reworking into newer works.[77] Thus, judges will need to retain full latitude to apply the idea-expression distinction and the exceptions of fair dealing or use or of free utilization. This latitude is also consistent with the principle of preference for laws favouring the free flow of information.[78]

In any event, article 13 of the TRIPs Agreement will prohibit limitations or exceptions prejudicial to the 'normal exploitation of the work' or the 'legitimate interests of the rightholder'. Admittedly, these criteria, drawn from the Berne provision on the reproduction right, are not closely tailored to other Berne rights that might apply in global networks.[79] Nonetheless, they preclude any arbitrary characterization of a right for the purposes of instituting a limitation or exception

---

74. *See* Bernard Edelman, 'La télédistribution dans les chambres d'hôtel', *Recueil Dalloz Sirey*, 1994, 27e Cahier, Chronique, 209.

75. *See supra* §2.1

76. *See* Geller, *supra* note 56, at 89-93; Ivan Cherpillod, *L'objet du droit d'auteur*, Lausanne, 1985, at 152-171.

77. *See* Geller, *supra* note 38, at 63-66.

78. *See supra* §2.3.

79. *Cf.* Geller, *supra* note 31, at 112-113 (critical reading of article 13 of TRIPs Agreement).

that would make little economic sense for rightholders. For example, law-makers could not plausibly characterize network dissemination as broadcasting or cable transmission to justify imposing legal licenses under article 11*bis*(2) of the Berne Convention.[80] In digital networks, especially in the on-demand delivery of works, end-users can be individually and interactively addressed, so that their reception of works may be easily licensed by contract. There is thus no economically justifiable reason for recourse to compulsory royalty rates, since there need be no 'absence of agreement' as required by article 11*bis*(2). Legal licenses would therefore contravene normal modes of network exploitation, to which the principle of preference favouring freedom of contract optimally applies.[81]

3.3. BACK TO CONFLICTS OF LAW

Any umbrella solution would then allow Berne countries some discretion in fashioning rights with regard to network dissemination. It accordingly would not yet achieve the utopia of a Berne revision that would standardize copyright laws internationally and thus avoid true conflicts between such laws. In any event, persisting variations in rights from country to country will continue to give rise to cases in which judges will confront possible conflicts between national copyright laws. Berne national treatment will then continue to require the choice of the law of the country where protection is sought.

Recall my argument that such a protecting country is best localized where judicial remedies have effect.[82] Nonetheless, in a complex case of transborder infringement, it might not be obvious in which country or countries, out of a number of possible protecting countries, specific remedies take effect. In that event, I submit, the goal set out in the Berne Preamble, namely protecting authors' rights 'in as effective and uniform a manner as possible', suggests the following principle of preference: apply the law best protecting the work at issue. For example, think back to our hypothetical case of Keaton's classic film work *The General*: an injunction to prevent access to the work would have effect both in United States, where it is transmitted from a database but not protected, and in France and Germany, where it is ultimately enjoyed and still protected. The copyright laws of France and Germany would then apply, but only to support injunctions against, and damages for, reception in these countries.[83]

On the analogy of satellite broadcasts, the European Commission has proposed to have the law of 'the country of origin', more precisely the country of transmission, applied at least to trans-Community network dissemination.[84]

---

80. *See also* Thomas Dreier, 'The Cable and Satellite Analogy', elsewhere in this book, at 58-61 (critique of analogy with cable retransmission in this regard).

81. *See supra* §2.2.

82. *See supra* §1.3.

83. *See generally* Geller, *supra* note 33, at §3[1][b][iii] (regarding choice of law and remedies in cases of transborder telecommunication).

84. *See* European Commission, *Green Paper: Copyright and Related Rights in the Information Society*, Luxembourg, E.U. Publ., 1995 at 41-42. *But cf.* German decision, Landgericht Stuttgart,

Factually, however, the analogy is far from convincing: while any broadcaster alone decides whether to transmit a work via satellite from any one country, end-users interactively trigger on-demand transmissions of works through any network, and they may do so from any number of countries at once in a network. There is also no necessary analogy between the fact that the broadcast via satellite originates from a studio or antenna fixed in a specific country and the fact that on-demand transmissions through any network take place from some computer controlling a database:[85] that computer, the so-called server, can be quite portable, or itself networked, across any number of countries in the network. Most importantly, legally, any rule tied to any country of origin or origination, for example, the country where the transmitting entity has business headquarters or where it organizes the transmission, would prompt pirates to establish their headquarters or 'to upload [works] from the least protective country possible' as long as countries differed in their levels of protection.[86]

The European Commission in turn asks: if a primary rule dictating the choice of the law of some 'country of origin' raises any difficulty, then why not devise a secondary 'safeguard' rule to apply the law of some other country to obviate that difficulty?[87] This manoeuvre is much like that of the Ptolemaic astronomers who compounded their primary hypotheses of formally perfect heliocentric circles with endless secondary hypotheses of epicentric circles on circles in order to fit their empirical observations. The difficulties of any primary rule, tying the choice of law to any single connecting factor fixed in geographical space, would only be compounded by new difficulties raised by secondary rules multiplying alternative factors of the same type. As a result, this manoeuvre would undercut any argument for the legal certainty of any such formally simple choice-of-law rule by creating a potentially complex set of exceptions that could swallow up the rule itself. Fixing on any single connecting factor cannot lead to legal certainty in cyberspace for the simple reason that it ignores the ultimately global scope of network exploitation covering many countries at once.[88]

Indeed, the very notion of 'a country of origin' is but an outmoded vestige of the last century. As defined by the Berne Convention, this notion has already become unworkable because of changes in its definition in the course of Berne revisions, as well as in national copyright terms.[89] Conceived on the paradigm of authorship and publication involving hard copies that can be localized geographically, this notion becomes misleading in the digital environment where

---

21 April 1994, *Zeitschrift für Urheber- und Medienrecht*, 1995, no. 1, 58 (Swiss broadcast relayed by satellite into Germany: court applies German law).

85. *Cf.* Dreier, *supra* note 80, at 63 (uncertainty of localizing infringing 'reproductions' in network, although this author seems to assume that any initial 'storage acts' necessarily 'only take place within one jurisdiction').

86. Ginsburg, *supra* note 4, at 322-323. *See also* Dreier, *supra* note 80, at 63 (difficulty of following satellite analogy absent harmonized laws).

87. *See, e.g.*, European Commission, *supra* note 84, at 42 (proposing safeguard rule for transmissions coming from outside the Community).

88. *But see* Ginsburg, *supra* note 4, at 337-338 (proposing complex system of alternative choice-of-law rules).

89. *See* Ricketson, *supra* note 32, at 210-219.

creation and dissemination can take place across cyberspace all at once. For example, if the country of origin is determined by the nationality of the author, where is this country when a team of authors from the four corners of the world create a work by collaborating over a global network? If it is determined by first publication, where is the country of origin when a work is first disseminated instantaneously in a hundred countries at once through a global network? Fortunately, Professor Ulmer prepared the way in the Paris Act for amputating this problematic notion from the Berne system.[90]

As explained above, Berne national treatment entails the choice-of-law rule applying the laws applicable in countries where infringement takes place.[91] It has been proposed here to consider these protecting countries as those where means of redress for infringement take effect. Thus construed, this rule will provide certainty to authors and their successors, for the simple reason that it focuses on the actual markets over which copyright is to give them control. Of course, media enterprises will need more complex contracts to assure themselves of rights for markets that, because of more powerful media, span more and more countries at once. Similarly, courts will eventually have to take account of a greater variety of laws in adjudicating cases of transborder infringement within global networks. The principle of preference proposed here, that is, the presumptive application of the most protective law, should hopefully facilitate this task. It could allow the plaintiff to sue on the basis of that law, placing the burden on the defendant of showing what other laws should apply.[92]

Conclusion

In the nineteenth century, there was a movement to institute a 'universal law of copyright (..) [in] a single code, binding throughout the world.'[93] In the twentieth century, Berne revisions have incrementally approached this utopia by compelling Berne countries to assure increasingly broader and stronger minimum rights. Media progress, which largely stimulated this revision process, is now digitally networking the world and, inexorably, necessitating still-more comprehensive minimum rights.[94]

I have here addressed the interim task of resolving conflicts of laws that will continue to arise as copyright law is harmonized, but not yet standardized, world-wide. Choice-of-law analysis has traditionally led courts to look to the territorial situs of the acts that copyright law theoretically entitles authors and their successors to control. However, in the shift from geographical space to cyberspace,

---

90. *See* Eugen Ulmer, 'Points de rattachement et pays d'origine dans le système de la Convention de Berne', 36 *Nordiskt Immateriellt Rättsskydd* 208 (1967).

91. *See supra* §1.3.

92. *Cf.* Berne Convention, art. 15 (codifying presumptions allowing plaintiffs named as authors or publishers to sue absent proof by defendants that they are not entitled to do so).

93. William Briggs, *The Law of International Copyright*, London, 1906, at 162.

94. *See* Geller, *supra* note 2, at 68-69.

I have argued, judges may better apply the laws in effect on the territories where remedies, in practice, can most adequately redress the violation of rights.

I have also made an interim proposal for declaratory Berne provisions. They should assure adequate means of redress for copyright throughout global networks pending a full Berne revision. They should also be coupled with a principle of preference that would apply the most protective copyright law providing a basis for such remedies in any given case absent any showing to the contrary. Whether courts follow this principle on the basis of treaty language or as a matter of judicial policy, it would lead them to inquire into rights most appropriate for protecting authors' claims in a digitally networked world. In any event, as default law-makers, judges will inevitably be the first to face what Dr. Boytha called the 'core problem' of international copyright: 'the dissolution of territoriality'.[95]

The test of these interim measures is whether they facilitate progress toward a full Berne revision. To start, they should cut short the squabbles resulting from the copyright provincialism that leads representatives of diverse legal cultures to insist on universalizing merely local solutions. Further, they should assuage the legitimate fears of media enterprises that, to use Professor Dommering's apt phrase, their copyrights will be 'washed away through the electronic sieve', that is, global networks.[96] Finally, they should give law-makers time to experiment on national levels with rights and remedies responsive to digital media.[97] At the same time, we will have the chance to rethink international copyright coherently for a digitally networked world.

95. György Boytha, 'Fragen der Entstehung des internationalen Urheberrechts', in: *Woher kommt das Urheberrecht und wohin geht es?*, Robert Dittrich (ed.), Vienna, 1988, 182.

96. Egbert J. Dommering, 'Copyright Being Washed Away Through the Electronic Sieve', elsewhere in this book, 1-11 *passim*.

97. *See*, e.g., Report (White Paper) of the Working Group on Intellectual Property Rights, *Intellectual Property and the National Information Infrastructure*, Washington D.C., 1995, at 211-236 (proposals to amend U.S. Copyright Act).

Copyright Exemptions Old and New: Learning from Old Media Experiences

*Dirk J.G. Visser**

> 'Developments in technology and society have come to the point where the purchase of the (..) equipment is within reach of large sections of the population. We see no grounds for a negative appreciation of this development as such. To many people the equipment would lose all attraction, if they were not permitted to reproduce today's artistic repertoire for their own personal use. A prohibition on such reproduction appears to us to be too drastic. Moreover, as experience in Germany has shown, the effective control of the observing of this prohibition, will present great practical problems. Proof of infringement can only be found through investigation of activities that usually go on inside the domestic circle, which in our opinion should not be encouraged'.[1]

These remarks were made by the Dutch Government during the discussion of the bill which changed the Dutch Copyright Act in 1972 in relation to audio tape recording equipment. In 1996 much of this seems to apply to PCs, modems and scanners. We do not seem prepared to prohibit them (politically this would be very unrealistic), and as a consequence we cannot expect their use to be prohibited either.

In this article I will look at some experiences of 'traditional' audio and video home copying and of (traditional) library privileges.

1. Home Copying

The above mentioned experience in Germany followed the famous home taping decision[2] of the German Supreme Court in 1955 which stated that:

> 'There is no general principle in copyright law that maintains that the claims of the copyright holder should stop short of the private sphere of the individual.'

In the years that followed, however, both the German courts and the legislator made it clear that the actual exercise of the right, in attempting to monitor or

* Research fellow, Department of Copyright and Information Law, Law Faculty, University of Leiden.

1. Second Chamber of Parliament 1972, L. de Vries, *Parlementaire geschiedenis van de Auteurswet 1912 zoals sedertdien gewijzigd* (Parliamentary history of the Copyright Act of 1912, as revised), The Hague 1989-..., 17.
2. Bundesgerichtshof (German Supreme Court), Judgement of 18 May 1955, *GRUR* 1955, 492.

control what goes on inside the home of the user, would indeed be an infringement of the private sphere. In 1964 the German Supreme Court decided[3] that the collecting society GEMA could not oblige sellers of home taping equipment to require all their customers to show their *Personalausweis*, and thus enable the collecting society to check whether these customers actually did obtain a license to use their home taping equipment (the collecting society had announced that it was planning to collect incriminating information on these buyers from neighbours, porters etc.).

Apparently there *is* a general principle that maintains that the *exercise* of an exclusive right should stop short at the private sphere of the individual.

A year later, in 1965, the German law was changed[4] in order to permit home taping, and a levy on home taping equipment, to be paid by the manufacturer or importer, was introduced. Later, the levy system was extended to include blank tapes.

Many countries followed this example. Whether the case against home taping was initially won in the courts,[5] lost[6] or never even tried as in the Netherlands, sooner or later[7] a levy system turned out to be the only option. With the exception of the United Kingdom, where in 1988 the legislator changed its mind at the last moment, exempting all home copying for the purpose of time shifting, without introducing a levy. In 1992 the United States introduced a levy system with a very limited scope, only covering digital audio tape recording.

As a consequence audio and video home taping were beyond control, not only for practical and technical reasons but also for reasons of privacy. Nevertheless, many believed the equipment and blank tape levy to be an acceptable alternative. On the one hand, VCRs were mainly used for time shifting purposes (it requires two VCRs to make a copy from a copy), and the quality and durability of the analogue tape recording were poor (at least not good enough to encourage second or third generation copying). On the other hand, levies could generate a reasonable amount of money to compensate the losses incurred by private copying. The levy seemed justified because these tapes and recorders were hardly used for other purposes than recording copyright protected material without permission of the rightholders. At least with audio taping, it was also relatively easy to distribute the money because, in all probability, the recording habits would follow the popularity of the music reflected by the sales figures of the CDs.

Within the terms of article 9(2) of the Berne Convention it may be argued that home taping does not conflict with the normal exploitation of the work, but does unreasonably prejudice the legitimate interests of the author, unless the prejudice is

---

3. Bundesgerichtshof (German Supreme Court), Judgement of 29 May 1964, *GRUR* 1965, 104.
4. Act dealing with Copyright and Related Rights (Copyright Act) of 9 September 1965, as amended to 9 June 1993, WIPO translation.
5. As was the case in Germany. See *supra* note 2.
6. As in the United States in the *Betamax* decision of the Supreme Court, 464 US 417 (1984).
7. *Cf.* Dutch Copyright Act of 1912, as amended to July 7, 1994.

eliminated or reduced to a reasonable level through a levy on recording equipment or material.[8]

As Paul Geller has observed: 'Fortunately, in practice, the method of deriving remuneration from means of effectuating mass uses, such as copy machines or blank-recording tapes, need not prejudice privacy interests'.[9]

2. Digital Equivalent

The predictable response of the rightholders to digital home taping has been to lobby for the abolishment of any home copying or fair use privileges as far as digital copying is concerned. Arguably, this would not require a change of the law, not even in the civil law countries, but could be achieved by interpretation of the law, with or without reference to article 9(2) of the Berne Convention.

Similar to the argument of the German Supreme Court, forty years ago, that audio home taping was not foreseen by the legislator of 1901 and that, therefore, such taping was not covered by the existing private copying exemption, it could be argued today that the exemptions of the sixties and seventies are not applicable to digital copying.

However, to me it seems likely that such a view may eventually have as little value as the German home taping decision of 1955. It is quite true that the legislators and judges of the ninety-sixties and -seventies did not, and could not, take into account the possibilities of digital copying when formulating the copying exemptions. Therefore there is no reason or justification to stick to these exemptions rigidly.

But is it, on the other hand, realistic and/or recommendable to prohibit all private digital copying[10]? Or is it just a matter of principle on the basis of which it will be possible to formulate appropriate licensing schemes? Are we to impose a levy on everything we can think of?[11]

Much depends, of course, on whether there is an acceptable way to exercise the right. The German audio taping experience has shown that an outright prohibition is not an option if there is no acceptable solution to its policing. Where

8. Committee of Experts on a possible protocol to the Berne Convention for the protection of literary and artistic Works, 2d session, Geneva, 10-17 February 1992, *Copyright* 1992, 72.

9. Paul Geller, 'Reprography and other processes of mass use', 38 *J. Cop. soc.* 31.

10. Cf. the Dutch Copyright Amendment Bill of 1992, Kamerstukken 22600; the bill was eventually rejected by the First Chamber of Parliament. As one member of the First Chamber remarked: 'A prohibition of electronic private copying in the narrow sense is impossible to police, will be breached on a massive scale, and may even render the legislator himself ridiculous'.

11. Cf. article 18 (3) of the Greek Copyright Act of 3 March 1993 (Law no. 2121): 'If the reproduction [for private use] is effected by technical means, including by the use of phonographic and film fixation equipment, magnetic tapes or other materials which facilitate the reproduction of phonograms or films, or by the use of photocopying machines, photocopy paper or a computer, a reasonable fee shall be payable to the creator of the work and to any rightholders of related rights. The fee shall be fixed at 6% of the value of phonographic and film fixation equipment and of magnetic tapes and other materials, at 4% of the value of photocopying machines and photocopy paper and at 2% of the value of computers.'

copying for private use within the private circle is concerned, the courts may well take the view that the privacy interest should (continue to) prevail, in spite of the consequences it may have for the interests of the copyright holders.

3. Library Copying and Copying on Demand

The following part of this article deals with something which in Germany and the Netherlands is covered by the same copyright exemptions as home copying, but is in fact something quite different, which in my opinion is reflected more appropriately by the separate status it has under British and American copyright law. Library copying and 'copying on demand' privileges (together with the first sale doctrine) constitute exemptions that combine the right to make or order copies for personal use on the part of one person or entity ('the public'), with the right to make the information available for this purpose, to provide this service or a 'do-it-yourself' opportunity on the part of another person or entity ('the library').

The important difference with the home copying exemption is that the latter does not give anyone the right to *supply* the information to others to tape or store. Nobody can successfully claim that he does not need permission to broadcast a film, because he is only giving viewers the opportunity to tape it at home. However, this is in a sense exactly what a library is allowed to do: it may make available all its books to the general public for them to photocopy or order copies to be made.

Library privileges also have quite a different foundation. Home copying exemptions are mainly introduced in the interest of privacy, whereas library privileges are based on a public interest: *access for all.*

Until the 1950s, library privileges where not much of an issue. Photocopying carried the risk of direct competition with primary publishing. This danger was limited, however, as libraries did not allow entire books that were still in print to be copied,and did not, at least not on a large scale, deliver photocopies of journal articles outside their premises. In some countries a remuneration was to be paid for this kind of copying, but in most countries it was left free altogether. Nevertheless, as libraries and publishers did not interfere with each other's 'share of the market' a reasonable balance was struck.

In the 1990's, however, libraries have started upgrading their document supply services to include the delivery of recently published material, sometimes in combination with on-line databases containing the current contents of scientific journals. These services will clearly compete directly with primary publishing. One problem is that in Germany and the Netherlands, according to the wording of the law, anything seems possible in this respect as long as no copies are made or kept in stock before they are ordered.

According to the publishers argue many of these document delivery practices are in clear violation of article 9(2) of the Berne Convention. As Paul Goldstein remarked in 1989: 'Cheap and easy photocopying taken together with widespread interlibrary loan and reproduction networks have effectively put modern libraries into the reprint business'.[12]

Libraries, at least in this country, do not to restrain themselves from providing copies of recent journal articles on demand, or operating an interlibrary loan system which has become a euphemism for digitizing and sharing expensive subscriptions over 'interlibrary loan networks'. However, they can hardly be blamed for this, as the number of new titles is still increasing faster than their budgets and their users keep asking for access to everything.

It seems that, eventually, libraries and publishers will want to provide nearly the same service in relation to the same product. The differences are that the libraries do not hold the copyrights, set prices below market value, and are sponsored by governments, whereas the publishers may (or may not[13]) own the copyrights, set prices commercially, and operate as commercial enterprises.

To some librarians it seems a logical development to go from making a photocopy in the library yourself, to ordering it by fax or email or accessing an on-line full text database. This view is too simplistic and ignores the interests of the copyright holders. We have to draw a line somewhere to determine what libraries are allowed to do.

3.1 STORAGE

Many copyright laws draw the line when it comes to the permanent storage on paper or in a database. Under most library privileges it is not permissable to make reproductions in advance and/or to have them in stock (in case someone orders them). The storage in a database is clearly a form of reproduction 'in advance', and is therefore usually not allowed. As a consequence digitizing is (if at all) only permitted from the moment a copy is ordered; the digitized copy must be deleted after delivery.

Under Dutch and German copyright law,[14] a library, or indeed anyone, is allowed to deliver copies on demand to anybody as long as an original (paper) copy is used to make the ordered copy from, and the copy is made after the request has been received. To a large extent the same seems to be true in the United Kingdom and the United States with regard to 'official' libraries.

In an age where photo- or electronic copies can be made at a moment's notice, and publishers hardly need to keep their publications in stock but provide 'printing on demand' services, one might well ask whether it makes any sense to draw the line at the making of copies in advance. The impact of document delivery on demand on the subscription market of a journal seems to be the same, whether or not the ordered copy is made in advance. At the same time it seems a waste if libraries would be compelled to delete the electronic image of an article (which is

12. Paul Goldstein, *Copyright Principles, Law and Practice*, Boston, 1989, 545.

13. There is much uncertainty on the question to what extent the publishers have 'electronic rights'.

14. *See* P.B. Hugenholtz & D.J.G. Visser, *Copyright problems of electronic document delivery*, Report to the European Commission (DG XIII), Luxembourg, 1995, 26, 38.

out of print, but highly in demand) after each delivery. Why should libraries not be allowed to digitize information in order to store it safely in a database and save space?[15] This fear to allow storage in a computer memory seems to spring from the idea many lawyers, judges and legislators seem to have that all control is lost once the information is stored in a database.[16]

In my opinion we should construe library privileges as exemptions to the right of communication to the public, as is done in the United States and the United Kingdom (and, of course, as exemptions to the reproduction right). However these privileges should only outline the quality, quantity and place of the exempted library information service. These rules should not interfere with or even take into account the preparatory activities of libraries, if there is no clear reason to do so.[17]

4. Dutch and German Case Law

At this moment, at least in Germany and the Netherlands, these preparatory activities seem to be the decisive factor, leading to rather unsatisfactory results, as two recent cases illustrate:

4.1 THE LITEROM CASE[18]

The first case concerned a CD-ROM produced by the Dutch Library Association (NBLC) containing 43.000 Dutch newspaper articles of literary criticism - without permission of the rightholders. This *LiteROM* was only made available on site in (non-profit) public libraries; users were only allowed the making of printouts of individual articles. In the libraries the CD-ROM replaced a traditional filing cabinet with photocopies of the same newspaper articles from which the users could make photocopies.

15. The rather paranoid but exemplary answer to that question given in a handbook on German copyright law (published in 1994!) is that databases are meant for distributing material, and consequently can not be considered 'archives': Fromm & Nordemann, *Urheberrecht*, 8th ed., 1994, 395: 'Archive sind nach sachlichen Gesichtspunkten geordnete Sammel- und Aufbewahrungsstellen für Geistesgut bestimmter Art, also Bibliotheken, Zeitungsarchive, Filmmagazine usw. Datenbanken gehören dazu nicht, weil sie nicht die bloße Sammlung und Aufbewahrung, sondern Weitergabe des Materials bezwecken (..)'.

16. Although this is not a very rational approach, part of it may be explained by the lack of clarity on what is actually allowed under copyright law after the information has been stored electronically. There is no doubt in my mind that the making available of a database either on site or on-line should be considered as an act of communication to the public, but so should the operation of a document delivery service. Whether we call this distribution, display or performance is of little importance.

17. These library privileges might include the obligation to pay some kind of remuneration to the rightholders (comparable to a public lending right). However, this has very little to do with copyright as an exclusive right.

18. District Court of The Hague, Judgement of 3 May 1995, *Mediaforum* 1995, B-76.

On 3 May 1995 the District Court of The Hague held that the making of this CD-ROM was an infringement of copyright and that the exemption for copying (on demand) for private study or use[19] did not apply.

4.2 THE INFOBANK CASE[20]

The second case concerned a commercial document delivery service run (and advertised) by a German bank. The service was operated on the basis of a traditional filing cabinet in which original newspaper clippings were kept, which were cut out by hand and filed every day. Some articles were photocopied to be filed under two different keywords, but the bank also had two subscriptions.

On 2 December 1994 the Court of Appeals of Cologne held that the operation of this commercial document delivery service was not an infringement of copyright because the exemption for copying (on demand) for private study or use[21] did apply.[22]

Both decisions reflect the 'iron rule' that one may not make copies (or store in a database) in advance, but as long as one makes the copies after one has received the request, one may advertise and commercialize one's service anyway one wants. This rule has obviously become obsolete due to technology.

Libraries should not interfere (too much) with or engage in the normal exploitation of the work (unless, of course, rightholders authorize them to do so[23]). Consequently, libraries cannot expect to be allowed to provide full text on line services to remote users in relation to recent material,[24] irrespective of the fact that they call this service 'mere viewing or browsing'. Such a service would probably interfere with the normal exploitation of the work. Neither should libraries be allowed to provide document delivery services of the same material without payment to the rightholders.

Libraries should continue to be free to supply their users who visit the library in person with paper copies (printouts or photocopies)[25] of individual articles for their private study or use (under the conditions set out in the British and U.S.

---

19. Article 16b of the Dutch Copyright Act of 1912.
20. Court of Appeals of Cologne, Judgement of 2 December 1994, *GRUR* 1995, 265.
21. Article 53 (2)(iv), German Copyright Act.
22. Cf. District Court of Frankfurt/Main, *ZUM* 1994, 438 (commercial document delivery *not* exempted); District Court of Munich, Judgement of 18 May 1995, not yet published (document delivery by university exempted).
23. We may well see a shift towards (academic) authors not transferring their electronic rights to publishers, but licensing them (non-exclusively) to libraries.
24. In this respect the 'Fair Use Statement' of the American Library Associations is probably unrealistic in sofar as it suggests that the public has a right to expect to read, listen to, view or browse through publicly marketed copyrighted material remotely (without any payment to copyright holders).
25. Of course, there is the danger that users will scan their paper copies in order to have them in digital form after all, but there is no way to prevent that from happening without infringing privacy.

library privileges). Users should be allowed to view, read and browse through all information available irrespective of the way the information is stored.[26]

As long as the user personally visit the library and only takes home the information in the form of a limited number of paper copies, all this should be allowed without the copyright holder's permission. These library privileges should not be overridden by restrictive terms in licenses as far as 'publicly marketed copyrighted material' is concerned.

Although users and libraries probably would like to be free to receive and deliver information in digital form outside the library, preferably through networks, this should not be allowed without a license. Neither should document delivery services to outside users be allowed without payment to the rightholders if the information is made commercially available in any other way.[27]

However, where on-line and other electronic delivery services are concerned, rightholders should remember that copyright (especially article 9(2) of the Berne Convention) 'does not protect any given media industry against the inroads of competing media, such as the mass availability of cheap photocopy or facsimile transmission devices'.[28] And, as it is far from clear whether journal publishers actually hold the 'electronic rights', authors may well choose to license those rights to libraries or other intermediaries instead.

Moreover, if rightholders refuse to license document delivery services or on-line databases by relying on national copyright provisions, thus preventing the appearance of a new product which they do not offer and for which there is a potential consumer demand, such refusal may well constitute an abuse of a dominant position under Article 86 of the EC Treaty.[29] The *Magill* case illustrates that under European competition law there are limits to the freedom of copyright holders to compel people to buy several separate products where there is a clear demand for a single combined product. An on-line database or a delivery service accessible for a reasonable price might well be such a product.

---

26. In my view, it does not make much difference whether a library provides stand-alone PCs with CD-ROM players, 'dumb' terminals with connection to remote databases, client/server combinations in local area networks, microfilms and reader-printers or interlibrary loan journals and photocopiers.
27. The delivery of information in digital form would bear a higher risk of large scale redistribution and would make it much harder for libraries to monitor the quantitative limitations of library privileges. Document delivery to (an unlimited number of) remote users would interfere with a normal exploitation of the work.
28. Paul Geller, *supra* note 9, at 31.
29. Cf. Court of Justice of the European Communities, Judgement of 6 April 1995, joint cases C-241/91 and C-242/91 (*RTE and ITP v. Magill TV Guide*), recital 54.

The Cable and Satellite Analogy

*Thomas Dreier**

1. The Cable and Satellite Model

Discussing the future of copyright in a digital environment, why would it be appropriate to examine the possibilities of a 'cable & satellite analogy', i.e. an analogy to the legal rules adopted by EC Directive 93/83/EEC of 27 September 1993 on the coordination of certain rules concerning copyright and rights related to copyright applicable to satellite broadcasting and cable retransmission?[1]

At first sight, the answer may not be all that obvious, since the Directive was adopted simply to regulate 'broadcasts transmitted across frontiers within the Community, (..) by satellite and cable'.[2] Distribution of radio and television programs via cable and satellite is an activity quite separate from the digital environment. It is a specific and limited means of distributing subject matter protected by copyright. It does not specifically concern distribution of protected subject matter in a digital environment.

However, in laying down the rules for transborder transmissions of programs and protected material contained therein, the Directive formulates some important new principles concerning both the place where a communication to the public takes place in a transborder situation (for satellite transmission) and the facilitation of the acquisition of an exclusive right (for cable retransmission). Obviously, the problems addressed by the Directive with regard to traditional radio and television programs bear some similarity to the problems encountered in the digital context. Here, likewise, we have to deal with difficulties in obtaining all the rights necessary in order to communicate a multimedia or online product across borders. The principles formulated by the Cable and Satellite Directive may prove to be so fundamental that their application by way of analogy may eventually be justified also within the larger context of the digital environment as such. It shall be the purpose of this paper to outline briefly the pros and cons of such an analogy (or such analogies).

Furthermore, since for the purposes of the Cable and Satellite Directive it is of no importance whether the program-carrying signals are in analogue or digital form, one will even have to ask to what extent the Directive is already applicable in

---

* Member, scientific research staff, Max-Planck-Institute for Foreign and International Patent, Copyright and Competition Law, Munich.

1. O.J.E.C. No. L 248 of 6 October 1993, 15 (cited as *the Directive*).

2. Directive, recital 3.

the digital environment by way of literal application, i.e. without the legal mechanism of an analogy.

2. The Cable Analogy

Let us first turn to the legal scheme created by the Directive for cable retransmission, since its direct applicability together with its applicability by way of analogy to the digital context proves to be much more limited than is the case regarding the legal scheme for satellite transmission.

2.1. LITERAL APPLICATION OF THE CABLE AND SATELLITE DIRECTIVE

In article 9 (1) the Directive prescribes that the exclusive right to authorize or refuse to authorize the cable retransmission be mandatorily exercised by collecting societies. It is the purpose of this provision to protect the cable operators, who 'cannot be sure that they have actually acquired all the .. rights'[3] covered by the agreements previously concluded with representatives of all groups of rightholders involved, against possible copyright infringement claims by outsiders. Incidentally, this new scheme works in favour of television viewers who are spared programs that might look like Swiss cheese.

In line with this, and according to its wording, the new rule only applies to the retransmission of 'television or radio programs intended for reception by the public'.[4] Although it is not defined in the Directive what exactly a 'program' is, it may nevertheless be deduced from the requirement of 'simultaneous, unaltered and unabridged retransmission' that in a program the order of its single components must necessarily be predefined in time by the program provider, very much as is the case with television and radio programs as we presently know them.

However, it follows that the cable part of the Directive cannot be directly applied to the on-line transmission of copyright-protected subject matter, such as it takes place in the case of data bases or other interactive information services, since as a result of the severed tie between a single component and its predefined position in a sequential order, these services no longer constitute 'programs' in the traditional sense.

Furthermore, it should be noted that the cable part of the Directive only applies to programs from another Member State.[5] The reasons for this are, according to the logic of the EC Treaty, that the EC cannot deal with matters of only internal effect in its Member States and that the EC especially did not want to

3. Directive, recital 10.
4. Directive, art. 1 (3), 8 (1).
5. Directive, art. 1 (3).

prejudice the much discussed question of cable retransmission within the direct reception area or the so-called service zone.[6]

2.2 THE PROS OF AN ANALOGY

To what extent can the cable solution of the Directive be applied by way of analogy, i.e. to what extent does the mandatory exercise of an exclusive right by collecting societies seem to present an adequate solution to problems arising within the digital environment?[7]

One may argue that such a solution seems appropriate whenever the rightholders cannot, or can no longer, individually exercise their exclusive rights. Indeed, quite recently the French legislature was the first to copy the cable model of the Directive and apply it to the reprography right.[8]

Furthermore, it should be noted that in respect of cable, the scheme also benefits those rightholders who have validly consented to the cable retransmission of their works and who would be adversely affected if only one single holder of a right in a single program component could block the entire retransmission.

Beyond this, from a user's point of view, and even more so from the general public's point of view, it is certainly rather tempting to argue that the solution of a mandatory exercise of exclusive rights should apply whenever the acquisition of all use rights necessary to provide a certain digital service proves to be too complicated, uncertain, and/or too costly. Here, in a rather vague way, the idea of a free flow of information is invoked, together with the public interest in having access to information and cultural material, and in obtaining the best info- and edutainment tools which are technically feasible.

From the rightholders' point of view, such a solution would, at least, be better than a legal license, a mere claim to remuneration or a cut back in the scope of the exclusive right altogether. After all, it leaves the collecting society with the power to negotiate, even if in most Member States this power will in practice be reduced to a larger or smaller degree by antitrust considerations.[9]

2.3 THE CONS OF AN ANALOGY

However, there are several points speaking against – at least an indiscriminate – analogy for the digital environment.

Firstly, conceptually speaking, to subject an exclusive right to its mandatory exercise by a collecting society means to reduce the exclusive right, i.e. to grant the author less than he or she had previously. Contrary to copyright doctrine, *droit*

6. Directive, recital 32.

7. For a discussion whether such an analogy is possible by way of interpreting the existing statutory language of the Directive, or only de lege ferenda, *see infra*, § 4.

8. Law no. 95-4 of 3 January 1995, J.O. of 4 January 1995, 120.

9. *See* Directive, art. 13.

d'auteur philosophy would only allow for such a reduction in order ultimately to strengthen the position of the author. At least, it would not seem possible to reduce an author's exclusive right so as merely to facilitate the licensing business of producers and commercial users or to have the end user pay less for the product offered on the basis of an author's creation. In cases where such a weakening of the exclusive right is accepted, for other reasons than to strengthen the position of the author, this will be done for political reasons that lie outside of the realm of copyright.

Indeed, the cable scheme established by the Directive was at least partly shaped by the media policy imperative of creating a *European audiovisual area*,[10] although it should be noted that in the case of cable, the contractual practice of all parties concerned had already largely anticipated the rule of the Directive. Likewise, it seems doubtful whether one might construe a general duty of one rightholder not to withhold an authorization if this would negatively affect other rightholders willing to authorize exploitation of their works; most likely, such a duty could only be established on a case-by-case basis. Furthermore, it would seem much easier in a digital than, e.g., in a print environment to block out a particular single component.

Secondly, attention should be drawn to the fact that in the traditional exploitation hierarchy of television and radio programs, cable retransmission in foreign countries clearly is an act not of primary, but of secondary exploitation of the material protected. Secondary exploitation acts may be governed by rules different from those governing primary exploitation, since in general less control is needed and the remuneration generated no longer needs to recapitalize the initial investment made. Consequently, any eventual analogy would most likely be limited to acts of exploitation which would appear as secondary (yet to be defined) in the digital environment.

It follows, thirdly, that for practical purposes even the majority of producers now plead in favour of free individual contractual negotiation. They have understood that any producer who today may benefit from a cutback in the initial author's exclusive right will suffer the same cutback tomorrow with regard to the rights in his own (online or offline) products. Any cutback, or even mandatory regulation of the exclusive right – be it rights assigned to the producers by the initial authors, or rights granted to the producers for their own activities – would diminish the control wanted within a primary exploitation context, and bring with it the risk that the remuneration obtained no longer covered the initial investment.

Fourthly, this is so because any solution of exercising rights via a collecting society has the twofold disadvantage that the rights can no longer be granted on an exclusive basis, and that the remuneration to be paid will have to be calculated in a rather general manner for certain groups of works and/or kinds of uses. It does not, however, allow for individual remuneration in relation to the particular commercial value of a particular work with regard to a particular use.

It follows, lastly, that the solution of exercising rights collectively – either prescribed by law, or by way of a voluntary gathering of rightholders – only makes

10. Directive, recitals 9, 12.

sense in two situations: where the use of the protected material may be characterized as an act of secondary exploitation (and where it is not possible, in general or only at unreasonable cost, to exercise the rights individually), or where the material as such is largely substitutable (as is the case of musical works with regard to their use as, e.g., background music).

3. The Satellite Analogy

Let us now turn to a possible satellite analogy. What does the Directive regulate, apart from satellite specific matters such as the equal treatment of Direct Broadcasting Satellites (DBS) and Fixed Service Satellites (FSS), provided individual reception of the signals is comparable to reception of signals by DBS? It decides the controversy over the so-called *Bogsch Theory*, namely the question whether a transborder satellite transmission of program signals only has to do with the law of the emission state or equally with the laws of all those states in which these signals may be received. The solution adopted – somewhat hidden in the definitions, art. 1 (2) (b) – comes in the form of a compromise: as a question of material law harmonization (and not of conflict of laws), it is decreed that the act of public communication relevant to copyright only occurs in the emission state (which, however, in order to avoid fraudulent evasion is defined as the 'state where (..) the signals are introduced into an uninterrupted chain of communication leading to the satellite and down towards the earth'[11]), and that there shall be a sufficiently harmonized level of material law protection throughout the Union.[12] Thus, the Directive creates both legal certainty and a legal environment favourable to satellite program providers.[13]

3.1 Literal Application of the Cable and Satellite Directive

Despite the fact that, in contrast to article 8 in the case of cable, article 2 of the Directive does not speak of programs, but rather obliges Member States to grant an exclusive right regarding 'the communication to the public by satellite of copyright works', both definitions and recitals make it quite clear that the satellite part of the Directive equally applies directly only to the satellite transmission of 'program-carrying signals' by 'broadcasting organizations'.[14] It may thus been concluded that, like in the cable context, 'broadcast' refers to traditional television and radio, and especially that the notion of 'program' presupposes a sequential order of material in time as defined by the broadcaster, which clearly distinguishes the

11. Directive, art. 1 (2) (b).
12. Directive, art. 2 - 4; *see also* recital 24.
13. *See* Directive, recitals 5, 7 and 14.
14. Cf. the definition of 'communication to the public' in the Directive, art. 1 (2) (a), (b), (d); recitals 3, 5, 7 ('broadcasting of programmes'), 8, 13, 14, 15 ('broadcasting rights').

object of regulation of the Directive from interactive digital network services, where the order of protected material consumed in time is determined not by the service provider but by the user of the service.

3.2 THE PROS OF AN ANALOGY

However, at first sight, the satellite solution adopted by the Directive may seem quite suitable to its application by way of analogy in the digital environment.[15]

Firstly, the situations are indeed rather similar: in both cases (satellite transmission of programs, and on-line communication of the contents of databases), protected subject matter is communicated from one source to several users, i.e. it is made available to the public. In practice, both these activities are – in view of the increasing use of telephone lines and after the dissolution of national telecommunications monopolies – increasingly transborder activities. It seems to be of no real importance for copyright purposes that so far most on-line activities use material cable links instead of immaterial satellite communication, since the transmission medium being used depends largely on technical and/or economic considerations and thus may vary over time.[16]

Secondly, quite similar to the case of satellite transmission of programs, transborder exploitation of protected works by on-line services brings with it both the legal uncertainty as to in which states the communication to the public takes place[17] and, were the Bogsch Theory to apply, the difficulty that rights would have to be obtained for all states from which the on-line service may be accessed. The latter difficulty seems even aggravated: whereas a satellite program provider can, by choosing an appropriately delimited satellite footprint, exercise at least a certain degree of control regarding the number and identity of reception states, on-line services may, by way of telephone and modem, be accessed from virtually any place in the world.

Thirdly, other than in the case of cable, as far as satellites are concerned we are dealing with acts of primary exploitation of protected material.

---

15. For a discussion whether such an analogy is possible by way of interpreting the existing statutory language of the Directive, or only de lege ferenda *see infra*, § 4.
16. However, it should be noted that national conflict of laws rules would probably apply the law of each state where the cable is running in the case of signal transmission by wire. To adopt a different solution, i.e. to apply only the law of the emission state in the case of signal transmission via satellite, would lead to an unequal treatment of economically similar activities. This concern is also raised by the EU Green Paper 'Copyright and related rights in the information society', COM(95) 382 final, of 19 July 1995, ch. 2, part 1, section I.3.
17. Assuming it is a communication to the public at all; note that due to the interactivity of the system, the users no longer use a particular protected work at the same time; *see also infra*, § 3.3.

3.3 THE CONS OF AN ANALOGY

However, likewise, a certain number of differences may be detected between the transmission of programs by satellite and the making available to the public of protected material via on-line services.

Firstly, due to the lack of simultaneous use of one and the same work already mentioned, it is not clear in all jurisdictions whether the offering of protected material via an on-line service does amount to a communication to the public. In case it does not (and unless a transmission right similar to the old French injection right is introduced), any analogy could only relate to other copyright-relevant acts which would most likely be those of storage at the one, and of reproduction at the other end of the line. However, on the one hand, it seems doubtful whether an analogy could indeed go this far, since reproduction acts at the user's end (be it display, storage or printout) are not undertaken by the on-line service provider; and on the other hand, an analogy would not seem necessary, since storage acts undertaken by the provider only take place within one jurisdiction anyway (that is if one excludes the technical reproductions at several intermediate locations of the network structure, which might indeed require a more careful analysis the outcome of which, however, largely would depend on the issue already familiar from the computer program context, namely whether or not such a technical reproduction is in fact subject to copyright or not). It should be noted that the satellite part of the Directive does not relieve the program provider of the burden of securing, by way of contract,[18] the broadcasting right from any single holder of rights in components of his program, as remote or as unknown as this particular rightholder may be.

Secondly, and this seems to be most important, the satellite model of the Directive mandatorily requires that more or less the same level of protection exists within all national states to which the satellite model applies.[19] Here, the present landscape of national copyright laws reveals enormous differences at almost all levels: it starts with the question already discussed namely whether or not the on-line offering of protected material to the public amounts to a public communication;[20] it continues with the legal uncertainty regarding the legal qualification of use acts, and it certainly does not end with the total disharmony regarding the exemptions to the exclusive use acts, to which article 9 (2) of the Berne Convention provides a proper, albeit rather vague limitation (for the reproduction right only). This is not to mention all the other discrepancies, for example regarding originality, initial ownership of rights, moral rights, duration and – most important – copyright contract rules which vary quite substantially throughout the world.

If the Satellite and Cable Directive can (more or less) live with these discrepancies within the EC, this is due to the existence of certain other harmonization measures and to the fact that, apart from private copying, protected

18. Apart from the very limited exception provided for in art. 3 (2) largely addressed to the existing Scandinavian system of extended collective licensing.

19. *See supra*, § 3 (before § 3.1). Cf. the subsidiary points of attachment in art. 1 (2) (d)(i) and (ii) of the Directive.

20. For harmonization in this respect with regard to satellites, *see* Directive, art. 2.

program material transmitted hardly gives rise to substantial subsequent use. This, however, is no longer the case in a digital environment, where any material transmitted can easily form the basis for new exploitation acts which are again subject to copyright. Just imagine the devastating effects of an analogy where the act of offering either does not amount to public communication in the state of origin, or where the material communicated can widely be reused in one of the reception states!

Thirdly, the Directive works on the assumption that the amount of payment to be made for the rights acquired corresponds to 'all aspects (..), such as the actual audience [and] the potential audience',[21] i.e. that economically speaking rightholders shall have no economic loss owing to the fact that from now on the transmission rights will only have to be acquired in the country of origin, and no longer – eventually – in all reception states of the transmission (of course, this assumption somehow contradicts the practical experience that as a rule, the total amount due is greater if paid on the basis of several claims for remuneration instead of one, even if a cake does not get bigger by being cut into slices). Such an assumption is only guaranteed where the number of those entitled to remuneration is either limited, or concentrated within one state, or sufficiently represented by collecting societies. However, this seems to be much more the case with regard to television and radio program content (e.g., music as the main contents of radio broadcasts is almost exclusively represented by collecting societies, and most film rights, including territorially split rights, are relatively easy to locate) than for protected subject matter in general.

Lastly, it may well be that the practical need for a solution analogous to the satellite solution is much smaller in the digital environment, since the provider of a commercial on-line service not only has to acquire a potential public communication right (if any), but also the reproduction right with regard to any single protected item intended for storage, and thus has to deal with all right holders, national and foreign, anyway. The same holds true regarding any rights necessary for acts to be undertaken by users, which the provider wants to make possible, and which are not covered in the reception state by an exception (such as the private use exception).

4. Outlook

Without doubt, the foregoing analysis to a large extent highlights only some major aspects. Furthermore, apart from discussing the analogy, it only deals with the status quo of the present copyright landscape. If one problem already consists in the legal uncertainty as to how the rules presently in existence are to be applied in a digital network environment (especially, to know what exactly are the copyright relevant acts), another problem consists in the anticipation of the future development of the system as such.

21. Directive, recital 17.

Here, three remarks seem to be called for. Firstly, as far as the analogy itself is concerned, it seems that only jurisdictions which allow for non-literal application of statutory language could possibly resort to it in the digital environment without any legislative changes having to be made. However, due to the fact that the Directive unequivocally speaks of transmission of 'programs', it is fair to assume that in all Member States any analogy discussed could only be adopted *de lege ferenda*, i.e. by way of legislative change.

Secondly, the discussion has shown that, at present, there seems to be but little room for either a cable or satellite analogy (an exception being a cable analogy for essentially substitutable material on a non-exclusive basis under rather generalized terms and conditions). Any introduction of the satellite analogy would mandatorily presuppose a series of accompanying harmonization measures, which could indeed give rise to reconsideration of the whole system as such. In doing so, one might theoretically again draw a distinction between harmonization within the EU and outside EU territory.[22] Of course, harmonization within the EU has its own logic driven by the both legal and factual process of creating a single market, and the Cable and Satellite Directive has reacted to it. However, the digital environment will almost by definition be a universal environment, which seems to preclude any unilateral or otherwise limited action. It is, of course, an open question as to which will be the most appropriate forum to achieve such harmonization, especially whether such harmonization can be achieved within the enlarged framework of a possible Berne Protocol.

Thirdly, any incorporation of a satellite analogy into the future harmonized digital copyright environment should likewise take into consideration the numerous identification, control and accounting possibilities offered by digital technology itself. Thus, it would seem both unnecessary and unjustified to curtail authors' rights in order to initiate and maintain the functioning of the future digital environment, where the same result could be achieved by technical means. Likewise, it might be unnecessarily complicated to maintain rules in a digital and technically controlled international environment, which was developed in times when exploitation of protected material was territorially oriented and in analogue form.

In essence, I believe it is too early to predict with a sufficient degree of certainty whether the possibilities offered by digital technique will indeed call for a satellite analogy, or whether, quite to the contrary, they will render the very question obsolete.

---

22. The EU Green Paper, *supra* note 16, also concludes that harmonization of material law protection standards is necessary before the satellite solution could be adopted as a general principle for digital work dissemination within the EU, and that protective clauses will have to be introduced in order to protect authors and owners of neighbouring rights.

The Copyright Approach to Copying on the Internet: (Over)Stretching the Reproduction Right?

*Jaap H. Spoor**

1. Introduction

As its name indicates, and although its full scope is considerably wider, copyright traditionally deals with copying. It does so through the reproduction right, which is generally considered to be one of its core prerogatives,[1] and which can be found in most, if not all national copyright laws. The national implementations of this right may vary to some extent, but the following characteristics are probably more or less universal: it is an exclusive right to reproduce the work in a material form.

Immaterial as the Internet[2] may seem from the outside, Internet operations nevertheless require almost continuous copying. All sorts of documents are uploaded to sites on servers, which involves their fixation on (mostly) hard disks. Whenever a user wishes to access such a document, signals will transmit it through an often wide range of intermediate computers to that user's computer, where it may again be fixed on disk. And even if the user merely wishes to consult the document on his screen without also copying it to a more permanent support, it must at least be temporarily stored in RAM memory. Are such copies subject to the reproduction right? If so, does that mean this right is stretched, or even overstretched?

Before discussing these questions in some more detail, I should like to make a few general remarks.

First, copyright only deals with protected works; works which are original and not (yet) in the public domain. Much, if not most of what is distributed over the net falls outside the scope of copyright, at least in practice, either because it is non-protected data, or because the right owners do not wish to limit distribution but prefer to encourage it, like in the case of shareware or news group contributions.

---

* Professor of Intellectual Property Law, Vrije Universiteit, Amsterdam; advocate, Trenité Van Doorne, Amsterdam.

1. Cf. Commission of the European Communities, *Green Paper. Copyright and Related Rights in the Information Society*, Brussels, 19 July 1995, COM (95) 382 final, 49: 'The right of reproduction is the core of copyright and related rights'.

2. Much of what is written below applies to electronic networks in general, not just to the Internet, but in the text I will mainly refer to the Internet.

That is a valid choice, but of course it can in no way restrict others, who wish to enforce the copyright in their own works, from claiming protection. This paper deals with the copyright in works which the right owners want to protect.

Second, even if the reproduction right is a core prerogative in copyright, it is not the only one, nor is it necessarily the one which is best adapted to dealing with Internet practice. It is not my intention to promote the reproduction right, let alone to promote it over all other prerogatives. The reproduction right just happens to be this paper's subject.

But it also is a well-known fact that once a right is in the statute book, right owners will try to enforce it in any situation which may arise, including situations which were never considered by the legislating authorities. This is certainly true for a classic prerogative like the reproduction right. That alone justifies a closer study of its application in an Internet context.

Finally, this is a vast, even virtually unlimited subject. I can do no more than discuss a few aspects, especially from an historic perspective. For one thing, the international dimension of electronic network reproduction and communication will be left almost entirely untouched.

2. The Reproduction Right

The reproduction right's exclusive nature is expressly laid down in article 9 (2) of the Berne Convention, which states that 'Authors of literary and artistic works protected by this Convention shall have the exclusive right of authorizing the reproduction of these works, in any manner or form'. The second paragraph allows the member countries 'to permit the reproduction of such works in certain special cases', but at once limits this faculty by making it a prerequisite 'that such reproduction does not conflict with a normal exploitation of the work and does not unreasonably prejudice the legitimate interests of the author'. Thus, it stresses the exclusive character of the right rather than limiting it.

Incidentally, it is rather remarkable that although earlier versions of the Berne Convention already contained provisions with respect to certain reproduction methods, such as phonorecords , it was not until the 1967 Stockholm revision that the general principle of article 9 was implemented. Perhaps in spite of being a core prerogative, when it comes to giving a more definite outline the reproduction right is less evident than it might seem to be. This is more or less confirmed by the fact that the Berne Convention does not define what is meant by 'reproduction'. The fact that the third paragraph expressly states that '[a]ny sound or visual recording shall be considered as a reproduction for the purposes of this Convention', can hardly make up for this lack of a more general definition.

Nor is this absence of such a definition accidental. In fact, the Stockholm conference proved unable to reach consensus on this point. Although the chairman of the responsible Main Committee, professor Ulmer, suggested that it should at least be clarified that 'reproduction' requires some form of fixation in material form, something which he feared otherwise might not be evident *a priori*, all such attempts failed, and probably not just for the view forwarded by the Spanish delegate Mr. Raya Mario who argued that everybody knows what reproduction means.[3]

A more likely explanation of the lack of consensus may also have been given by Mr. Raya Mario, where he added that to define 'reproduction' might be hazardous. Over time, the interpretations of reproduction have reflected technological and other changes. Now that copyright has entered the electronic era, new shadows start to surface.

Although the Convention does not prescribe an interpretation of 'reproduction', and the member countries therefore remain more or less free to interpret this notion, the mainstream interpretation stresses that reproduction requires some form of 'fixation in material form'; cf. e.g. article L 122-3 of the 1992 French Intellectual Property Code: 'La reproduction consiste dans la fixation matérielle de l'oeuvre par tous procédés qui permettent de la communiquer au public d'une manière indirecte'[4]; cf. also the U.S. Copyright Act definitions of 'copies' and 'phonorecords' which together can be considered to form the equivalent of 'reproduction'.[5] The U.S. Copyright Act also clarifies that '[a] work is "fixed" in a tangible medium of expression when its embodiment in a copy or phonorecord , by or under the authority of the author, is sufficiently permanent or stable to permit it to be perceived, reproduced, or otherwise communicated for a period of more than transitory duration'.[6]

3. Reproduction on the Electronic Highway

The French or U.S. definitions of reproduction need not necessarily correspond with other countries' interpretation of 'reproduction', but they certainly have sufficient authority to serve as a starting point when considering what goes on on the Internet.

As mentioned before, Internet and other electronic transmissions more or less consist of documents being copied from one computer to another all the time. Uploading, net-surfing, user groups, ftp or other downloading and archiving involve endless copying. Given the wide variety of operations on the net, ranging from e-mail or consultation on demand to automatic distribution of uploaded documents to all members of news groups, details of the operations may, of course, vary. Often, the transmitted data will also be temporarily stored on intermediate

3. Stockholm Conference reports, nr. 664.
4. This definition is identical to the one which was given in article 28 of the 1957 French copyright Act.
5. U.S. Copyright Act, Section 106 (1). According to Section 101 '"Copies" are material objects, other than phonorecords, in which a work is fixed by any method now known or later developed, and from which the work can be perceived, reproduced, or otherwise communicated, either directly or with the aid of a machine or device'; '"Phonorecords" are material objects in which sounds, other than those accompanying a motion picture or other audiovisual work, are fixed by any method now known or later developed, and from which the sounds can be perceived, reproduced, or otherwise communicated, either directly or with the aid of a machine or device'.
6. U.S. Copyright Act, Section 101.

computers, such as the access provider's servers. Internet demand for many documents, be it by anonymous ftp, gopher or WWW, is such that many servers temporarily copy ('mirror') everything their users consult on the net. As soon as one looks at a document, the server will make a copy and keep it for a short period, as chances have it that another user in the same area may shortly wish to consult the same document, and there will then be no need to obtain it once more from the original database, perhaps continents away: it's already available right here.

It is open to doubt whether such copies meet the requirement that they are sufficiently permanent or stable to permit the work to be communicated for a period of more than transitory duration. Copies which are made on intermediate servers and nodes during transmission may therefore well remain outside the scope of the reproduction right. But whatever the form of operation may be, it will always involves copies to be made on both ends of the line. Even when one simply e-mails a document to somebody else without keeping a copy, unlike with traditional mail it is not the material support that is transmitted; a fresh copy is made available each time.

There can be no doubt that the hard disk copies at both ends of the line – the uploader's server and the end user's computer – meet the statutory definitions of 'reproduction'. Copies in RAM may be more volatile, but nevertheless they will also satisfy the requirement quoted above that they are 'sufficiently permanent or stable to permit [the work] to be perceived, reproduced, or otherwise communicated for a period of more than transitory duration'.

Both the U.S. White Paper and the EC Green Paper accept these conclusions cursorily and almost as a matter of fact. The U.S. White Paper states that '[i]t has long been clear under U.S. law that the placement of copyrighted material into a computer's memory is a reproduction of that material (because the work in memory then may be, in the law's terms, "perceived, reproduced, or ... communicated ... with the aid of a machine or device")'.[7]

It certainly is true that this is clear under US law. Whether it also has *long* been clear is at least open for debate, since the doctrine according to which copies in RAM memory are reproductions is of rather recent origin. In fact, it is a clear instance of (earlier) stretching of the reproduction right. Nor does the U.S. White Paper mention the wide, and certainly not uncontested implications of this doctrine, viz. that the mere *use* of a copyright work, which used to be free, may no longer be free since its use will always require some form of reproduction in the digital environment.

Copyright traditionally also provides for exceptions to the reproduction right, e.g. for private use or educational purposes. Both the White Paper and the Green Paper suggest that these exceptions should be closely scrutinized and, perhaps, abolished where electronic network reproduction is concerned.[8]

In all, it seems clear that the reproduction right is indeed being expanded. Before discussing whether this right is also overstretched, however, and notwithstanding the tremendous chasm which separates the electronic highway

7. Report (White Paper) of the Working Group on Intellectual Property Rights, *Intellectual Property and the National Information Infrastructure*, Washington D.C., 1995, 64-65.

8. *Cf.* White Paper, *supra* note 7, 73 ff.; EC Green Paper, *supra* note 1, 52.

from 19th century printing, from a technological point of view as well as where its impact is concerned, it may be worthwhile to give some attention to the way in which the reproduction right and its central concept – reproduction – have developed over time.

4. Historical Development of the Reproduction Right

4.1 FROM EDITIONS TO SINGLE COPIES

The early copyright statutes essentially focused on acts of exploitation, especially through printing. Cf. article 1 of the 1793 French Copyright Decree, which gave 'authors of writings of all kinds, musical composers, painters and draughtsmen' the exclusive right to 'sell, have others sell and distribute' their works. The scope of that right may be derived from article 3, which declared liable to seizure 'all copies of editions printed or engraved without the authors' formal permission in writing'. Similar examples from other countries could be quoted as well.

'Editions' perhaps does not necessarily require copies to be produced in large numbers, but it nevertheless suggests a certain scale of copying. As time went by, however, not only the publishing right was extended to new and other methods of fixation than printing and engraving, but it was also increasingly recognized that the number of copies is more or less irrelevant. Even hand made single copies, if made for profit, were also held to infringe. This was especially relevant where single copies of paintings or musical scores were involved, since such copies were often made by hand at that time.

The scope of what was considered infringement was widened in another respect as well: copies no longer needed to be identical to the original; the reproduction right would also cover copies of translations and other adaptations, although for some time no clear distinction was made between the translation as such and the copies thereof. As Pouillet put it: *traduire, c'est contrefaire* (translating [without permission] is counterfeiting).[9]

The circumstances under which the right applies was also broadened. In 1907 Pouillet described as the prevailing opinion that actual, or at least potential, damage is required for a finding of infringement. In other words, the infringer's actions must be shown to affect the right owner's market negatively. Pouillet, however, criticized this view as being too narrow. In his view, copyright being a property right, any commercial use of the work must be considered infringing, whether it be destined for the same market as the original edition or for some different application.[10]

Together, all this led to a more abstract and at the same time more encompassing concept of what may be relevant exploitation, and the view that the 'droit d'édition' did cover any form of copying a work for profit made headway.

9. E. Pouillet, *Traité théorique et pratique de la propriété littéraire et artistique et du droit de représentation*, 3d ed., Paris, 1908, no. 533.

10. Pouillet, *supra* note 9, no. 471.

4.2 PHONORECORDS AND ANCILLARY COPIES

As new technologies developed, the scope of the reproduction right increased. One of the more fundamental steps was the clarification through several court decisions that phonorecords , although containing performances, do not as such fall under the performing right but belong to the scope of the reproduction right, or *droit d'édition*, as it was then still called in France. At the same time, this finding also implied that an object from which the work can only be perceived with the aid of a machine or device could still be a reproduction. Conversely, after some hesitations, for instance in German Court cases, *broadcasts* were finally made the object of the performing right or a corollary thereto, not of the reproduction right.

Still another noteworthy development concerned the position of what may be called *ancillary copies*. In the German *Gottfried Keller* case, which was decided in 1923, a publisher had made printing plates and galley proofs in preparation for an edition which he intended to publish as soon as Gottfried Keller's novels would fall in the public domain, and the question arose whether these plates and proofs were themselves reproductions. The German Supreme Court came to a negative answer, again on the ground that printing plates in general cannot as such be used to enjoy the work, and that it would be unreasonable to come to a different decision where the galley proofs were concerned.[11]

According to modern doctrine, at least under the 1965 German Copyright Act, this situation has changed; ancillary copies now are also considered to be reproductions. Although they do not as such satisfy the interest of the public, they are nevertheless objects wherein the work is embodied, and that alone is enough to make them reproductions. What counts is the fact that the work has been embodied on a material support; not actual exploitation.

This position should not be understood as merely focusing on the statutory wording instead of at the interests at stake. In fact, this interpretation is probably primarily triggered by the feeling that, if protection is granted for a certain term, right owners must be able to enjoy it fully. Since exploitation cannot take effect right from the start, when the work is created, but has to be prepared first, the same should apply to competing exploitations after the term of copyright has expired.

4.3 PRIVATE COPYING: AUDIO AND VIDEO

The development of end-user accessible reproduction technology also widened the scope of reproduction in another respect. Until then, at least for all practical purposes, copyright only had to deal with 'acts of exploitation'. Even if most copyright statutes provided for a conceptually broad reproduction right, at the same time they made exceptions for small-scale copying for private or personal use, which was generally[12] considered permissible.

---

11. Reichsgericht (German Supreme Court), Judgement of 7 November 1923, *RGZ* 107, 277.
12. Although not without exceptions. Thus, the Belgian 1886 Copyright Act did not provide for a private use exception; F. van Isacker, *De exploitatierechten van de auteur* (The author's exploitation rights), Brussels, 1963, 180.

Photocopying and home taping, however, rapidly threatened or even actually began to interfere with the normal exploitation of copyright works. Although the 1901 German Copyright Statute expressly allowed making single copies for personal use, in the 1955 *Gema v. Grundig* case, the German Federal Supreme Court ruled that private (audio) copying by magnetophone could not profit from this exemption.[13] In its fundamental judgment the Court set out that the impact of (then) modern recording technology was such that it affected the right owner's interests, and that where the author's protection conflicts with the user's private sphere the former must come first, since without the author's creative labour the work would not have been available for copying in the first place.

The U.S. Supreme Court came to a different result in its *Betamax* decision[14]: home taping was considered not to be necessarily infringing. A major motive for this Court, however, lay in the fact that people often merely tape television broadcasts for time-shifting purposes, i.e. in order to watch the program at a moment which suits them better; not as a substitute for prerecorded tapes which they might otherwise have bought or hired.

The reasoning of the *Gema v. Grundig* Court led to considerable debate, yet it is more or less mirrored in the second paragraph of article 9 of the Berne Convention, which was adopted twelve years later and which stipulates that exceptions to the reproduction right may not interfere with the normal exploitation of the work.

Legal doctrine is fairly divided as regards the limits of copyright, and in fact always has been. While back in 1907 Kohler wrote that to make hand-written copies for personal use should be considered permissible 'as human life needs its freedom, and thought and what comes with it should no more be withdrawn from man than air and light',[15] half a century later[16] Van Isacker expressly stated that even such hand made copies are infringements:

> 'We believe the only sound conclusion would therefore be that the reproduction, regardless of whether it will have a strictly private or a public destination, under all and any circumstances remains subject to the author's previous consent. The fact that the author in most cases will never be aware of a truly and in every respect private reproduction and therefore almost never will be able to prevent it, is a practical obstacle which however has nothing to do with the legal principle'.[17]

---

13. Bundesgerichtshof (German Supreme Court), Judgement of 18 May 1955, *GRUR* 1956, 492.
14. *Sony Corp. v. Universal City Studios, Inc.*, 464 U.S. 417 (1984).
15. J. Kohler, *Urheberrecht an Schriftwerken und Verlagsrecht*, Stuttgart, 1907, 171: 'Man kann jemandem nicht verbieten, ein Schriftwerk für sich abzuschreiben, sofern das Abschreiben eben nür eigenpersönliche Zwecke haben soll. Auch hier liegt der Grund darin, dass das menschliche Leben seine Freiheit haben will, und dass Gedanken und Gedankenverbindungen dem Menschen ebensowenig entzogen werden sollen, wie Luft und Licht.'
16. Although half a century divides Van Isacker from Kohler, the 1886 Belgian Copyright Statute which formed the basis for Van Isacker's comment was in fact older than the German Literary Copyright Act of 1901.
17 'De enige gezonde conclusie schijnt ons dan ook te bevestigen dat de reproduktie, om het even of ze een strikt private of publieke bestemming zal ontvangen, steeds en in alle omstandigheden

It is open to doubt whether this practical obstacle really has nothing to do with the legal principle, and even more whether this 'only sound conclusion' does indeed represent the 'legal principle', except under the 1886 Belgian Copyright Act. It certainly is interesting to note what happened after the *Gema v. Grundig* judgment. Now that home taping formally required consent, Gema offered a licensing scheme to the public, and it seems that thousands of owners of tape recorders actually requested and were granted a license at some 12 German marks a year. However, as tape recorders became cheaper and more popular, compliance (or rather the lack of it) developed into such a problem that a different approach was followed in the new 1965 Copyright Act. Under the new regime, home taping for private use is no longer infringing, while a 5 % levy is added to the price of the hardware in order to compensate the right owners. Some years later, it was supplemented with a blank tape levy.

4.4 REPROGRAPHY

Similar developments have taken place in the field of reprography. Here too, the statutory reproduction right generally was wide enough to cover all forms of reprography, or if it was not, it could be expanded so as to cover it. This is precisely what happened in The Netherlands, where until 1972 the Copyright Act permitted to make one or just a few copies of a work, provided they were destined for the copying person's private use. The 1972 revised Act, however, considered reprography as a threat to authors and publishers and essentially limited permissible reprography to articles or small portions of books, such copies to be used in certain situations only; besides, the Act provided that equitable remuneration should be paid to the right owners.

Remuneration schemes, however, proved hard to implement, while year after year copying grew more popular, both within and outside the statutory limits. In 1995, a bill which essentially should have subjected all relevant photocopies to the remuneration scheme failed in the Senate; mainly because the administrative obligations for owners of photocopying equipment were considered outrageous while safeguards against unjustified right owner demands[18] were seen as insufficient; but also because the Senate questioned whether all and any copies made from protected material should be subject to remuneration, regardless of their function or impact.

This is just how it went in The Netherlands; the situation may be different in other countries. Still, more in general, the experiences in this particular sub-domain of the reproduction right do not seem very inspiring.

---

onderworpen blijft aan de voorafgaandelijke instemming van de auteur. Het feit dat de auteur in de meeste gevallen een werkelijk en in alle opzichten private reproduktie nooit zal kennen en derhalve nagenoeg nimmer zal kunnen verhinderen, is een praktische moeilijkheid, welke aan het juridische principe echter vreemd blijft.' Van Isacker, *supra* note 12, 180.

18. Such rights to be exercised exclusively by the *Stichting Reprorecht* (the Dutch RRO), on behalf of authors and publishers.

4.5 SOFTWARE COPYRIGHT

The last development (and extension) of the reproduction right which should be mentioned here concerns software copyright; and more in particular the loading of computer programs in a computer's internal memory. Software copyright has profoundly influenced copyright law, and may well continue to do so over the next decades. This is not only true for the very fact that software has received the status of a copyright work, but for many aspects of how it is protected as well.

It is not surprising that, once the discussion as to the status of computer software had subsided, it also was universally accepted that software copies on floppy or hard disks are reproductions. Such copies can rightly be compared to CDs or even phonorecord copies of musical works; the fact that one needs some machine in order to display or hear the works is no reason not to call them reproductions. But merely loading a program in internal memory is not quite the same thing. Stored in RAM, if anywhere, the program serves but one goal: to make the computer do its job. It is rarely, if ever copied from RAM to another support, except perhaps elsewhere in the same RAM memory; it is not even saved at the end of the session, but simply erased; and while it may probably be displayed on the screen and studied page by page, in practice this is quite rare and certainly not done by any ordinary user (except where the user interface is concerned). For the rest, the program code simply controls the internal process.

Moreover, the computer may merely load in internal memory such parts and pieces of the program as are needed at a certain moment, and those parts need not necessarily always consist of copyrightable subject matter. Still, once the question arose whether loading a program into the computer's internal memory can also be seen as reproduction, the debate did not so much deal with this *fixation* aspect: when do we consider a work to have been fixed on a material support? Instead, it mainly focused on the fact that applying the reproduction right to RAM storage does amount to granting rights for the actual *use* of a copyright work; a thing which copyright had never done before. Once that objection had been brushed aside as being simply too doctrinary, it was also accepted that loading a program in RAM amounts to reproduction.

Yet this is not surprising if one looks at what was at stake. Loading a program in RAM needed to be controlled if software copyright was to offer effective control at all. One server may serve a whole battery of PCs, enabling all of them time and again to use the program. The impact of loading a program in RAM simply is so great that some right had to deal with it. Now that copyright had been chosen as the tool for software protection, the reproduction right certainly was closest at hand, and ready to be stretched if there needed to be any stretching.

5. A Few Lessons from History

5.1 INDEPENDENCE OR CONTROL

Over a century ago the Belgian copyright scholar Paul Wauwermans explained the difference between the public performance and display rights on the one hand, and the reproduction right on the other, by stressing that the author may choose between two alternatives: he may either transfer a copy to the user or have the work performed. In the latter case, 'the listener will only take home recollections, thoughts, merely intangibles'.[19] It follows that, in contrast to performances, copies are tangible objects which (so to say) one can take home.

Nowadays it is difficult to imagine how a century ago musical or theatrical performances often were events not to be missed, as it might be years before one would get another chance to hear that same symphony performed or see that same play on stage. Gramophone, CD and television have drastically altered all that. But although television even brought the cinema to the home, it was not until in our time that video-recording made time-shifting possible, thus also removing the constraints of time with respect to the exploitation of movies.

The importance of all this reproduction technology for copyright practice can hardly be overestimated. Copies stand for *independence*. Where public performances are concerned, the customer has to be in the right spot at the right time. *Please, honey, don't be late, I want to be there when the band starts playing*[20] nicely sums up the customer's position where performances are concerned. Moreover, he probably also will have to buy a ticket first. In contrast, one may read a book, listen to a record or watch a video whenever one likes. Copies free the user from limits of place and time. They also free him from the right owner's control: he may use the copy time and again without having to buy another ticket. If the author is to have his due, he must therefore at least be able to exercise control over copies being made.

In order to reach this goal, the evolution of the reproduction right follows and reflects technological development. As new technologies are invented and mature, printing is first generalized to reproduction, and time and again the characteristics of the reproduction right are adapted and widened. At the same time, exceptions to the right are abolished or limited. Today, the reproduction right may more or less cover any fixation, no matter how technically sophisticated and ephemeral, provided it is durable enough to enable some form of use or further communication of the work, so as to give the right owners as much control as possible over the exploitation and use of their works. Over and again, *control* is the key word, and

19. P. Wauwermans, *Le droit des auteurs en Belgique*, Brussels, 1894, 219: 'Ou bien l'auteur cède une reproduction matérielle de son oeuvre, transmet à celui avec qui il veut se mettre en communication intellectuelle un exemplaire du livre, une copie du tableau. Il exercera, pour atteindre ce but, le droit de multiplication, d'édition, de reproduction. Ou bien il cherchera à faire jouir de son oeuvre par des procédés d'exécution: l'auditeur n'emportera que des souvenirs, des pensées, rien que d'immatériel. C'est le droit de représentation, d'exécution musicale ou dramatique'.

20. Quoted, I believe, from Irving Berlin's *Alexander's Ragtime Band*.

any fixation, no matter how ephemeral, may be considered relevant if to label it 'reproduction' can help right owners to stay in command; especially if such copies enable the user to access the work.

5.2 END-USER REPRODUCTION

The reproduction right has done quite well where protected works are reproduced professionally and in comparatively large numbers. For one thing, infringements are easier to trace, while transaction costs are relatively modest. Widespread small-scale reproduction like home taping and reprography, on the other hand, has proved much harder to regulate, at least in practice. Where users make their own copies, one could almost say *they* are in control, instead of the right owners.

The problem is further enhanced by the fact that in the field of home taping and reprography it is all but impossible to devise satisfactory remuneration schemes. Such payments as are made never seem to be even remotely related to the copies one actually makes and, to make things worse, the money can only be distributed along extremely general lines, which have little or nothing to do with the copying as such. Moreover, the cost of collecting and distributing the money is considerable, at times even appalling. Such considerations do not encourage end-users' compliance with the statutory rules. To the extent that the reproduction right aims at control, it therefore has not done particularly well in this area.

5.3 COPIES AS TRANSACTION OBJECTS

There is yet another angle which deserves attention. In the 'classic' situation where one buys a book or record, the copy not only embodies the work, it also forms the object for a transaction whereby the user acquires access to the work while at the same time paying for it. The royalty often forms part of the price, and while the copy moves from the publisher towards the user, the royalty so to say moves in the opposite direction towards the right owner. This may not always be true, and it may not be the essence of the reproduction right, but it nevertheless may help explaining why the reproduction right worked quite satisfactory in the classic situation where publishers printed editions consisting of thousands of copies, while it seems to be so much of a problem now. The traditional copy not only embodies the work, it also is an instrument which demonstrates the right owner's consent, and which through its being sold facilitates royalty payments.

Moreover, it also gives the buyer the feeling that he really is acquiring something for which he is willing to pay. In other words, while the law states that *any fixation* of a work in material form is a reproduction, the reproduction right's success in practice may at least be enhanced where reproductions are truly *tangible* objects, which are produced by a professional third party who markets them, and where sale or rental leads to some form of relationship between right owner and end-user.

Incidentally, it can be pointed out that there is only a very loose relation between the royalty which may form part of the copy's price and the copied work. After all, one has to pay more for a bound copy than for a paperback of the same novel. Nor is there a direct relationship between the price one pays and the extent to which the copy may be used. A book may be read time and again or lent to a friend without additional payment being required. In other words: a *per copy* price is not necessarily also a *per use* price.

6. Overstretching the Reproduction Right?

In several respects, copies in electronic networks are different from their traditional counterparts. On the Internet copies are no longer transported, they are simply produced on demand, or even without demand, while they are as easily discarded again. In a way this recalls the now long obsolete practice of Indian tribes, who on their errands on arrival in a new camp used to make baskets and other useful products, only to throw them away when the journey was resumed, for it was easier to produce them whenever they were needed than to carry them all the way all the time.

Nevertheless, the making of copies understandably remains a point of focus. On the net transmission may be the goal, but copies are the tool, and traditionally copyright focuses on tools at least as much as on goals. For two centuries the reproduction right has adapted itself to all kinds of technological developments; it is only logical that this should happen once more with electronic networks. Given the impact of the Internet, where anyone may upload anything, public domain or not, for commercial reasons or out of sheer enthusiasm, while anything which has been uploaded may spread through the net like a virus, it is not surprising that the reproduction right is applied to these copies.

Nor is it unreasonable. After all, although their numbers may be much larger, Internet copies serve the same ends as traditional copies, i.e. to permit access to protected works. As said before, if copyright owners are to have their due, they must at least be able to exercise control over copies being made where such copies enable others to access the work. The fact that one transmission often involves a whole range of reproductions being made does not so much alter the principle.

Probably most people will accept that the reproduction right should apply to uploading, given its potential for eventually communicating protected works. The main itch concerns copies which the end user makes; not only user downloads, but first of all RAM copies made during consultation. Such reproductions do not feel like copies, although they meet the current definitions for reproduction. They also seem harmless but may nevertheless form a severe protection gap if they should fall outside the scope of copyright altogether. Here, the desire for control clashes with the compliance problem described above with respect to home taping and reprography. While the Internet's potential for massive communication seems to require even more control than earlier technology, at the same time the net's extremely distributed small-scale end user reproduction brings such control further out of reach than ever, if experiences with home taping and reprography are anything to go by.

Conclusions

Nevertheless, two of the conclusions from the historical review given above may perhaps help in somewhat bridging this gap between control and compliance. First, in at least one respect there is an essential difference between the more traditional methods of end-user reproduction and electronic network copying. Home taping and reprography are impossible to regulate through a per-transaction license, while networks have at least the potential for such licensing. Documents can contain codes which identify the right owner as well as the work, and which can be used for licensing purposes. I certainly do not support systems where any copy made on-line is automatically reported back to the right holder, but the potential for voluntary licensing is extremely welcome.

This brings us to the second point. As mentioned above, traditional copies such as books and records can as a rule be used over and again without additional payments being required. If right owners wish to make electronic network licensing a success, perhaps they should not be too touchy about any separate copy that is made. If users are left a reasonable amount of freedom and are given value for money as well, compliance may turn out to be less of a problem than with traditional end-user copies. What is needed most are practical solutions to make copyright on the Internet effective without making it threatening or needlessly interfering; such as campus licenses which allow certain user groups to access entire databases, instead of making users pay per document they actually consult.

Seen from this historical perspective, the present application of the reproduction right to electronic networks does not seem unreasonable or overstretched. The net even may permit effective licensing for end-user copying. For the time being, there seems to be no need for specific legislation with respect to electronic network reproduction.

Adapting Copyright to the Information Superhighway

*P. Bernt Hugenholtz**

1. Towards the Information Superhighway

> '... within the foreseeable future we will have computer systems in which thousands or even millions of authors' works – books, articles, pictorial works, maps, music, plays, recordings, motion pictures, and other forms of artistic expression – are permanently stored in a single copy. These computer systems will be linked, by wire or laser beams or communications satellites or some other method, with other computers throughout the world. These in turn will be linked with viewing screens in public institutions and in private homes and businesses. Any work from this great body of authorship could instantly be inspected by anyone in reach of a viewing screen, and that person could obtain a copy of any or all of the works merely by pressing buttons. In many cases the demand and need for printed copies will completely disappear'.[1]

More than 25 years have passed since Barbara Ringer predicted the advent of the digital networked environment and the profound impact this would have on the law of copyright. In 1996 much of Barbara Ringer's prediction has materialized. Today, more than 25 million computer owners are linked on a global scale by the Internet, the forerunner of the information superhighway. Internet users all over the world have direct access to vast quantities of text, data, maps, photographs, computer games, still and moving images, and sound recordings. Spectacular advances in network fidelity, data compression and storage capacity will enable the Internet (or any other computerized telecommunication network) to eventually carry nearly the complete Berne Convention catalogue of works. Moreover, the digital environment will enable traditionally distinct categories of works to merge into new breeds of works containing information in a plurality of 'modes', so-called *multimedia* works.

Indeed, the advent of the information superhighway has not taken the copyright community entirely by surprise. The copyright problems of

---

* Associate Professor, Institute for Information Law, University of Amsterdam; advocate, Stibbe Simont Monahan Duhot, Amsterdam. This paper is based on studies prepared for the European Commission (DG XIII and DG XV) in 1994 and 1995.

1. B. Ringer, 'The Use of Copyrighted Works in Information Storage and Retrieval Systems', German translation in: *GRUR Int* 1968, 18.

computerized information storage and retrieval systems have been studied ever since the early 1970's.[2] Problems relating to the dissemination of copyrighted works through cable networks are equally well researched. Moreover, 'multimedia' works have been in existence, albeit in a somewhat primitive form, for many years; video games and moving pictures are well-known examples of 'multimedia' works *avant la lettre*.

So, one might conclude, we have seen it all before: the arrival of the information superhighway is an evolutionary, not a revolutionary development. The existing copyright system has proven to be flexible enough in the past. There is no need for radical changes in the future; never change a winning team.

Arguably, this down-to-earth approach would make a sensible and pragmatic short-term solution. If the European Software Directive[3] has proven anything, it is that legislators should not overreact to the problems presented by new information technologies. In the long run, however, this conservative approach will probably not suffice. The development of the information superhighway is, admittedly, a gradual process. But the combined effects of mass digitalization, networking on a global scale, and information delivery on demand, will eventually require more than just piece-meal changes to the present copyright system. The emerging digital networked environment is affecting the very economic underpinnings of the present copyright system. In the end, a thorough rethinking of the copyright paradigm will probably be inevitable.[4]

No such exercise will be undertaken in this article. Its main purpose is to suggest short term solutions, primarily from a European perspective, to some of the most pressing copyright problems of the digital networked environment. The focus of this paper, then, will be on the scope and limitations of the existing catalogue of protected rights (§§ 2-4). How do the various acts of network communication (digitization, uploading, transmission, browsing, viewing, downloading) fit into the current system? Is there an imminent need for redefinition or clarification of the exploitation rights? Will existing copyright exemptions survive in the new environment? Does the good-old 'old media' exhaustion rule come into play?

Prior to these discussions, I will make some more general observations on the nature of the 'information superhighway', as it affects – or may affect – the law of copyright, both in theory and practice.

---

2. *See* e.g. E. Ulmer, *Elektronische Datenbanken und Urheberrecht*, Munich, 1971; D. Goose, *Die urheberrechtliche Beurteilung von elektronischen und Mikrofilm-Datenbanken*, Berlin, 1975; P.B. Hugenholtz, *Auteursrecht en information retrieval. Verveelvoudiging en openbaarmaking in het computertijdperk*, Deventer, 1982; P. Katzenberger, 'Urheberrechtsfragen der elektronischen Textkommunikation', *GRUR Int* 1983, 895; F. Gotzen, 'Grandes orientations du droit d'auteur dans les états-membres de la C.E.E. en matière de banques de données', in: *Banques de données et droit d'auteur*, Paris, 1987, 85; A. Lucas, *Le droit de l'informatique*, Paris, 1987, 289; *Les nouveaux moyens de reproduction*, XXXVII Travaux de l'Association Henri Capitant, Journées néerlandaises, Paris, 1988; M. Vivant (ed.), *Lamy droit de l'informatique*, nos. 1563-1617.
3. Directive of the Council of the European Communities of 17 May 1991, O.J.EC L 122/42.
4. *See* Egbert J. Dommering, 'Copyright being washed away through the electronic sieve', elsewhere in this volume.

1.1 THE INFORMATION SUPERHIGHWAY

In this article, the '(information) superhighway' shall be short-hand for the digital networked environment of the near future. The superhighway is neither a new product, nor a new service, nor a new type of network. It represents the integrated, broad-band, high-speed, general-purpose telecommunications network of the coming century. The superhighway will not be a single physical network, but a conglomerate of local, regional, national and transnational telecommunications infrastructures, interlinked to form a global information superhighway.

From a technical perspective, the superhighway is not homogeneous. The necessary physical links will be provided by copper wires, optical fibres, radio links and satellites, or a combination thereof. In the superhighway a variety of existing telecommunications infrastructures, such as the telephone network, cable networks, satellite networks and broadcasting stations will converge. The infrastructure of the superhighway will not be operated by a single, monopolistic telecommunications operator. It will not be a monolithic network; parts of it will be controlled by operators under a state monopoly, other parts by private companies. Users and information providers will probably not deal with these network operators directly; access and service providers will provide the necessary telecommunications services and facilities.

The superhighway will be a broad-band network, permitting the communication of data, text, audio, video and images at high speed and high fidelity. As an integrated 'network of existing networks', the superhighway will carry both digital and analogue signals. In contrast to most existing cable networks, the superhighway will permit interactive, two-way communication. Information can be uploaded and downloaded to and from any point in the network; consumers will be able to receive information on individual demand. Conversely, information users may become information providers as well.

Will tomorrow's superhighway be the Internet of today? Perhaps. Clearly, many aspects of the above-mentioned definition presently apply to the Internet. However, the Internet's limited bandwidth does not, as yet, make full scale audio and video services (either broadcast or on-demand) a realistic option. These technical limits notwithstanding, most of the copyright problems discussed in this article exist – and require solution – in the context of the Internet as well.

1.2 CONVERGENCE

The emerging superhighway and the multimedia programs it will carry, exemplify the general trend towards convergence in the telecommunications and information industry. This tendency can be perceived on different levels.

Convergence of 'platforms'

In analogue times, different modes of communications required dedicated 'platforms'. For switched voice telecommunications (POTS: 'plain old telephone service'), narrow-band networks were used, which were traditionally operated by state-controlled PTTs. Radio and television programs were disseminated over hertzian waves or, in a later stage of development, via broad-band cable networks. Similarly, for various forms of off-line communications genre-specific media were employed. Printed paper carried text or photo's, vinyl records carried sound, celluloid film carried moving pictures.

In the emerging digital environment, the medium is gradually being 'liberated' from the message. PTT-operated telephone networks will soon carry full-motion video programs. Cable networks will provide interactive programming and person-to-person voice and data communications. Compact discs will carry motion pictures and all sorts of interactive multimedia programs. Traditional print media are giving way to electronic delivery systems as the preferred platform for disseminating text and data.

This convergence of 'platforms' directly affects the structure of the present copyright system. In the digital environment the existing borderlines between the different genres of works are becoming blurred and hard to maintain. This is problematic, since the present copyright system does not protect each genre equally; in most European countries, e.g., a computer program is better protected than, say, a novel.[5] Moreover, in many countries the rightholder's exploitation rights are defined in platform or genre specific terms: right of printing, right of broadcasting, right of cable distribution, etc.

Convergence of roles

As the Internet experience clearly demonstrates, traditional actors in the communications process (information producer, provider, publisher, intermediary and user) will take on new roles in the digital networked environment. The Internet is structured as an 'open platform model', as opposed to the 'broadcasting model' of most existing mass media. On the Internet authors may freely disseminate their works without the intervention of traditional publishers: authors are becoming 'publishers'. Moreover, digital technology enables users to actively search and manipulate information available on the network: users are becoming authors. Furthermore, traditional intermediaries, such as university libraries, may take on new roles as information providers: intermediaries are becoming publishers as well. This convergence of roles may eventually affect the existing system of rights allocation in copyright and neighbouring rights legislation.

1.3 COMMUNICATING ON THE SUPERHIGHWAY: A CHANGE OF PARADIGMS?

The digital networked environment of the superhighway represents a change of paradigms for the traditional copyright industries. Mass circulation of copies carrying identical information products is replaced by transmission of customized

5. Pursuant to the European Software Directive, *supra* note 3, most copyright exemptions that apply to ordinary 'writings', e.g. for private copying, are not valid in respect of computer programs.

information on demand. In this process, the 'public sphere' between information provider and information user is gradually dissolving.[6] The act of 'publishing' thereby loses much of its original connotation. The increasingly 'private' nature of information distribution on the superhighway is amplified by the increasing use of encryption techniques.

Information on demand

The superhighway infrastructure enables users to actively communicate with information providers: *interactivity*. Users can retrieve information of their choice from information banks at innumerable points on the network. Conversely, publishers and other information providers will 'customize' information to accommodate specific user demands, employing detailed 'user profiles' drawn up from previous usage patterns. In this process of interactive and customized information usage, the information product will gradually lose its 'concrete' form of expression. Instead, the product will merely serve as a source file for an infinite variety of derivative information products on demand.

Interactivity and customization combined will make existing (or future) legal distinctions between 'stand-alone' and collective works (such as audiovisual works and databases) difficult to maintain. On the superhighway, the collective work will rarely be consumed in its entirety. Instead, the interactive user will use only the most useful (customized) 'bits and pieces'– the 'nuggets' of the treasure trove. For this reason alone, creating a separate 'multimedia' work category would be ill advised.

It is expected delivery on demand will gradually replace 'broadcasting'(the simulcasting of information to a passive audience) as the principal communication pattern of the superhighway. In the future, unlike today's Internet, proprietary information will probably no longer 'roam around freely over the net'.[7]

Metering

The intelligence built into the superhighway will enable information providers to precisely monitor and control the individual user's information consumption. Whereas in the present world of physical copies, royalties are calculated on a per-copy basis, on the superhighway royalties can – and will – be charged per actual use. A per-use ('pay-as-you-go') royalty scheme may be either time-based or volume-based; of course, flat rate schemes are possible as well.

---

6. Th. Dreier, 'Copyright digitized: philosophical impacts and practical implications for information exchange in digital networks', WIPO Worldwide Symposium on the Impact of Digital Technology on Copyright and Neighbouring Rights, Harvard University, 31 March - 2 April 1993. WIPO Publication No. 723 (E), Geneva, 1993, 187, at 198.

7. Allen N. Dixon & Laurie C. Self, 'Copyright protection for the information superhighway', *EIPR* 1994, 465, at 466.

Direct licensing

Many rightholders believe (or wish to believe) that the built-in intelligence of the superhighway will enable them to grant and administrate licenses to individual users themselves. Works disseminated over the superhighway will carry identifying 'tags', inviting prospective users to (automatically) contact right owners, or 'permission headers', pre-determined licensing conditions to which users may agree in real time.[8] 'Self-administration of rights' might gradually replace collective licensing or collective administration of rights. Thus, the digital networked would bring back to rightholders what they (nearly) lost in the age of mass copying: the power to transact directly with information users.

Encryption

Encryption of information-carrying signals is already customary in some branches of the information industry: satellite-to-cable broadcasting, subscription television, pay television, etc. To other branches, such as the book trade, encryption is totally alien. The computer software industry retains painful memories of the market failure of the 'copy protection' schemes applied in the 1980's. Consumers simply refused to buy computer programs containing anti-copying algorithms or devices. At present, copy protection has become all but extinct.

Many in the information industry predict that encryption (on various levels) will eventually replace copyright law as the principal means of protection on the superhighway. According to the oft-quoted Charles Clark, 'the answer to the machine is in the machine'.[9] However, the recent experiences of the software industry indicate that, perhaps, it would be imprudent to solely rely on technical solutions.

Ironically, the implementation of encryption technology is being hampered, in many countries, by existing or proposed restrictions under public telecommunications law, for reasons of public security, to use encryption hardware devices or encoding software.

2. Exploitation Rights on the Superhighway

Copyright owners are protected by a bundle of exclusive exploitation rights. National legislators have applied different methods in defining the catalogue of exclusive rights, enumerating the various 'restricted acts'. In some countries, copyright laws provide for rather detailed, media-specific definitions of the restricted acts. In others broader, and more abstract, notions of 'reproduction', 'distribution' and 'communication to the public' are applied.

Either way, the exploitation rights serve as abstractions of the various acts that constitute exploitation from an economic point of view. Many restricted acts

8. 'Technological strategies for protecting intellectual property in the networked multimedia environment', *The Journal of the IMA Intellectual Property Project* 1994, Vol. 1, no. 1.

9. Charles Clark, 'The Answer to the Machine is in the Machine', elsewhere in this book, 139.

are patterned after existing modes of exploitation: publication in book form, public performance, broadcasting, etc. However, the digital networked environment of the superhighway represents a radical change in the way copyrighted works are exploited. Mass distribution of copies or signals carrying identical information is replaced by transmission on individual demand of customized information.

Thus, the existing set of exploitation rights, as defined in national or international legal instruments, does not necessarily reflect the manner in which protected works are communicated in the digital networked environment. The advent of the superhighway, therefore, presents legislators with a choice: either expand or modify existing 'old media notions'[10] or redefine the catalogue of restricted acts, taking into account the peculiarities of the new environment.

In examining these rights legislators (and courts) should not, in my opinion, focus on technological detail, but follow the *normative approach* inherent in the law of copyright. Existing rights and limitations are not merely technical, descriptive notions, but purpose-oriented; they must be applied and interpreted accordingly.

Communicating copyrighted works on the superhighway may involve one or more of the following acts:

- digital reproduction, adaptation
- temporary storage
- providing on-line access
- point-to-point transmission
- broadcasting
- dissemination in closed user groups
- decoding
- screen display or use

2.1 DIGITAL REPRODUCTION AND ADAPTATION

There is general agreement that the storage of a protected work in a digital medium amounts to a *reproduction* (copy) within the meaning of article 9 (1) of the Berne Convention. The words 'in any manner or form' in this provision are clearly meant to cover all methods of reproduction, including storage in electronic digital form. Clearly, there is reproduction whenever protected works stored in digital form are *uploaded* or *downloaded* to or from a host computer or server. Uploading and downloading will result in copies of the work being permanently stored in the server's and/or end user's computers. Of course, any further duplication of the digitally stored work will be considered a subsequent act of reproduction.

Under normal circumstances, converting a work into a digital format will not, as such, result in an *adaptation* or other alteration. The conversion process does not alter the composition or form of expression of the work; the converted file is a reproduction, not an adaptation, translation or transformation. Arguably, the same

10. Paul Geller, 'The Universal Electronic Archive', 25 *IIC* 54 (1994).

is true for any comparable act of data compression, decompression, encoding or decoding.

Of course, this is different if the work is digitally reworked or manipulated; the manipulated work will, indeed, qualify as an (unauthorized) adaptation. It goes without saying that digital manipulation bears the risk of infringing moral rights as well.

2.2 TEMPORARY STORAGE

In various stages of its journey through the digital network the work will be temporarily stored, either in whole or in part. Every act of transmission will involve one or more acts of loading the work in a (volatile) computer memory. In the process of being routed through the network, the work is constantly being 'stored and forwarded'. Furthermore, the acts of downloading and screen display may involve subsequent acts of temporary storage of (parts of) the protected work.

Opinions differ as to whether temporary storage qualifies as an act of reproduction. Article 4(a) of the Software Directive[11] and articles 5(a) and 7(2)(a) of the recently adopted European Database Directive[12] all refer to 'temporary reproduction'. The Software Directive seems to take an especially broad view of the reproduction right; according to its article 4(a), the protected acts include:

> '... the permanent or temporary reproduction of a computer program by any means and in any form, in part or in whole. In so far as loading, displaying, running, transmission or storage of the computer program necessitates such reproduction, such acts shall be subject to authorization of the rightholder.'[13]

However, under close scrutiny article 4 (a) of the Directive does not guarantee an exclusive right of loading, displaying or running the protected program; these acts must 'necessitate such reproduction'. This definition leaves a certain latitude to national courts and legislators in determining the scope of the notion of 'reproduction'.[14]

At present, in many countries the copyright status of temporary storage is unclear. An exception is the United Kingdom; under Section 17 (6) of the Copyright, Designs and Patents Act (CDPA) '[c]opying in relation to any description of work includes the making of copies which are transient or are incidental to some other use of the work.' In contrast, Section 101 of the United States Copyright Act distinguishes between merely 'transitory' storage and more

---

11. *Supra*, note 3.
12. Directive 96/9/EC of the European Parliament and of the Council on the Legal Protection of Data Bases, Brussels, 11 March 1996.
13. Under article 5 (1) of the Software Directive no authorization for these acts is needed 'where they are necessary for the use of the computer program by the lawful acquirer in accordance with its intended purpose (..)'.
14. *Cf.* Bundesgerichtshof (German Supreme Court), Decision of 20 January 1994 ('Holzhandels-programm'), *Computer und Recht* 1994, 275. The Court left expressly undecided the question of whether the act of running a computer program is restricted under the Software Directive.

permanent or stable forms of reproduction. This follows from the definition of the term 'fixed' used in the definition of 'copies' in Section 101:

> 'A work is "fixed" in a tangible medium of expression when its embodiment in a copy or phonorecord, by or under the authority of the author, is sufficiently permanent or stable to permit it to be perceived, reproduced, or otherwise communicated for a period of more than transitory duration.'

Perhaps, not all forms of temporary storage should be treated equally under copyright law. Acts of short-lived copying as mere byproducts of a technical communication process, such as the 'store-and-forward' mechanisms used on the Internet and other digital networks, should not be qualified as acts of reproduction. A similar argument can be made in respect of screen display; see below at § 2.7.

2.3 PROVIDING ON-LINE ACCESS; DELIVERY-ON-DEMAND

What makes the superhighway infrastructure really different from existing broadcasting or cable networks is its capacity for two-way communication. By linking an existing information bank to a publicly accessible host or server, the information contained in the information bank becomes instantly available to the (general) public. Does this amount to a restricted act? Probably not under the Berne Convention. The Convention does not provide for a general *right of communication to the public*, such as the Dutch 'recht van openbaarmaking'.[15]

Providing on-line access and disseminating works over networks are acts of exploitation that do not fit nicely in those national laws that list the protected acts in a platform-specific manner. The copyright status of electronic delivery on demand appears to be especially problematic in Germany. Electronic delivery-on-demand probably does not qualify as either 'distribution', 'broadcasting' or other act of communication restricted by the German Copyright Act. By contrast, the performance right in France, including a broadly defined right of 'télédiffusion', appears to be especially well adapted to the digital environment.[16]

Many national legislators fail to deal with the mere act of making a work *accessible* (by electronic or other means) to the public. In this respect, the Spanish Copyright Act is a notable exception. Under article 20 § 2 (h) of the Spanish Act 'communication to the public' includes 'public access to computer databases by means of telecommunication, where such databases incorporate or constitute protected works.'[17]

---

15. Dutch Copyright Act, article 12.
16. Article L-122 (2) of the French Copyright Act; *see* A. Lucas & H.-J. Lucas, *Traité de la propriété littéraire et artistique*, Paris, 1994, no. 338. *See* for a general overview of the law in EU and EFTA Member States: P.B. Hugenholtz and D.J.G. Visser, *Copyright problems of electronic document delivery: a comparative analysis*, Report to the Commission of the European Communities, Luxembourg, 1995.
17. Article 20 § 2 (h) Law on Intellectual Property, no. 22, of 11 November 1987, as amended on 7 July 1992 [WIPO Translation].

According to the European Commission's preferred interpretation of the Directive on rental and lending rights,[18] the delivery-on-demand in a networked environment could amount to an act of 'rental' or 'lending'.[19] From an economic perspective, this broad interpretation (or extension) of the rental right is, perhaps, understandable. Indeed, the superhighway has the capability of substituting the distribution of physical copies by on-line delivery on demand. Moreover, the solution proposed by the Commission is attractive in so far as that it 'automatically' harmonizes an exclusive right of electronic delivery-on-demand on the European level.

However, the Commission's electronic rental right is conceptually flawed. Systematically, the rental right has its origins in the exhaustion doctrine, which – the Commission assumes – should not be applied to any rights of transmission. The rental right is devised as an exception to the exhaustion rule.[20] It would be systematically unsound to simply transplant this right into the digital networked environment, where physical copies no longer are distributed. Therefore, application of the Directive to electronic delivery-on-demand would not appear to be justified.

2.4 POINT-TO-POINT TRANSMISSIONS, CLOSED USER GROUPS

Under current copyright law, the act of transmitting a protected work over the network does not as such amount to a restricted act, unless the transmission is part of a broader process involving reproduction or communication to the public.

Here too, a normative approach is called for. The rationale of the right of communication to the public is, primarily, of an economic nature; copyright owners must be protected against acts of exploitation outside the private sphere.

Under current copyright law, the act of transmitting a protected work over the network does not as such amount to a restricted act, unless the transmission is part of a broader process involving reproduction or communication to the public. 'Point-to-point' transmissions of protected works (e.g. involving two computer users connected by a modem or exchanging messages by e-mail) is basically no different from sending letters by ordinary mail, and should be treated accordingly.

How then can (unrestricted) point-to-point transmissions be distinguished from electronic delivery services that, in principle, should fall within the scope of the specific rights? Following the normative approach previously advocated, we should not focus on merely technical acts of digital transmission. Arguably, the right of communication to the public might be triggered by the act of publicly offering (the transmission of) a protected work. Thus, rightholders would be

18. Council Directive 92/100 on rental and lending rights and certain rights related to copyright in the field of intellectual property, O.J. EC no. L 346 of 27 November 1992, 61.

19. Commission of the European Communities, *Green Paper. Copyright and Related Rights in the Information Society*, Brussels, 19 July 1995, COM (95) 382 final, 58-59. *See* J. Reinbothe and S. Von Lewinski, *The EC Directive on Rental and Lending Rights and on Piracy*, London, 1993, 41-42.

20. *See infra* § 4.

protected against – even unsuccessful – delivery services, whereas point-to-point transmissions of an incidental or private nature would remain outside the scope of copyright.

Closed user groups and local area networks add complexity to the problems of defining the scope of existing exploitation rights. The question arises whether offering or transmitting a protected work to a closed user group qualifies as a communication to the *public*. In this context the notion of 'public' is critical.

National copyright laws do not apply the notion of 'public' in a uniform manner. The copyright status of secondary cable distribution is an interesting example. In some countries, such as The Netherlands,[21] all forms of cable distribution beyond the circle of family and friends are considered restricted acts. In other countries, such as Austria,[22] cable retransmission by means of small community antenna systems is exempted from the broadcasting right.

2.5 BROADCASTING

Even though delivery-on-demand will eventually be the preferred communication pattern on the superhighway, acts of 'broadcasting' information will still be common in the digital networked environment. Broadcasting is a common phenomenon on the Internet; electronic mail boxes are filled each day with unsolicited information simulcast from a single source to a plurality of users.

In respect of alphanumerical data and texts, acts of 'superhighway' broadcasting are probably not covered by any specific Berne Convention minimum right. Article 11 BC is applicable only to dramatic, dramatico-musical and musical works. Article 11*bis* BC concerns either primary over-the-air broadcasting or secondary wireless or cable distribution. Article 11*ter* BC refers to 'recitations'; article 14(1)(ii) BC to cinematographic adaptations. Even so, superhighway broadcasts will, in most cases, be considered acts of broadcasting, cable distribution, public performance or communication to the public by wire protected under national copyright laws.

Encrypted signals can be 'communicated to the public', assuming the codes are made available to a user group that is sufficiently 'public'. Compare article 1 (2)(c) of the European Satellite and Cable Directive:[23]

> 'if the programme-carrying signals are encrypted, then there is communication to the public by satellite on condition that the means for decrypting the broadcast are provided to the public by the broadcasting organization or with its consent.'

---

21. Hoge Raad (Supreme Court of the Netherlands), Judgement of 24 December 1993 (*Centraal Antennesysteem et al. v. BUMA*), [1994] 3 Ent.L.R. E-43.
22. Article 17 (3), Austrian Copyright Act.
23. Council Directive 93/83 on the coordination of certain rules concerning copyright and rights related to copyright applicable to satellite broadcasting and cable retransmission, O.J. EC no. L 248 of 6 October 1993, 15; cf. Section 6 (2) of the United Kingdom CDPA 1988.

Needless to say, the *absence* of encryption in a disseminated work should not be regarded as a forfeiture of copyright protection or an implied license to redistribute or reproduce the work.[24]

2.6 DECODING

Decoding encrypted information in a digital environment will, under normal circumstances, amount to an act of reproduction. A copy of the encrypted work is produced, unless the decoding is achieved in real-time, e.g. by using special decoding hardware, and the decoded file is not (temporarily) stored in or after the process. The act of decoding *as such* is not normally a restricted act, either under the Berne Convention or under national copyright laws.

A notable exception is the Software Directive; article 4 (b), read in conjunction with article 6, provides for a (conditional) right to prevent *decompilation*. Moreover, Article 7(1)(c) prohibits the unauthorized possession of or trade in computer software decoding devices. Similar prohibitions, aimed at preserving telecommunications secrecy or preventing computer crime, exist in many national telecommunications or computer crime laws. Arguably, copyright law is not the appropriate vehicle for such provisions; the trade in decoding devices is not an act of exploitation or use of the protected work.

Moreover, encryption techniques and other forms of technical protection are not instruments of protecting intellectual property – i.e. the work as such. They are merely means of protecting the signals or physical objects that carry information, be it copyright protected or not. Technical protection schemes are content-neutral; legal enforcement measures, therefore, belong to quite a different realm than copyright.

2.7 SCREEN DISPLAY

In the 'paper' world, the act of reading a document or viewing a television program does not qualify as a restricted act. This may be different in the digital networked environment. By displaying an electronically delivered document on a user terminal, part of the document is temporarily stored in the RAM memory of the user's computer, unless the user is equipped with a 'dumb' terminal (lacking memory facilities). Thus, screen display may be considered a (partial) reproduction of the work. Moreover, screen display may qualify as a 'public display', 'communication to the public' or comparable act, whenever a plurality of users watch the same computer terminal or screen.

Whether or not screen display amounts to a (partial) reproduction of the work displayed, is a contested issue. Arguably, qualifying screen display as reproduction would be a – technologically inspired – overstretching of the reproduction right.

24. P. Gyertyánfy, 'Conflicts and changes. The new technologies in the protection and administration of copyright', WIPO Harvard Symposium, *supra* note 6, 157, at 164.

The mere reception or consumption of information by the end user has traditionally remained outside the scope of the copyright monopoly.[25] The transition into the digital networked environment does not, as such, seem to justify such a radical extension of the exclusive right. Arguably, the right of privacy and the freedom of reception guaranteed in articles 8 and 10 of the European Convention on Human Rights would be unduly restricted by such an all-encompassing right.

Proponents of an exclusive right of screen display, however, argue that the screen display of a protected work is comparable to an act of 'printing' in the paper world.[26] Indeed, a work wholly or partly displayed on screen can be permanently stored or printed; thus the display can serve as a source file for subsequent (unauthorized) acts of copying.

In all, the copyright status of screen display appears to be a crucial question. Should the copyright monopoly include a *use right* in the digital networked environment? For computer programs, article 4 (a) of the Software Directive seems to point in that direction. In my opinion, we should be careful not to automatically extend this rule to *all* categories of works in new environment.[27] Freedom of reception considerations may, perhaps, not carry much weight in respect of computer programs; the superhighway will eventually carry the very works (political and literary commentary, journalistic expression, etc.) for which article 10 of the European Convention on Human Rights was written.

3. Limitations and Exemptions

National copyright laws are very different in defining the statutory limitations (exemptions) to the restricted acts. Some legislators provide for lengthy, hard-to read and hard-to-apply, detailed sets of copyright privileges, such as the United Kingdom's breathtaking set of library privileges.[28] Other laws contain only minimal exemptions, employing general notions of 'private use'. Most European copyright laws contain at least the following limitations:

- copying for personal (scientific, educational or private) use
- library privileges
- educational and scientific exemptions
- special rules for reprographic reproduction
- freedom of quotation
- freedom of news reporting

25. P.B. Hugenholtz, 'Convergence and Divergence in Intellectual Property Law: The Case of the Software Directive', in: Willem F. Korthals Altes, Egbert J. Dommering, P. Bernt Hugenholtz & Jan J.C. Kabel (eds.), *Information Law towards the 21st Century*, Deventer/Boston, 1992, 319, 323.
26. *See* 'The Printed Word', Preparatory document for and report of the WIPO/UNESCO committee of governmental experts, Geneva, 7-11 December 1987, *Copyright*, 1988, 74, § 182-191.
27. *Cf.* EC Green Paper, *supra* note 19, 51-52.
28. Sections 32-41 CDPA; see Hugenholtz & Visser, *supra* note 16, at 54-55.

The present system of copyright limitations presents users of copyrighted works with a bewildering array of detailed rules and regulations, most of which were written in a pre-electronic era. The existing set of limitations is especially hard on users and producers of *multimedia* works. In respect of multimedia works several incompatible regimes concur: reprography, home taping, computer software and/or database protection, etc. Which set of limitations will prevail in a given situation, is entirely unclear.

The inflexibility of current platform specific limitations combined with the expanding right of reproduction threatens to upset the traditional balance between copyright protection and user freedoms. Not surprisingly, libraries, intermediaries and users are pressing for the preservation of copyright limitations in the digital environment. This concern is reflected in the Green Paper of the NII Working Group on Intellectual Property Rights:

> 'As more and more works are available primarily or exclusively on-line, it is critical that researchers, students and other members of the general public have opportunities *on-line* equivalent to their current opportunities *off-line* to browse through copyrighted works in their schools and public libraries.'[29]

Right owners, on the other hand, argue that many of the existing limitations should *not* be preserved in the new environment. Existing statutory licenses for photocopying, home taping and other mass private reproduction, do not reflect a fundamental 'freedom to copy'. These statutory licenses have been introduced for merely practical reasons; no individual licensing of mass private reproduction was considered feasible. According to right owners, all this is changing in the digital networked environment. As licensing practices developed in the database publishing industry seem to indicate, licensing individual electronic usage is becoming a reality. From the right owner's perspective, in the digital environment the 'normal exploitation' of a work, as protected under article 9 (2) of the Berne Convention, would include *each and every act of use*.

There is merit in both arguments. Consequently, it would be too facile to recommend a mere restatement of existing limitations and exemptions. The rationale of many existing limitations may not justify simply converting them to the digital environment. Instead, we must differentiate. Exemptions having their origins in market failure (i.e. the inability of copyright owners to transact directly with users) deserve critical review and, perhaps, should not survive in the new environment.

However, many existing copyright exemptions do *not* exist because of market failure, but in order to protect human rights and basic societal needs. Copyright exemptions are not, necessarily, exceptions. Exemptions are instruments in finding the necessary balance between property rights in information and safeguarding the public interest. Private copying exemptions are principally aimed at protecting the individual's private sphere. Library privileges, archival exemptions, rights of news reporting and quotation rights are intended, inter alia, to safeguard our cultural

29. Preliminary Report (Green Paper) of the Working Group on Intellectual Property Rights, *Intellectual Property and the National Information Infrastructure*, Washington D.C., July 1994, 133.

heritage and foster the free flow of information. Other exemptions protect basic academic freedoms or serve essential educational purposes. These exemptions must, indeed, be preserved, as much as possible, in the digital networked environment.

Moreover, if the digital use right, mentioned above, would become reality, there are convincing arguments for *extending* the scope of existing exemptions in order to regain the necessary balance. Rights and exemptions are somehow intertwined; if the scope of rights increases, it may be necessary to broaden the exemptions accordingly.

4. Exhaustion of Rights

One of the most pressing problems to emerge from the previous paragraphs is the potential proliferation of exclusive rights pertaining to acts of digital communication. Applying a broad notion of 'reproduction', *every* such act – including transmission, reception and use – would be restricted. Arguably, a copyright of such an all-encompassing nature would be counterproductive and unduly restrictive to the information trade.

Moreover, an 'all-inclusive' copyright would be difficult to reconcile with basic European Union freedoms. The dissemination of information through the superhighway will not stop at national boundaries. In many cases the information provider will be located in one Member State, whereas the end user will be located in another Member State. In addition, the server or host might be located in a third Member State. If every act of disseminating a protected work through the network would qualify as a restricted act, the freedom to provide transborder information services might be severely hampered by exclusive intellectual property rights exercised on a national territorial basis. This would undermine the creation of a European information market.

In reviewing the scope of the exclusive right, we should take a close look at the 'exhaustion'(i.e. first sale) principle: does it apply in the digital networked environment? At present, copyright laws in many Member States provide for a right of distribution in respect of material copies of the protected work. Once these copies have been brought into circulation by or under license of the copyright owner, subsequent (secondary) acts of distribution, rental not included, fall outside the scope of the copyright monopoly (*national exhaustion*).

A similar exhaustion rule has been developed by the European Court of Justice in respect of transnational distribution of goods protected by intellectual property rights (*European exhaustion*).[30] According to the Court's interpretation of Articles 30 and 36 of the EC Treaty, absent harmonisation of intellectual property rights at the community level, the 'specific subject-matter' of intellectual property does not justify the exercise of distribution or importation rights on a per-country basis. Thus, the distribution right is exhausted in the entire Union, whenever a

30. *Cf.* e.g. European Court of Justice, Judgement of 20 January 1981, Cases 55/80 and 57/80 (*Membran & K-Tel*), 2 *CMLR* 44.

product is put on the market in a Member State by or under license of the rightholder. In other words, the distribution right can be exercised only once: in the Member State where the copies are first circulated, the 'country of origin'.

4.1 EXHAUSTION THEORIES

Of course, the exhaustion doctrine in copyright law has its roots in 'the technological paradigm of printing'.[31] Should this principle be applied in a similar manner in the digital networked environment? Prior to answering this question, we shall take a brief look at the rational underpinnings of the exhaustion rule[32]:

Ownership theory

According to this theory, the exhaustion principle reflects a trade-off between rights of intellectual property and property rights in physical goods. Property rights in protected goods would be unduly restricted if distribution rights were to remain intact after the goods are put on the market with the copyright owner's consent.

Freedom of commerce theory

By the same token, the free trade of goods would be excessively restricted if no exhaustion existed. This is essentially the reasoning underlying the European exhaustion rule developed by the Court of Justice.

Legal security

Market players have a legitimate interest in knowing the copyright status of goods being traded on the market. Since no public record of valid copyrights presently exists, legal security requires exhaustion after the initial (licensed) transaction.

Remuneration theory

Under this theory copyright owners are adequately compensated for the initial act of putting the protected goods on the market. Copyright owners do not 'deserve' additional compensation for any subsequent acts of distribution. However, upon critical examination, this 'theory' does not offer much guidance. If exhaustion would not apply to the distribution right, the copyright owner would no longer need to be fully compensated for the initial (first) sale. The copyright

31. Cf. U.S. Congress, Office of Technology Assessment, *Intellectual property rights in an age of electronics and information*, Washington D.C., 1986, 205.

32. Ulrich Joos, *Die Erschöpfungslehre im Urheberrecht*, Munich, 1991, 51-68.

owner might, then, decide to amortize his investment over a string of primary, secondary and subsequent acts of distribution.

Legislative tool

Some scholars do not consider the exhaustion principle a 'principle' at all.[33] Exhaustion is merely a legislative tool, an easy and elegant way of restricting the exclusive right of distribution in the general interest. Instead of applying a general exhaustion rule, legislators would be free to opt for more specific instruments in curtailing the distribution right.

Application to the digital networked environment

Without assessing the relative value of the various exhaustion 'theories' described above, it is obvious that not all theories are equally relevant to the digital networked environment. Clearly, the (prevailing) property theory cannot serve as a reference point. On the superhighway the exercise of intellectual property rights in respect of secondary 'distribution' does not directly affect any property rights in physical goods.

On the other hand, the 'commerce theory' offers a strong argument for extending the exhaustion rule to the new environment. In the not too distant future, much of the national and intra-community 'physical' information trade will we replaced by information exchanges over the superhighway.

Arguably, the 'legal security' argument carries relatively little weight in respect of digital distribution of works. The digital environment facilitates the identification of disseminated works – and their copyright status. Status information, possibly including licensing conditions, can be carried by the work itself in so-called permission headers or software envelopes.[34]

The true value of all these arguments, as they relate to the digital networked environment, will become clear only after generally accepted trade customs have developed. If the present, rather anarchistic etiquette of the Internet would become the prevailing norm on the information superhighway, the commerce theory and the legal security argument would make a strong case in favour of applying the exhaustion principle in the digital networked environment. On the other hand, if the superhighway were to conform to the emerging trade customs of the electronic publishing industry, these arguments would carry little weight.

Not surprisingly, rightholders are adamantly opposed to the idea of applying the exhaustion principle to the digital network. Thus, both the U.S. White Paper and the EC Green Paper flatly reject any application of the exhaustion principle to the superhighway.[35]

---

33. D.W.F. Verkade & J.H. Spoor, *Auteursrecht*, Deventer, 1993, 163.

34. *See supra* note 8.

35. Report (White Paper) of the Working Group on Intellectual Property Rights, *Intellectual Property and the National Information Infrastructure*, Washington D.C., 1995, 95; EC Green Paper, *supra* note 19, 48.

4.2 EXHAUSTION OF THE BROADCASTING RIGHT

Most copyright laws in the European Union confine the exhaustion rule to acts of *physical* distribution. Germany is a notable exception; according to the German Supreme Court, the rule is a fundamental principle of copyright law, that applies to *all* exploitation rights. Accordingly, the (immaterial) broadcasting right is exhausted by secondary cable distribution under certain specific circumstances. In its decision of 7 November 1980 (*Gema/Deutsche Bundespost*),[36] the Bundesgerichtshof decided that copyright owners may not exercise their broadcasting rights in respect of cable transmissions in 'shadow areas', where the initial hertzian broadcast cannot be received because of physical impediments. The decision of the Bundesgerichtshof has been harshly criticized in German literature; many scholars believe it to be in conflict with article 11*bis* of the Berne Convention.

On the European level, the Court of Justice has refused to apply the well-established European exhaustion rule to secondary cable transmissions. In its two decisions in the *Le Boucher* case,[37] the Court considered that the broadcasting right of a film producer was not exhausted by the licensed primary broadcast in a neighbouring Member State. The rightholder could therefore legitimately oppose the unauthorized retransmission of the film via cable networks. The Court of Justice observed that 'the right of a copyright owner and his assigns to require fees for any showing of a film is part of the essential function of copyright in this type of literary and artistic work'.

It is interesting to note that the Court in *Le Boucher* focused on the economics of exploiting the work at issue (i.e. film). Films are exploited on a per-performance basis; therefore, application of the exhaustion rule would effectively destroy the copyright. Even though *Le Boucher* does not take into account alternative modes of exploitation of cinematographic works (video, rental, pay-per-view), the decision contains a strong argument against extending the exhaustion rule, whether on the national or European level, to the digital networked environment. Presumably, the prevailing mode of exploitation on the superhighway will be delivery on demand; copyright owners will be remunerated *per use* ('pay-as-you-go'). If exhaustion would be applied, on-demand program delivery services would not be copyright protected after the initial act of making the program publicly available (i.e. 'retrievable').

---

36. German Supreme Court (Bundesgerichtshof), Judgement of 7 November 1980 (*Gema/Deutsche Bundespost*), *GRUR* 1981, 413.

37. European Court of Justice, Judgement of 18 March 1980, Case 62/79 (*Coditel v. Ciné-Vog Films*), *RIDA* 105 (1980), 156; European Court of Justice, Judgement of 6 October 1982, Case 262/81 (*Coditel v. Ciné-Vog Films II*), *RIDA* 115 (1983), 120.

5. Conclusions

Paradoxically, most modern copyright laws have more problems in adapting to the new electronic media than their 'antiquated' counterparts. Traditional *old media* exclusive rights and limitations are mostly defined in platform-independent ways, thus accommodating not only traditional print and other analogue media, but also many of the electronic media of the present and the future. By contrast, legislators attempting to keep up with current technological development are faced with narrowly defined, platform specific rights and limitations, that can not be easily stretched to fit in the digital networked environment.

The previous chapters have amply demonstrated that applying 'old media' notions to the new environment does not always yield satisfactory results. The replies to the European Commission's questionnaire on the information superhighway (in preparation of the DG XV hearing of 7-8 July 1994 in Brussels) indicate that most rightholders prefer to make only piecemeal changes to the copyright system.[38] Respondents have suggested to 'clarify' the existing catalogue of rights so as to include the acts of transmission, uploading, downloading, public display and access. A similar approach is evident in the pending Berne Protocol proposals.

This 'minimalist' approach is not favourably looked upon by copyright doctrine. According to Geller the advent of the superhighway calls for more radical changes to the present copyright system. Geller does not subscribe to the view that current copyright notions are adequate or would need only piecemeal amending:

> 'I therefore question the ultimate wisdom of trying to adapt Berne provisions to networked archives by giving definitional first-aid to such basic, but limited notions.'[39]

Indeed, it seems inevitable that the digital networked environment will eventually necessitate more radical changes to the copyright system. Arguably, a long-term revision of the copyright system is necessary – not only to insure adequate protection to rightholders, but also to protect the legitimate interests of users of protected works. Overstretching 'old media notions', such as the right of reproduction, obviously bears the risk of overprotection.

Contours of a new law

Any future over-all revision of the copyright system must take into account the specific nature of the communication process of the digital networked environment, as well as the peculiar economics of providing, distributing and using information on the network. In the future, exclusive rights on the superhighway must no longer be (solely) based on expanded notions of copying and reproduction, but be redefined so as to become 'network-oriented'.[40]

38. *Replies from Interested Parties on 'Copyright and neighbouring rights in the Information Society'*, European Commission (DG XV), Brussels, 1995.
39. P. Geller, *supra* note 10, 58.
40. *Cf.* Dommering, *supra* note 4, *passim*.

Thus, the new law must be built on a sound analysis of the economics of digital network dissemination. Unfortunately, many legislators and scholars seem to be losing sight of the economic underpinnings of the existing set of exploitation rights. A dogmatic preoccupation with merely technical acts of reproduction may result in an unwanted proliferation of the copyright monopoly.

Moreover, the new law must be made 'multimedia proof' as much as possible. The emerging multimedia environment is rapidly making technology specific rulemaking, either within or outside the framework of intellectual property, obsolete. As heterogeneous categories of works, specific media and technologies 'converge' into a homogeneous multimedia environment, existing regulatory distinctions between specific work categories, media or technologies will be increasingly difficult to maintain.

Finally, the new law must respect fundamental rights and freedoms of users and intermediaries. In this context, it is unfortunate that considerations of informational privacy and freedom of expression are virtually absent from the European Commission's Green Paper. Clearly, these basic freedoms are at stake, if, as the Green Paper seems to suggest, the economic rights of rightholders were to be stretched to comprise acts of intermediate transmission and transient reproduction, as well as acts of private viewing and use of information.

Even so, a clear picture of the future of copyright in the digital environment does not emerge from the previous discussions. This should come as no surprise. The superhighway is a multi-purpose, multi-user, multimedia environment, capable of delivering in a variety of ways almost the complete Berne Convention catalogue of works. The copyright problems of the superhighway, then, are the problems of the entire information and entertainment industry. To these there are no quick and easy answers. In the context of this article, only a few of these problems have been addressed, with a special view to offering short-term solutions to the European legislator.

Moreover, one important fact should not be overlooked. Even though the superhighway has become the buzz-word of the nineties, it does not, as yet, exist. The closest thing to the superhighway presently in existence is the Internet – hardly a suitable laboratory for studying copyright in the digital environment. Since copyright problems are directly related to market conditions, it would be simply premature to propose more than minor changes to the present copyright system.

As the European Commission rightly observes, 'regulation [must] not simply respond to isolated requests for action on a one-off basis'[41] The information superhighway may, in the future, merit certain radical changes to the copyright system. At present, the omnipresent superhighway has yet to be paved; no pressing need for immediate action, either on the national, European or global level, therefore exists.

41. EC Green Paper, *supra* note 19, 33.

Short-term regulatory measures

In examining (and, possibly, redefining) the catalogue of exploitation rights, legislators and courts should follow a *normative approach*. Rather than an 'overstretched' right of reproduction, the right of communication to the public, as it exists in many countries (albeit in different forms), appears to be a suitable and flexible instrument for protecting intellectual property on the information superhighway. Instead of focusing on merely technical (intermediate) acts of reproduction and transmission, the right of communication to the public is conceptually linked to the essence of the economic right, i.e. *making protected works available to the public*.

How, then, should today's legislator find the necessary balance between copyright, freedom of services and essential user freedoms? Instead of the all-or-nothing approach of the exhaustion rule, two alternative solutions are possible. The first is to accept that most communication on the superhighway will involve a plurality of restricted acts. The interests of right owners and users would, then, be accommodated by carving out more or less broadly defined limitations and exemptions. The (inevitable) cumulation of exclusive rights would be offset by expanding the existing set of limitations. In so far as these limitations would directly concern acts of 'necessary' transmission or use of information, these exemptions might not be overridden by contract. The legitimate software user's right to produce a back-up copy of the computer program, guaranteed under article 5 (2) of the Software Directive, serves as an example.

Alternatively, one might decide to directly curtail the exclusive right, for instance by excluding various acts of usage from the reproduction right, so as to avoid unwanted overprotection. From a systematic perspective, the latter solution is more attractive – and certainly more elegant.

If a European or global 'superhighways' legislative initiative were contemplated at this point in time, the following short-term regulatory measures might be contained therein:

- Grant to copyright owners a broadly defined, exclusive right of communication to the public[42] (by any means now known or to be developed) in respect of all categories of works. This right should cover, at least, the following restricted acts:
    a) 'broadcasting', i.e. simulcasting to the public via wire or wireless means; and
    b) making a work publicly available on demand, by wire or wireless means.
- The act of screen display and related acts of temporary storage may not be restricted by copyright, in so far as these acts are necessary for private viewing, and do not qualify as communication to the public.

42. To be sure, this broad right of communication to the public must not be confused with the limited right protected under articles 11, 11*bis* and 11*ter* of the Berne Convention. The compulsory licensing provision of article 11*bis* (2) would, therefore, not apply.

- Acts of temporary storage may not be restricted by copyright, in so far as these acts are necessary for transmitting a work, and do not qualify as communication to the public.
- Last, not least: preserve essential copyright exemptions.

Intellectual Property and the National and Global Information Infrastructures

*Bruce Lehman**

This seminar is right on target – we must learn to understand the complex problems that these new technologies present, to understand the necessity to protect and administer copyright in the global information society, and to understand that there is much that can be done to ensure the proper protection of intellectual property. As the world's economy evolves to rely more on trade in information products and services, and as technology changes at an ever increasing pace, maintaining strong protection for intellectual property will be even more important to the continued growth of the global information society and the intellectual property industries that will support that growth.

Modern copyright law is the creature of technological change – from Gutenberg's movable type to digital audio recorders, and everything in between – photocopiers, radio, television, videocassette recorders, cable television and satellites. Today, information technologies – computer hardware and software, and communications technologies, such as cable, are coming together and creating an enormous impact on the ways that copyrighted works are created, reproduced and disseminated. The convergence of these technologies is leading us inexorably to the creation of the global information society.

Digital Technology

Digital technology is not the first and, probably not the last challenge to copyright owners' ability to authorize or prohibit the reproduction, adaptation, distribution, public display and performance of their works. For instance, the introduction of audio cassette recorders created problems for copyright owners. But, while copies of sound recordings were cheap, they were also certainly lower in quality than the original. This was the case until the introduction of *digital* audio recorders, which make reproductions just as cheaply as the analog recorders, but with no degradation in sound quality. The U.S. Congress responded to this very real threat to sound recording copyright owners by enacting the Audio Home Recording Act of 1992, which combined legal and technological safeguards.

Advances in digital technology and the rapid development of electronic networks and other communications technologies raise the stakes much higher.

---

* Text of speech, 6 July 1995. Bruce A. Lehman is U.S. Assistant Secretary of Commerce and Commissioner of Patents and Trademarks; Chairman, Working Group on Intellectual Property Rights, Information Infrastructure Task Force.

Any two-dimensional work, text, photographs, art works, etc. can be 'digitized'– translated into the series of zeros and ones that are digital code. The work can then be stored and used in that digital format. This dramatically increases:

- the ease and speed with which it can be copied;
- the quality of the copies (both the first and the hundredth); the ability to manipulate and change the work; and
- the speed with which copies of it – both authorized and unauthorized – can be 'delivered' to the public.

Works also can be combined easily with other works on a single medium, such as a CD-ROM, creating multimedia works that cause a blurring of the lines between different types of works. All would agree that an interactive multimedia CD-ROM with text, sounds, and still and moving images is a work, but is it a literary work or an audiovisual work or something else entirely? Answers to these questions will have effects on the availability of intellectual property protection internationally.

High-speed, high-capacity electronic information systems – the information superhighways – make it possible for one individual, with a few key strokes, to deliver perfect copies of digitized works to scores of other individuals virtually anywhere in the world. Users can 'post' or upload a copy to a bulletin board or other service where thousands upon thousands of individuals can download it – or print out unlimited 'hard' copies on paper or disks. This convergence of information and communications technologies is changing dramatically how people and businesses deal in information products and services, and how works are created, owned, distributed, reproduced, displayed, performed, licensed, managed, presented, organized, sold, accessed, used, and stored.

The Global Information Infrastructure

To ensure that U.S. Government policies will be in place to cope with this revolution, President Clinton created the White House Information Infrastructure Task Force to work with Congress and the private sector to develop comprehensive telecommunications and information policies to articulate and implement the Administration's vision for the National Information Infrastructure (NII) – the U.S. information superhighway that will connect to the Global Information Infrastructure (GII).

As Chairman of the Information Infrastructure Task Force's Working Group on Intellectual Property, I have overseen the process of taking a fresh look at U.S. copyright law and international protection in the context of digital technology and the GII. We have issued a 'Green Paper' on how our copyright law will adapt to the NII and made some preliminary recommendations for modest changes to the law to ensure it would meet the needs of the NII. We held extensive public hearings on the Green Paper and solicited written comments. We are now analyzing the comments and are studying what changes may be necessary in our recommendations. Indeed, we expect to issue our 'White Paper' this August recommending necessary adaptations of our copyright law and policies to ensure the broadest possible availability of the GII in all countries as well as the appropriate protection for creators' rights.

The GII has great potential. It should provide greater access to a wider variety of information, education and entertainment products to more people faster and more economically than currently possible. But this will not happen if the copyright owners of those products do not have adequate protection against infringement. They will *not* be willing to put their copyright interests at risk by allowing access to their work via the electronic superhighways if appropriate systems – both domestically and internationally – are not in place to ensure access and to deal with the threat to copyright owners' ability to control the exploitation of their works in the digital environment.

These issues are not limited to the United States or to any one country and its intellectual property laws. Millions of users are already on the Internet in virtually every country of the world. But the GII will be much more than the Internet; it will be a high-speed, interactive, broad-band telecommunications system capable of transmitting text, sound, images and video at a rate faster than the telephone-based Internet. Hundreds of channels of 'television' programming and thousands of volumes of 'books' will be available in homes and businesses throughout the world.

The United States was among the first to undertake a national effort to study and understand the public policy issues that underlie the continuing evolution of such a system and what measures, if any, the Government should take to encourage its rational and effective implementation. The lessons that we learn in this task will be of great use to others as they examine their own national policies and a truly world-wide information infrastructure is established.

Berne Protocol

Clear and effective norms for the protection of intellectual property rights must be put in place now – before users of the system develop habits that do not respect intellectual property. Many of these norms are already being discussed in the World Intellectual Property Organization (WIPO). WIPO is working to establish a Possible Protocol to the Berne Convention for the Protection of Literary and Artistic Works and a Possible New Instrument for the Protection of Performers and Producers of Phonograms. We have also initiated discussions on GII-related issues with the G-7 ministers who have agreed that all countries, not just the G-7, must work toward setting legal and technical standards. To that end, the Ministers endorsed cooperation in international fora, and particularly, the WIPO to achieve agreement on a *mutually* beneficial system of dealing with the critical intellectual property issues before us.

As we move toward a world where dissemination of entertainment and information products through on-demand delivery services over interactive digital networks is the norm, it may be necessary to harmonize levels of protection under our disparate systems of copyright, authors' rights and neighbouring rights, and we must consider ways to bridge the gaps among these systems.

If the GII as well as national NIIs are to flourish, then we must protect the intellectual property rights of the sectors of our economies that create and build these infrastructures and that provide the content which flows through these new technologies. To do this, intellectual property rights must be granted in national legislation fully on the basis of national treatment for *all* rights and benefits. There is, however, some controversy over the scope of the national treatment obligation under the Berne Convention and its application to what some may regard as newly created rights and subject matter. Similar questions arise under other international copyright and neighbouring rights conventions.

The United States is committed to making progress in WIPO toward improving international protection for works protected by copyright, for authors' rights, and for the subject matter of neighbouring rights. We want to build upon the intellectual property norms that were set in the Agreement on the Trade Related Aspects of Intellectual Property (TRIPs). This is essential, especially in view of the needs to deal with the intellectual property issues associated with the GII. The transition into a world-wide information society demands both a narrowing of the focus on specific issues in the cases of the Berne Protocol and the New Instrument, and a broadening of the WIPO efforts to encompass the digital world in both areas.

In the world of the GII with its digital distribution systems and multimedia works, distinctions among the rights of authors, producers and performers that are the basis for the separation of copyright and neighbouring rights are rapidly becoming irrelevant. This new information society is already resulting in the creation of new industries and new jobs resulting in economic growth and exports which ultimately will benefit authors, producers and performers. Governments need to consider carefully the implications of the GII for their national economies and their copyright systems. The work in WIPO is essential for the GII in order to set sound policy, and select the essential elements of the present Berne Protocol and New Instrument texts and work toward reaching international agreement on them.

One issue common to both the Berne Protocol and the New Instrument is inclusion of the TRIPs enforcement provisions (Articles 41 through 61). While there may be some justification for their inclusion, care must be taken to ensure that any enforcement obligations in these Agreements are consistent with the relevant TRIPs articles, and with the interpretations of that text that may be given by dispute settlement in the World Trade Organization. Additionally, we will have to continue to look into the possibility of including provisions on the use of technical security measures and on prohibiting devices and services that may be used to defeat technical security measures so that we will be able to protect both the content and any copyright management information associated with such systems.

One of the most important issues we face in setting international norms is defining the nature of a dissemination or a transmission of a work in digital format; is it a public performance, an act of reproduction, or a distribution? Can it be all at the same time? How do rules concerning the right of importation apply in a digital environment? Just as these questions are critical in the domestic context, they are equally acute in the context of international treaties and the harmonization of levels of protection. We believe that the concept of a digital 'transmission' right should be included both in the Berne Protocol and the New Instrument, perhaps as a separate right, as an aspect of a distribution right, as part of a right of communication to the public, or as an aspect of the reproduction right. While this is an issue that needs much further discussion, the United States believes that including such a right is an important part of the Berne Protocol and New Instrument and is necessary to meet the needs of intellectual property protection in the emerging GII.

The Berne Protocol and the New Instrument should also include provisions to prohibit decoders and anti-copy prevention devices and services as well as a prohibition on the fraudulent inclusion of rights management information and the fraudulent removal or alteration of such information.

National Treatment

To permit the effective development of the GII, national treatment must be the basis for protection in any intellectual property agreement. At an absolute minimum, national treatment must apply to the minimum obligations established in any agreement in WIPO. The author or rights holder should be able to realize fully the economic benefits flowing from the free exercise of his or her rights in any country party to the Protocol or New Instrument. We continue to believe that, in respect of any work, this is required by Article 5 of the Berne Convention. To do otherwise in either a Berne Protocol or another agreement on copyright protection would be contrary to Article 20 because it would be a derogation of rights existing under Berne and not be an Agreement to 'grant to authors more extensive rights than those granted by the Convention, or contain other provisions not contrary to this Convention' as provided for under Article 20. To the extent that we have agreed that the principles of the New Instrument should follow those of the Berne Convention, to do otherwise in respect of related rights, would be contrary to the letter and the spirit of the Convention.

U.S. copyright legislation has granted rights that some may regard as new rights – rental rights in computer programs, sound recordings, and musical works embodied in sound recordings – exclusively on the basis of national treatment. The United States has instituted a system of royalties on blank digital audio recording media and digital audio recorders. Benefits from these rights have all been granted on the basis of full national treatment. We believe that this is consistent with our obligations under the Berne Convention and other international intellectual property and trade treaties and agreements.

Following the U.S. Supreme Court Decision in the case of *Feist* there is increasing concern in the United States that many valuable, factually-oriented databases may be denied copyright protection, or that courts may determine infringement in ways that severely limit the scope of copyright protection for databases. Some further consideration of the issue of providing for a *sui generis* unfair extraction right to supplement copyright protection may prove to be useful. How a right, such as the unfair extraction right proposed in the EU Database

Directive, could protect both copyrighted and uncopyrightable databases should be carefully evaluated and given serious consideration.

Additionally, the issue of multimedia works will take on an important international dimension. If these are regarded at the international level as works in a new, separate category, the issue of their coverage under the existing conventions and the rule of national treatment will be open to debate. If, however, as current discussions seem to indicate, they are subsumed into the existing categories of works, establishing meaningful rules internationally will be simplified.

Further study to determine what other rights may need to be adapted to the emerging digital environment are underway both in domestic and international fora. However, some issues merit identification here, and one of those is the level of protection to be accorded to sound recordings.

Many believe that the time has come to bring protection for performers and producers of sound recordings into line with the protection afforded to the creators of other works protected under the Berne Convention. This includes providing high-level standards for rights and benefits granted on the basis of national treatment. This is necessary for a number of reasons. First, there is no just reason to accord a lower level of protection to one special class of creative artists. Second, the extent of international trade in sound recordings makes it imperative that standards of protection be harmonized at a high level. Third, and perhaps most importantly, the digital communications revolution – the creation of advanced information infrastructures – is erasing the distinctions among different categories of protected works and sound recordings and the uses made of them.

Concerns have been raised over the extent and scope of moral rights in the world of digital communications. Some believe that the ability to modify and restructure existing works and to create new multimedia works makes strengthening international norms for moral rights more important than ever before. Others take the view that any changes to international norms for the protection of moral rights must be carefully considered in the digital world. We agree with this view. Careful thought must be given to the scope, extent and moral rights in respect to digitally fixed works, sound recordings and other information products.

There are issues such as digital fixation, storage and delivery that will need to be taken into account in the New Instrument. There are also questions concerning the scope of rights and the right owners that might be covered by the New Instrument. To the extent possible, definitions in the New Instrument should be identical to those in the Berne Protocol. Otherwise, differences in phrasing could lead to differences in interpretation, and jeopardize the 'bridging' of the New Instrument with the Berne Convention and the Protocol. Many of these issues are critical to the United States and other countries.

Conclusion

These are some of the issues that we must focus on in the near term in our work in WIPO. The digital era is bringing dramatic changes in intellectual property and the application of intellectual property law – such dramatic changes that it has been suggested that the differences that have divided us from our counterparts in some civil law countries may become irrelevant. In the new digital world, technologies are merging and are resulting in new multimedia works, rapidly blurring the lines between types of works – and types of rights – leaving the transmission right somewhere between the performance and distribution rights. In the long run, there is a clear need to build bridges between the copyright and *droit d'auteur* systems to meet the challenges of these new technologies and to pave the way for a smooth transition into the new global information society.

Only by such cooperation will all of the world, regardless of its legal system or its stage of development, share in the benefits that will flow from these technological marvels.

Towards a Global Solution: The Digital Agenda of the Berne Protocol and the New Instrument

The Rorschach Test of Digital Transmissions

*Mihály Ficsor**

1. 1886, 1896, 1908, 1928, 1948, 1967, 1971

There used to be a certain regular pattern in the series of revisions of the Berne Convention. The international copyright community, in the first century of the history of the Convention, found it necessary to update the standards at least every twentieth year. Although certain modifications were introduced just to make the relevant norms simply more perfect and more detailed on the basis of the experience obtained through the application of the Convention and national copyright laws, the main objective of the various revisions was, in general, the adaptation of the existing norms or the adoption of new norms in response to the challenges of new technologies.[1] The latest, the 1971 Paris revision of the Convention was, however, an exception: it only addressed the specific cultural, social and economic problems of developing countries; no updating of the general copyright norms was on its agenda.

Thus, we can say that the last true substantive revision of the Berne Convention took place in 1967. The alarm clock of the Berne Union, duly set, in keeping with the well-established 20-year rhythm, was to ring in 1987. It certainly did. The international copyright community, however, this time pushed down the 'snooze' button and, with a somewhat bad conscience, pretended to continue sleeping. It pretended to, but it actually did not. And quite soon, it still got up, full of energy – although in a kind of schizophrenic mood.

This was so because, by the end of the 1980's, the situation of the Berne Convention, became quite paradoxical. The new technologies did not produce so many and such important changes in the history of the Convention between its adoption in 1886 and its twin-revisions in 1967 and 1971 as during the period that

---

* Assistant Director General of the World Intellectual Property Organization (WIPO).

1. For example, the following questions were dealt with at the various revision conferences: in 1986 mechanical reproduction; in 1908 photographic works, cinematography; in 1928 cinematography, radiodiffusion; in 1948 cinematography, radiodiffusion, mechanical reproduction; in 1967 television.

had elapsed since 1967-71. Nevertheless, for a long while, it was a sacrosanct principle followed by the international copyright community that the Berne Convention should not be touched, it should not be revised, and even no question about a possible revision should be raised. A revision was considered dangerous and hopeless; dangerous because nobody was able to predict the outcome of a revision; it might produce unexpected and undesirable results, and it might even decrease the level of protection provided in the Convention; and hopeless because, under Article 27(3) of the Convention, unanimity would be needed for a revision which, with the great number of member countries of the Berne Union, did not seem realistic to achieve.

'Guided development'

The absence of a new revision did not mean, however, that the international copyright system did not develop during the 1970's and 1980's. It did, but it followed an alternative route; the route of 'guided development,' in the sense in which Sam Ricketson referred to this form of development in 1986 in his well-known book on the Berne Convention: 'In essence, "guided development" appears to be the present policy of WIPO, whose activities in promoting study and discussions on problem areas have been of fundamental importance to international copyright protection in recent years.'[2]

WIPO convened a series of meetings and prepared a number of studies and documents dealing with the impact of new technologies. Some of the meetings took place during the 1970's, but the truly intensive activities started at the beginning of the 1980's. In the first stage, the new uses of works and the various computer-related questions were on the agenda, such as storage of protected works in computers and computer-produced works (in 1980 and 1982); cable television (in 1980, 1981 and 1983); copyright protection of computer programmes (in 1983 and 1985); private copying (in 1984); rental and lending of phonograms and videograms (in 1984); and direct broadcasting by satellites (in 1985).

Following this series of meetings, attention was focused on the various categories of works. The following categories were discussed, in chronological order: audiovisual works and phonograms (in 1986); works of architecture (in 1986); works of visual art (in 1986); dramatic, choreographic and musical works (in 1987); works of applied art (in 1987); the 'printed word' (covering the various sub-categories of writings, except computer programmes, and also extending to questions concerning the protection of data bases, in 1987); and photographic works (in 1988).

In parallel to the meetings concentrating on the various new uses and on the different categories of works, also some important aspects of the exercise, administration and enforcement of rights were discussed, such as the status of works created by employed authors (in 1981 and 1986); collective administration of rights (in an international forum, in 1986; the program then was continued in various ways and, in 1990, led to the publication of an important WIPO study

2. *See* Sam Ricketson, *The Berne Convention for the protection of literary and artistic works: 1886-1986*, Deventer, 1986, 919.

offering detailed guiding principles for national legislation) and the means of fighting piracy (a Committee of Experts, meeting in 1988, discussed detailed model provisions for national legislation, the further consideration of which was, however, suspended, pending the outcome of the Uruguay Round negotiations at GATT).

Although this period of 'guided development' had brought positive results, at the end of the 1980's, it became clear that mere guidelines and recommendations no longer offered sufficient guarantees for the harmonious development of copyright. In the absence of binding international norms, there was increasing danger that national legislators would choose differing solutions to new problems, that this would lead to increasingly divergent trends in the international system of copyright and neighbouring rights, and that this, in turn, would also undermine the delicate balance between the minimum level of protection determined by the Berne and Rome Conventions, on the one hand, and the principle of national treatment, on the other.

The preparatory work on a WIPO Model Law on Copyright was the last effort of WIPO to respond to the new challenges before its Governing Bodies decided in favour of preparing new binding international norms for the protection of copyright and neighbouring rights. The Committee of Experts convened to prepare the Model Law held three meetings, in 1989 and 1990, and worked out model provisions which were considered generally applicable in the countries party to the Berne Convention. The text of the Model Law was finalized by the International Bureau and was ready for publication, but it has not been published. At the request of various governments, it was set aside, pending the outcome of the preparatory work on a possible protocol to the Berne Convention.

2. Towards a Protocol to the Berne Convention

The Governing Bodies of WIPO took the decision to prepare a possible protocol to the Berne Convention at their September-October 1989 sessions.[3] The preparation of a protocol was proposed, in a way, to avoid the pitfalls of revising the Convention and still to update the international copyright norms. As the Committee of Experts established to do the preparatory work noted correctly, at its first session the terms of reference for the protocol would not require a revision of the Convention and the protocol could rather take the form of a special agreement, in keeping with Article 20 of the Convention.[4] The special agreement formula seemed attractive at least for two reasons: first, because, from the very notion of a special agreement, it followed that for its conclusion unanimity was not required, and, second, because Article 20 of the Convention only allows such agreements 'in so far as [they] grant to authors more extensive rights than those granted by the Convention, or contain other provisions not contrary to this Convention,' and, thus, the danger of decreasing the existing level of protection could be avoided.

3. *See* WIPO AB/XX/2, Annex A, item PRG 02(2).
4. *See* WIPO document BCP/CE/I/4, § 11-72.

The project of the Berne Protocol was first included in the 1990-1991 programme of WIPO and was retained in the 1992-93, 1994-95 and 1996-97 programmes.[5]

2.1 PREPARATORY WORK

The first two sessions of the Committee of Experts were held in November 1991 and in February 1992, and the work of the Committee, in keeping with the original terms of reference, extended to all new questions of copyright protection.[6] The terms of reference of the Committee of Experts were, however, modified by the Assembly of the Berne Union in September 1992, in deciding:

(i) the establishment of two Committees of Experts, one for the preparation of a Possible Protocol to the Berne Convention and another for the preparation of a Possible New Instrument on the protection of the rights of performers and producers of phonograms;

(ii) that the issues to be discussed by the Committee of Experts on a Possible Protocol to the Berne Convention would be (only) the following ten:

(1) computer programmes,
(2) databases,
(3) rental right,
(4) non-voluntary licenses for the sound recording of musical works,
(5) non-voluntary licenses for primary broadcasting and satellite communication,
(6) distribution right, including importation right,
(7) duration of the protection of photographic works,
(8) communication to the public by satellite broadcasting,
(9) enforcement of rights, and
(10) national treatment,

(iii) that the Committee of Experts on a Possible Instrument for the Protection of the Rights of Performers and Producers of Phonograms would discuss all questions concerning the effective international protection of the rights of performers and producers of phonograms.[7]

The third session of the Committee of Experts on the Berne Protocol and the first session of the Committee of Experts on the 'New Instrument' (this is the generally accepted short reference to the 'possible new instrument on the protection of the rights of performers and producers of phonograms') were convened on the basis of the above-quoted decision for two consecutive weeks, in June-July 1993.[8] The latter Committee was unable to complete the discussion of

5. *See* WIPO documents AB/XX/20, § 152 and § 199; AB/XXII/22, § 197; AB/XXIV/18, § 224-231 and § 283-284; AB/XXVI/2, item 03(1).

6. *See* particularly the questions relating to digital technology, discussed in § 3 *infra*..

7. *See* WIPO document B/A/XIII/2, § 22.

8. *See* WIPO documents BCP/CE/III/2 and 3; INR/CE/I/2 and 3.

the memorandum prepared by the International Bureau, and the discussion was therefore completed at a second session of the Committee in November 1993.[9]

The preparatory work of the Berne Protocol and the 'New Instrument', at the beginning, was somewhat slowed down at the request of various countries, which – quite understandably – wanted to avoid any possible interference of this work with the TRIPs negotiations in the GATT Uruguay Round. The WTO Agreement, along with the TRIPs Agreement, was signed in April 1994, and this created a new atmosphere also for the Berne Protocol and 'New Instrument' projects. At the fourth session of the Berne Protocol Committee and the third session of the 'New Instrument' Committee in December 1994, a political will seemed to be present on the part of the participating government delegations to speed up, and preferably conclude as soon a possible with success, the preparatory work. Another important development was that the need for new norms in response to the challenges of digital technology – an issue which had not been addressed in the TRIPs negotiations and had been only partly dealt with by the two Committees before – became the centre of attention. There was agreement that the two Committees should deal with all aspects of the impact of digital technology on copyright and neighbouring rights.[10]

The latest sessions of the Committees (the fifth session of the Berne Protocol Committee and the fourth session of the 'New Instrument' Committee) were held jointly in September 1995. Following the decisions of the previous sessions, the governments of WIPO member countries and the European Commission had been invited to make proposals, on the understanding that those proposals would serve as the basis for discussions. The International Bureau received three sets of proposals: from the European Community and its Member States, from the United States of America and from Australia. Those proposals were reproduced and distributed, along with a comparative table prepared by the International Bureau.[11] Later the Governments of South Africa and Argentina also submitted comments.[12]

The discussions at the joint sessions of the two Committees further underlined the sincere intention of the participating governments to accelerate the preparatory work and to try to reach agreement on the contents of the Berne Protocol and the 'New Instrument' as quickly as possible. The Delegation of the United States of America even proposed that a diplomatic conference or diplomatic conferences should be foreseen for the adoption of the two new treaties as early as at the beginning of the second part of 1996.

2.2 RESULTS

It cannot be said, however, that these sessions of the Committees have produced spectacular results. As far as the Berne Protocol is concerned, the discussions still

9. *See* WIPO document INR/CE/II/1.

10. *See* WIPO document BCP/CE/IV/3, § 10-27.

11. *See* WIPO documents BCP/CE/V/3 and 4; INR/CE/IV/3 and 5.

12. *See* WIPO documents BCP/CE/V/6 and 7; INR/CE/IV/7.

took place on the basis of the above-quoted ten-point agenda, which seemed to be out-of-date, which contained in itself certain contradictions and which showed a serious lack of harmony with the agenda of the 'New Instrument' Committee.[13]

The Committee (i) reached a fairly definite agreement on treaty language concerning computer programmes and databases, which, however, was more or less the same as the language included in the TRIPs Agreement;[14] (ii) supported, in general, the recognition of a general distribution right which would be exhausted with first sale, but it was divided as to the question of whether exhaustion should have national and regional effect or international effect, and, consequently, it was also divided in respect of whether or not the recognition of an importation right would be justified;[15] (iii) agreed that a rental right should also be provided for, but the positions of the various delegations differed to a great extent concerning the coverage of such a right;[16] (iv) decided to continue discussions on the abolition of compulsory licenses for sound recording of musical works and for primary broadcasting, but certain countries were not prepared yet to join the consensus on such abolition;[17] (v) agreed that the term of protection of photographic works should be the same as the general term of literary and artistic works;[18] (vi) left out satellite broadcasting as a separate item of the agenda;[19] (vii) generally agreed that the Berne Protocol should contain provisions on the enforcement of rights adopting the relevant provisions of the TRIPs Agreement with some *mutatis mutandis* type changes, but the United States of America did not share this agreement;[20] and (viii) postponed (again) any substantive discussion on national treatment considering that, first, the contents of the Protocol should be outlined and that this issue might only be discussed in a meaningful way afterwards.[21]

As regards the 'New Instrument' Committee, we may say that it is even farther away from any tangible results. To start with, there is no agreement yet as to whether such an instrument is needed at all. Opinions are also very much divided as to the coverage of the possible instrument, namely whether or not it should also extend to the rights of performers in audiovisual fixations of their performances.[22]

In respect of the details, there seems to be fairly general agreement (i) on the need to recognize moral rights for performers along the lines of the provisions of

---

13. It contained contradictions, for example, in listing the right of rentals as a right independent of the right of distribution, and was heavily limited, while the 'New Instrument' agenda covered all possible issues.
14. *See* WIPO document BCP/CE/V/4, 4-5; BCP/CE/V/9-INR/CE/IV/8, § 55-58.
15. *See* WIPO document BCP/CE/V/9-INR/CE/IV/8, § 241-311.
16. *See supra* note 15, id.
17. *See supra* note 15, § 59-70.
18. *See supra* note 15, § 81-83.
19. *See supra* note 15, § 84.
20. *See supra* note 15, § 354.
21. There was no substantive decision on this issue at the joint session; the Chairman's proposal to this effect was adopted.
22. *See supra* note 15, § 16-47 (general discussions).

Article 6*bis* of the Berne Convention, with obvious *mutatis mutandis* changes;[23] (ii) on the adoption of provisions concerning the rights of performers in their live performances (but this agreement only covers what is already provided for in the TRIPs Agreement, and does not cover, for example, the extension of the provisions to audiovisual fixation of live performances);[24] (iii) on the extension of the term of protection of performers and producers of phonograms to 50 years;[25] and (iv) on the abolition of formalities as conditions of protection.[26] Concerning the rights of distribution, importation and rental and concerning national treatment, the situation is the same as in the case of the Berne Protocol.[27] As far as certain other basic rights are concerned – particularly the rights of performers and producers of phonograms in respect of the public performance, communication to the public and broadcasting of the fixations of their performances and phonograms, respectively – no silver lining appeared at the end of the discussions which would offer hope for any emerging agreement.[28]

There was a separate discussion about the so-called *digital agenda* of the two Committees, but, as characterized by the Chairman, it was only of a general discussion of an introductory nature. It was assumed that a more detailed and more concrete discussion would take place at the next sessions of the Committees. We shall deal with that discussion in §§ 3 and 4 below.

The Committees decided[29] that their next joint sessions would take place from February 1 to 9, 1996. The governments and the European Commission have been invited to send to the International Bureau of WIPO treaty-language proposals on issues under consideration, other than computer programmes and original databases, which would serve as bases for discussions. Furthermore, at the request of developing countries, regional consultation meetings will also take place on the Berne Protocol and the 'New Instrument'. The Committees adopted a recommendation, according to which the competent Governing Body of WIPO[30] should be convened after the meetings of the two Committees in February 1996, 'should the work be sufficiently advanced to decide on the convocation and date of one or more diplomatic conferences for the conclusion of the appropriate treaties.'

The Committees also noted in their decisions that 'the discussion of all issues considered appropriate to be dealt with at this stage in the evolution of the use of new technologies, in particular new information infrastructures, are advancing in parallel in both contexts. Consideration of supplementary *sui generis* protection of databases continues,[31] without prejudice to copyright protection and without yet determining the form of a possible treaty.' This interpretation of the terms of

23. *See supra* note 15, § 86-142.
24. *See supra* note 15, § 143-187.
25. *See supra* note 15, § 240.
26. *See supra* note 15, id.
27. *See supra* note 15, id.
28. *See supra* note 15, § 188-239.
29. *See supra* note 15, § 356 and § 376.
30. In this context, the competent Governing Body is the General Assembly of WIPO.
31. *See also supra* note 15, § 351-353.

reference of the Committees might have been considered somewhat liberal, but (i) such implicit extension of the terms of reference was useful and necessary; and (ii) since this was reported by the Director General to the Governing Bodies of WIPO at their September-October 1995 sessions, and since those Bodies noted the report without any opposition, no doubt may emerge about the legitimate nature of the extension.[32] Thus, the way is open to embrace the entire 'digital agenda.'

In light of these developments and decisions, it may not be exaggerated to state that the next sessions of the two Committees will be decisive for the future of the Berne Protocol and the 'New Instrument,' for regulation of the most urgent issues of the impact of digital technology on copyright and neighbouring rights, and, in a way, for the healthy development of the international system of the protection of these rights.

3. Impact of Digital Technology: WIPO Activities

WIPO has devoted substantial attention to the impact of digital technology on copyright and neighbouring rights in recent years. The first significant event organized by WIPO on this topic was the WIPO Worldwide Symposium on the Impact of Digital Technology on Copyright and Neighbouring Rights, held at Harvard University in March-April 1993.[33] A second gathering of experts focusing on the challenges of digital technology, the WIPO Worldwide Symposium on the Future of Copyright and Neighbouring Rights, was organized in the new wing of the Louvre in Paris in June 1994.[34] The third similar event, the WIPO Worldwide Symposium on Copyright in the Global Information Infrastructure, took place in May 1995 in the National Centre of Arts in Mexico City.[35] As a result of those meetings, some general directions emerged for the development of new international norms to ensure appropriate, efficient protection and management of copyright and neighbouring rights in the digital environment. The WIPO World Forum on the Protection of Intellectual Creations in the Information Society, which will take place in Naples, in the Palazzo Reale, from October 18 to 20, 1995, after the finalization of this paper, hopefully will produce similar results in the present, crucial period of the preparatory work of the Berne Protocol and the 'New Instrument.'

WIPO, of course, does not restrict its activities to these brainstorming-type events. In the last two years, the International Bureau of WIPO has convened a series of consultation meetings with the representatives of interested non-governmental organizations, where concrete, practical aspects of the exercise, management and enforcement of copyright and neighbouring rights in the digital environment were examined (such as digital identification numbers with related databases, encryption-decryption systems, digital rights-management systems). In

32. *See* WIPO document AB/XXVI/19, § 205-242.

33. *See* WIPO publication No. 723(E).

34. *See* WIPO publication No. 731(E).

35. The material of the symposium was published in November 1995.

June 1995, at the request of the interested organizations, this series of meetings was transformed into a WIPO Consultation Forum for Non-Governmental Organizations on the Protection and Management of Copyright and Neighbouring Rights in Digital Systems, which will be convened regularly; and the Governing Bodies of WIPO, at their September-October 1995 sessions, also decided to set up a WIPO Standing (Intergovernmental) Advisory Committee on the Intellectual Property Aspects of the Global Information Infrastructure, the task of which is to give guidance for the implementation and application of appropriate norms at the national level and monitoring internationally relevant developments concerning the protection, management and enforcement of rights in the digital environment.

3.1 TOWARDS A 'DIGITAL AGENDA'

The most important activity of WIPO in this field, however, relates to the clarification of the existing international copyright and neighbouring rights norms and the establishment of possible new norms in response to the challenges of digital technology, which is carried out by the above-mentioned Committees working on the preparation of the Berne Protocol and the 'New Instrument'.

When, in 1989-90, the preparatory work (at that time, only on the Berne Protocol) started, the possible implications of digital technology for copyright and neighbouring rights were already perceived, but the 'digital revolution' was not yet at such full speed as today, and, thus, it was not yet so much in the focus of attention of the international community as now in the middle of the 1990's. When, in 1992, the idea of our Harvard symposium, mentioned above, emerged, still quite significant time and energy was needed to persuade certain people around us that it was worthwhile devoting, *horribile dictu*, an entire three-day symposium on this 'funny' topic. And today? We have just calculated recently, that, if we in WIPO accepted all the invitations to the various international, regional, and national meetings discussing the copyright and neighbouring rights issues of digital technology, each of our colleagues in the copyright sector of the International Bureau would have to be away all the time to attend, as an average, 1.6 meetings per day.

For the above-mentioned reasons, it is understandable that, at the first sessions of the Berne Protocol Committee, digital technology as such was not yet on the agenda. Nevertheless, before the restriction of the terms of reference to ten items (described above) took place, the Committee still discussed various issues that now may be considered, directly or indirectly, parts of the 'digital agenda,' such as expert systems and other artificial intelligence systems, computer-produced works, storage of works in computer systems, private reproduction with special attention to digital reproduction, the right of public display, and the definition of 'public' in respect of public performance, public display and communication to the public.[36]

36. *See* WIPO document BCP/CE/I/3 and BCP/CE/II/1.

All these items were, however, deleted from the terms of reference, as discussed above, in 1992, as proposed by certain countries.[37] It was a paradoxical situation that, while the documents to be prepared by the International Bureau for the Berne Protocol Committee were not supposed to extend to any issues other than those covered by the heavily restricted terms of reference, the documents to be prepared for the newly established 'New Instrument' Committee were supposed to deal with 'all questions concerning the effective international protection of the rights of performers and producers of phonograms.'[38]

Therefore, it was the memorandum of the International Bureau, prepared for the first session of the 'New Instrument' Committee, which first addressed more extensively the issues raised by the rapidly spreading application of digital technology (such as digital reproduction and manipulation, sampling, digital copy-protection and copy-management systems, digital broadcasting and other digital communication to the public) and contained treaty-language proposals for the updating of the international norms on the protection of the neighbouring rights concerned.[39] The above-mentioned proposals made by the International Bureau concerning the issues raised by digital technology for the rights of performers and producers of phonograms were transferred for a 'second reading' by the Committee at its session held in December 1994, without major changes, for further discussion.

The International Bureau, in its memorandum prepared for the June 1993 session of the Berne Protocol Committee held on the basis of the ten-point terms of reference, in a way, 'smuggled back' certain issues relating to digital technology; namely, under the item of the right of distribution, it proposed that a right of rental should 'survive' the first sale of copies, *inter alia*, in case of the rental of any works in digital format (such as on CD-Roms), and, under the item of enforcement of rights, it suggested that provisions be included obliging countries party to the Protocol to introduce measures against those who manufacture, import or distribute devices to defeat or circumvent copy-protection, copy-management and encryption systems.

As mentioned above, the December 1994 sessions of the two Committees brought about a breakthrough in the preparatory work of the Berne Protocol and the 'New Instrument'. Those were the first sessions held after the conclusion of the TRIPs Agreement; it was already clear which issues had not been solved through the Uruguay Round negotiations and had thus been left to the Berne Protocol and 'New Instrument' projects. There seemed to be quite general agreement that the most important and most urgent questions to be answered to related to the impact of digital technology on copyright and neighbouring rights.[40]

At those sessions, the most thorough discussion took place on the legal nature of digital transmissions, and the views of the delegations differed to a great

---

37. The 'certain countries' were mainly those industrialized countries that formed the so-called Stockholm Group.
38. *See* WIPO document A/B/A/XIII/2, § 22; item (viii).
39. *See* WIPO document INR/CE/I/2.
40. *See* WIPO document BCP/CE/IV/3, § 10-27.

extent;[41] these views are dealt with in § 4, below, in detail. The other issue fairly intensively discussed was the inclusion of possible provisions obliging countries party to the Berne Protocol and the 'New Instrument' to offer protection (and appropriate sanctions) against those who manufacture, import and distribute any device, or offer any service, the only or primary purpose or effect of which is to defeat or circumvent any device or system applied for the prevention of violations of exclusive rights. There was fairly general agreement that such provisions were necessary,[42] although certain details (such as the need for appropriate language offering guarantees against 'overprotection' through technical means[43] were identified as requiring further discussions. The Delegation of the United States of America also stressed that similar provisions were justified for the protection of rights management information which would be indispensable for an appropriate management of rights in a digital environment.[44]

At its December 1994 session, the 'New Instrument' Committee, in addition to the issues mentioned above, also dealt with further questions relating to the application of digital technology, such as certain definitions which might have to be reconsidered so that they could be duly applied in a digital environment ('performers,' 'phonograms,' 'publication,' 'reproduction,' 'public');[45] the need for recognition of moral rights for performers;[46] and a right of adaptation for performers and/or for producers of phonograms[47] to offer appropriate protection against certain forms of digital manipulation; and, the proposed strengthening of the rights of performers and producers of phonograms in respect of 'traditional' digital broadcasting and other 'traditional' digital communication to the public ('traditional' meaning that the broadcasting or the communication to the public is not in the form of an on-demand, interactive transmission).[48]

3.2 NATIONAL STUDIES

As mentioned above, the discussion of the 'digital agenda' at the joint sessions of the Berne Protocol Committee and the 'New Instrument' Committee still was of a general, preliminary nature. As proposed by the Chairman of the two Committees, under that agenda, the questions relating to digital transmission/digital delivery and to the technological protection and rights management systems were discussed. The reasons for which the discussion was not – and could not be – more specific were the following. The deadline for the submission of proposals for the joint sessions of the two Committees was June 20, 1995. At that time, certain studies

41. *See supra* note 40, § 47-58.
42. *See supra* note 40, § 87-96.
43. *See supra* note 40, particularly § 92.
44. *See supra* note 40, § 88.
45. *See* WIPO documents INR/CE/III/3, § 28-42; INR/CE/III/3 Suppl.
46. *See supra* note 45, § 80-92.
47. *See supra* note 45, id.
48. *See supra* note 46, § 64-79.

being carried out in various industrialized countries were already in a more or less advanced stage; however, the positions, in general, were not sufficiently final so that the countries concerned might have been able to submit concrete proposals on the key issues, particularly on the most complex issue: the issue of digital transmission/digital delivery.

Perhaps, the only exception was the report of the Copyright Convergence Group published in Australia in August 1994,[49] which contained very precise provisions as to how the Copyright Act of Australia should be amended in response to the challenges of digital technology. It was in harmony with this that the most specific proposal concerning how digital transmissions should be regulated in the Berne Protocol was submitted by the Government of Australia.[50]

The Japanese 'Green Paper' had also been published before the deadline for the submission of proposals (in February 1995),[51] but the Government of Japan did not submit proposals to the September 1995 sessions of the Committees. The reason for this probably was that the paper was still really 'green' in the sense that, although it thoroughly discussed the questions involved, it did not offer final proposals, but rather various alternatives which still required further discussion.

The Green Paper of the Commission of the European Communities[52] was published nearly a month after the deadline for the submission of proposals (on July 19, 1995). Furthermore, although containing a deep analysis of the issues raised by digital technology and outlining certain options, its objective was not to propose definite solutions but, for the time being, rather only an appropriate basis for consultation among the Member States of the European Community.

Finally, the White Paper of the United States of America,[53] was published only on September 9, 1995, which was the second day of the joint sessions of the two Committees. It did contain specific provisions concerning the amendment of the United States legislation and it was distributed to the participants in the joint sessions on the same day, but, of course, it was not possible to use it as a basis for discussion at those sessions.

The discussions at the various sessions of the two Committees, and the quite diverging ideas and proposals included in the above-mentioned reports and studies indicate: (i) that the legal characterization and regulation of digital transmissions will be a key issue in the forthcoming, accelerated preparatory work of the Berne Protocol and the 'New Instrument'; (ii) that an agreement on this issue would be indispensable for the success of the Berne Protocol and 'New Instrument' projects; and (iii) that still great efforts are needed so that such agreement might be achieved. The final part of this paper is devoted exclusively to this issue.

---

49. Copyright Convergence Group, *Highways to Change. Copyright in the New Communications Environment*, August 1994, Copyright Commonwealth Australia, ISBN 0642208166.

50. *See* WIPO document BCP/CE/V/3, § 27-32.

51. Report on Discussions by the Working Group of the Subcommittee on Multimedia Copyright Council. Study of Institutional Issues Regarding Multimedia, Agency for Cultural Affairs, Tokyo.

52. Commission of the European Communities, *Green Paper. Copyright and Related Rights in the Information Society*, Brussels, 19 July 1995, COM (95) 382 final.

53. *Intellectual Property and the National Information Infrastructure*, Report (White Paper) of the Working Group on Intellectual Property Rights, Washington D.C., 1995.

4. Digital Transmission: What Rights Will Apply?

When this paper discusses the questions relating to 'digital transmission,' that is transmission (or 'delivery') of works and objects of neighbouring rights in computer networks, such as the Internet,[54] from one computer to another computer (or to various other computers). Consequently, this notion does not cover 'traditional' broadcasting and 'traditional' communication to the public by wire or by wireless means.

It seems that this kind of digital transmission/delivery is like a *Rorschach test* for those who deal with copyright and neighbouring rights: everybody sees something else in it. The result of this test may reveal a lot about the circumstances, interests and intentions of the person who offers this or that legal characterization of such a transmission; it may indicate the law of which country has been taken into account for such characterization; it may indicate the nature of the activities of the person involved (for example whether he is an author, a producer, a publisher or a representative of a performing rights society); and it may very clearly indicate the relevant interests taken into account and the objectives intended to be achieved.

Let us review the various candidates – the various possible rights – to encompass digital transmissions at the level of international copyright and neighbouring rights norms.

4.1 NO RIGHTS

This option may hardly be considered seriously. Nevertheless, there are some who argue that no copyright and neighbouring rights protection is needed in computer networks, like the Internet; the operators and users of such networks are sufficiently qualified and responsible to settle everything on the basis of their own ethics – the so-called *netiquette* – and they do not need nor want the intervention of the law.[55]

This position may be justified as long as the Internet and similar networks are used as a forum for special interest groups exchanging views and information among each other (information in the basic sense of the word, not extending to works protected by copyright) and, perhaps, by certain scientists and scholars who traditionally do not care so much for copyright protection of their publications, but much more for their names being in circulation, their works being referred to and mentioned in footnotes and other references as frequently as possible and, through this, for being recognized by their colleagues and for being 'remunerated', for example, through invitations to participate in certain scientific and scholarly programmes as speakers, experts, contributors to studies, etc. However, this position is unrealistic and untenable as soon as the productions of the publishing, entertainment and information industry, or works or objects of neighbouring rights

54. For a description of the Internet experience, *see* U.S. White Paper, *supra* note 53, 179-182.

55. For a description of such views, *see* U.S. White Paper, *supra* note 53, 15

created with the objective of being remunerated, are used in a computer network, and, in such a context, it does not deserve serious consideration.

4.2 RIGHT OF REPRODUCTION

It seems that the right of reproduction is a very strong candidate for a widespread and efficient application in digital networks, and in a digital environment, in general.

The list of those acts which are considered to be reproduction is long and impressive, and includes, but is not limited to, the following:

- inclusion of a work or object of neighbouring rights in any off-line, digital storage device (such a CD-ROM) is reproduction;
- scanning of a printed work is reproduction;
- any other digitization of a work or object of neighbouring rights is reproduction;
- uploading a work or object of neighbouring rights is reproduction;
- downloading a work or object of neighbouring rights is reproduction;
- storage – even temporary storage – of a work or object of neighbouring rights in a computer memory is reproduction.[56]

The last statement – on temporary storage – requires, however, some further analysis and comment.

Temporary storage

The technical description of digital transmissions may offer quite big surprises for those who use a user-friendly computer network, as a kind of 'black box,' for such acts as browsing, viewing pictures, watching audiovisual creations, listening to sound recordings, that is, without any intention to make and keep any copy of any protected material. It will be explained to them that each of those acts, which they probably do not perceive at all as an act of reproduction, does involve making at least temporary copies of at least certain parts of the protected material in the internal memory of their computers. Of course, if a copy is really made, even temporarily, there is no reason not to recognize the act as an act of reproduction.

So that we may speak about a copy, and a reproduction, the work or object of neighbouring rights should, however, be *fixed* at least temporarily. And it seems that some doubts may emerge whether everything appearing in, or going through, a computer memory might truly be considered a fixation. For example, even those who are the strongest advocates extending the concept of reproduction to the various acts involved in digital transmissions refer to 'intermediate reproduction' arising along the chain of transmission as a possible case that might not be covered by this concept.[57] The Japanese Green Paper, though including a proposal to recognize temporary storage in electronic form as reproduction, also refers to

56. *See* U.S. White Paper, *supra* note 53, 65-66; European Commission Green Paper, *supra* note 52, 50; Japanese Green Paper, *supra* note 51, 9-10.

57. *See*, for example, the European Commission Green Paper, *supra* note 52, 50.

certain doubts whether transitional storage may always be considered fixation and, thus, reproduction.[58] The text and the legislative history of the Copyright Act of the United States of America also indicate certain limits of what may still be considered as a fixation; as the White Paper refers to this[59]: 'A simultaneous fixation (or any other fixation) meets the requirements if its embodiment in a copy or phonorecord is "sufficiently permanent or stable to permit it to be perceived, reproduced, or otherwise communicated *for a period of more than transitory duration*".[60] Works are not sufficiently fixed if they are "*purely evanescent or transient*" in nature, "such as those *projected briefly* on a screen, shown electronically on a television or cathode ray tube, or *captured momentarily in the «memory» of a computer.*"'[61] (It is worthwhile noting the word 'memory' in quotation marks, those marks apparently referring to the fact that, although we speak of the memory of a computer, that memory, in the cases mentioned, does not actually 'memorize' – does not fix – what is captured by it momentarily.)

Nevertheless, it seems to be clear that it would not be justified to deny the characterization and qualification of an act that involves fixation, even if for a very short time, as reproduction, in the fear of 'overstretching' the application of the right of reproduction. This would be in conflict with Article 9(2) of the Berne Convention under which '[a]uthors of literary and artistic works protected by this Convention shall have the exclusive right of authorizing the reproduction of these works, *in any manner or form*' (italics added).

Screen display

The International Bureau of WIPO has represented this position consistently in the various documents it has prepared, *inter alia*, on this issue. For example, in the memorandum prepared by the International Bureau of WIPO for the Committee of Governmental Experts on the Printed Word, the meeting of which was held in Geneva in December 1987, the so-called 'reproduction theory' was presented in respect of display of works on a screen. The position expressed and the arguments presented by the International Bureau were the following:

> 'The display of writings or graphic works on a screen differs in nature from the performance of a dramatic, dramatico-musical or musical work, the recitation of a literary work and the communication to the public or broadcasting of such a performance or recitation as well as from the performance, communication to the public or broadcast of a cinematographic work. The essence of the difference is that, when writings and graphic works are displayed on a screen, they are *fixed* for a shorter or longer time, while in respect of the above-mentioned other uses that is not the case. The fixation takes place at least for the time which is necessary for reading the text and studying or enjoying the graphic work

58. *See* Japanese Green Paper, *supra* note 51, 9-11.
59. *See* U.S. White Paper, *supra* note 53, 28.
60. United States Copyright Act, section 101; italics added.
61. House Report, 53 (repr. in 1976 U.S.C.C.A.N. 5666-67), quoted in U.S. White Paper, *supra* note 53, at 28; italics added.

concerned. What appears on the screen is actually a copy of the work (or a part of it), usually in page format.

If it is true – and it seems to be true – that the display of a writing or a graphic work on a screen is reproduction and the presentation of the work is a copy, such a display is necessarily covered by the right of reproduction. The relationship between the storage of the work in the computer system (as a copy) and the screen display of the same work (as another copy) is similar to the relationship between a printing plate and the printed copies. The preparation of the printing plate does already qualify as the reproduction of the work and, of course, both that reproduction and the making of printed copies are covered by the right of reproduction. It is another matter that the preparation of the plate and the making of the copies can be – and actually are – considered as two stages of the same use, and usually both stages are covered – explicitly or implicitly – by the same authorization. When a writing or a graphic work is stored in a computer system for the purpose of making it available to the public through display on screens, the two acts of reproduction can be – and actually are – considered as two stages of the same complex use and usually the same authorization covers both (the authorization may also extend to another possible reproduction, namely to the hard-copy reprographic reproduction of the same work).'[62]

The views of governmental experts were quite divided concerning these ideas at that meeting. Several delegations said that they did not consider such a display a reproduction 'because the copy of the work was not obtained in a tangible form,' while several other delegations were in favour of further study qualifying display as reproduction, and some of the latter delegations underlined that 'it was not a further condition that the reproduction be in a tangible and lasting form; uses of programmes run in computers could be a good example of such short-term fixations which were recognized as reproduction of the work concerned.'[63]

In view of the large division among the positions of the various governments on this issue, the International Bureau, in its first series of proposals submitted to the Berne Protocol Committee, proposed the recognition of a specific right of public display.[64] At the second session of the Committee, where this proposal was discussed, the same division of views was manifested as to whether or not such a display was a temporary reproduction and, thus, already covered by the right of reproduction.[65] As mentioned above, the right of display was left out from the terms of reference when these were heavily restricted in 1992. It is another matter that, now that all questions relating to digital technology are considered to be covered again, it may, of course, be discussed again.

For the present subject matter, however, what is relevant from the above-mentioned discussions on the legal characterization of screen display is the question of whether or not what is only temporarily fixed in any manner

62. *Copyright*, February 1988, 77.

63. *Cf. supra* note 62, 82.

64. *See supra* note 36, first document, § 105-107.

65. *See supra* note 36, second document, § 91.

whatsoever, including in an intangible form, may be considered reproduction. This issue was also directly addressed by the same first series of proposals submitted by the International Bureau of WIPO. It was proposed that any storage in a computer system (irrespective of the duration of the 'storage') be recognized as reproduction.[66] The views were divided also on this issue, particularly on whether or not 'running' a computer program – and thus its temporary storage in a computer – should be considered as reproduction.[67]

A year later, when, at the first session of the 'New Instrument' Committee, the same proposal of the International Bureau – for the recognition of the storage, even temporarily, in electronic form[68] – was discussed in the context of the rights of performers and producers of phonograms, there seemed to be a more general recognition that temporary storage must be considered reproduction, but still there were some delegations which did not agree with this.[69] The level of difference among the various positions on this issue was maintained more or less at the same level at the third session (December 1994) of the 'New Instrument' Committee, where the definition of 'reproduction' was discussed again.[70]

Therefore, it seems that still further efforts are needed for the clarification of the notion of reproduction in respect of temporary storage/fixation of works and objects of neighbouring rights so that the right of reproduction may obtain complete recognition and may serve copyright and neighbouring rights protection at its full capacity in a digital environment.

In addition to this, the issue of exceptions to, and limitations on, the right of reproduction should also be reconsidered. Probably, it would not be appropriate to try to work out new international norms, at least for the time being; however, it should be made certain that Article 9(2) of the Berne Convention is duly interpreted and applied in accordance with the new conditions. It seems clear that, with the increase of copying in private homes and offices, instead of obtaining copies through the traditional public channels, private reproduction, in many more cases than before, must not be free, and also that, since such reproduction may become part of one of the most important ways of exploiting works, if not the most important one, the right of reproduction must not even be reduced to a mere right of remuneration (also taking into account that technological means combined with centralized management of rights offer appropriate alternatives to maintain an exclusive right).

Relationship with other acts

Still, the right of reproduction, even after all the necessary clarifications, may not be the only right to fully encompass copyright and neighbouring rights protection in digital networks.

---

66. *See supra* note 36, first document, § 72-72.
67. *See supra* note 36, first document, § 48-57.
68. *See supra* note 39, § 28(f).
69. *See* WIPO document INR/CE/3, § 79.
70. *See* WIPO documents INR/CE/III/3, § 38; INR/CE/III/3, Suppl.

First, certain acts may qualify as reproduction, but in a way that the reproduction in a computer memory may only be incidental to, or, to put it in another way, may only be an indispensable intermediary step towards, another act – or another aspect of the same act – that is more relevant in the case of the given use of the work: for example, communication to the public (or, under the national laws of certain countries, 'public performance'). Certainly, if an act of communication to the public takes place, there is no reason to deny the application of that right (and only apply the right of reproduction) just because the communication to the public takes place through a temporary reproduction of the work or object of neighbouring rights in a computer memory. If both communication to the public and reproduction take place, both the right of communication to the public and the right of reproduction must be applied. It is up to appropriate contractual practice to take into account the close relationship of the two acts or the two aspects of the same complex act.

Second, in respect of digital transmissions, special considerations may emerge concerning the relationship between the right of reproduction and a (possible) right of distribution. In this respect, it may be an extremely important factor from the viewpoint of legal policy that reproductions made in an extremely great number of private homes and offices all over the world may not be appropriately monitored and controlled; at the same time, it seems much easier to monitor and control the activity of those (the service providers and/or the 'content' providers) who upload the works and objects of neighbouring rights in a digital network and thus make – or at least make available for making – such reproductions. The result of the latter activity is similar to the result of distribution of (tangible) copies, and thus it is justified to consider the applicability of the right of distribution in this respect.

4.3 RIGHT OF DISTRIBUTION

The above-mentioned memorandum prepared by the International Bureau of WIPO for the Committee of Governmental Experts on the Printed Word, the meeting of which was held in Geneva in December 1987, described the relationship between the right of reproduction and the right of distribution in the case of transmissions in computer networks as follows:

> 'The model of traditional (printing) reproduction of writings and graphic works is that the distribution of copies takes place *after* reproduction. In the case of computer storage and transmission to the public – for screen retrieval – of writings and graphic works, the process if different: the distribution takes place *during* the reproduction of the copies. While in the case of traditional reproduction techniques (such as printing), it can be questioned whether the right of distribution follows from the right of reproduction (in certain countries the answer is affirmative, and it seems to be correct), in the case of electronic distribution – or, as it is frequently called, "electronic delivery" – where distribution is part of the reproduction process, [and it could be equally said: where the reproduction is part of the distribution process] the recognition of a

> kind of implicit right of distribution (..) based on the right of reproduction seems to be inevitable.'[71]

This position of the International Bureau was based on the so-called *reproduction theory* discussed above, which related to the legal characterization of screen displays, but which, as also discussed, might be considered applicable and valid for any other cases where copies are produced through transmission. The proposals included in the United States White Paper mentioned above seems to follow similar considerations. Under the Copyright Act of the United States of America, the exclusive rights of the copyright owner include the distribution of copies or phonorecords of the copyrighted work to the public by sale or other transfer of ownership or by rental, lease, or lending.[72] This right is substantially restricted by the 'first sale' doctrine under which, notwithstanding this right, 'the owner of a particular copy or phonorecord lawfully made under this title, or any person authorized by such owner, is entitled, without the authority of the copyright owner, to sell or otherwise dispose of the possession of that copy or phonorecord.'[73]

The White Paper proposes that a digital transmission should be covered by the right of distribution under the United States Copyright Act as follows:

> 'The Copyright Act gives a copyright owner the exclusive right "to distribute copies or phonorecords of the copyrighted work" to the public. It is not clear under the current law that a transmission can constitute a distribution of copies or phonorecords of a work. Yet, in the world of high-speed, communications systems, it is possible to transmit a copy of a work from one location to another. This may be the case, for instance, when a computer programme is transmitted from one computer to ten other computers. When the transmission is complete, the original copy typically remains in the transmitting computer and a copy resides in the memory of, or in storage devices associated with, each of the other computers. The transmission results essentially in the distribution of ten copies of the work. However, the extent of the distribution right under the present law may be somewhat uncertain and subject to challenge. Therefore, the Working Group recommends that the Copyright Act be amended to expressly recognize that copies or phonorecords of works can be distributed to the public by transmission, and that such transmissions fall within the exclusive distribution right of the copyright owner.'[74]

The White Paper also suggests that it be clarified that the 'first sale' doctrine and the related restriction of the right of distribution is not applicable when copies are distributed by 'transmission'.[75] The arguments given for the exclusion of the application of the 'first sale' doctrine in the case of digital transmissions are as follows:

---

71. *See supra* note 62, 77.
72. *See* United States Copyright Act, section 106 (3).
73. United States Copyright Act, section 109 (a).
74. *See* U.S. White Paper, *supra* note 53, 213.
75. *See* U.S. White Paper, *supra* note 92.

> 'This provision of the first sale doctrine limits only the copyright owner's distribution right; it in no way affects the reproduction right. Thus, the first sale doctrine does not allow the transmission of a copy of a work (through a computer network, for instance), because, under current technology *the transmitter retains the original copy* of the work while *the recipient of the transmission obtains a reproduction of the original copy* (i.e., a *new* copy), *rather than the copy owned by the transmitter*. The language of the Copyright Act, the legislative history and case law make clear that the doctrine is applicable only to those situations where the owner of a particular copy disposes of physical possession of that particular copy. (..)
>
> If the owner of a particular copy transmits a copy to another person without authorization (either from the copyright owner or the law), *such a transmission would involve an unlawful reproduction of a work, and the first sale doctrine would not shield the transmitter from liability for the reproduction nor for the distribution.* Under the first sale doctrine, the owner of a particular copy of a copyrighted work may distribute it, but may not reproduce it.'[76]

These arguments indicate that the authors of the White Paper see the relationship between the right of reproduction and the right of distribution in a way very similar to what is reflected in the above-quoted analysis of the International Bureau of WIPO. It seems that it is recognized that what is actually transmitted is not a copy (and certainly not the copy of the transmitter) but electronic signals as a result of which new copies are obtained by the recipient. Thus, the expression in the White Paper 'to distribute copies (..) to the public (..) by transmission' may also be considered as shorthand for 'to distribute copies (..) to the public (..) by reproducing such copies through transmission.'

It is obvious, however, that what may be a perfect and workable solution in the Copyright Act of the United States of America, may not be equally applicable at the international level. To start with, for example, the Berne Convention does not recognize a general right of distribution; it only provides for such a right in respect of cinematographic works (see Articles 14(1)(i) and 14*bis*(1)). Thus, if we intended to use the right of distribution at the international level in the same way as it is proposed to be used under the United States Copyright Act, as a first step, the Berne Protocol and the 'New Instrument' should introduce a general right of distribution to extend to all categories of works and objects of neighbouring rights. There is a good chance that this may happen; both Committees seem to support the recognition of such a right.[77]

This is, however, not yet sufficient. A second step is also needed. The right of distribution should be construed in a way that it also extends to the distribution of copies of works and objects of neighbouring rights by making such copies through transmission (any other appropriate word or expression synonymous with 'transmission' may also be used) with an appropriate clarification that the possible provision on the exhaustion of distribution right does not cover this case. It seems

76. *See* U.S. White Paper, *supra* note 53, 92.

77. *See supra* note 15, § 279.

that this second step may not be easy in the context of the Berne Protocol and the 'New Instrument.' The discussions by the two Committees on the right of distribution has indicated quite strong resistance to the extension of the right of distribution beyond the transfer of ownership or possession of *tangible* copies.

The report of the fourth session of the Berne Protocol Committee (December 1994) reflects this as follows:

> 'The overwhelming majority of the delegations that took the floor on this issue were of the opinion that the right of distribution should be restricted to cover distribution of physical, tangible copies only.'[78]

> 'Among the delegations that opposed the extension of distribution rights to cover immaterial distribution, the majority indicated that they considered the right of communication to the public, in conjunction with the right of reproduction, as the relevant rights applicable to digital transmission and copying at the receiving end. Some of these delegations indicated that they were aware that these rights might not cover all situations, and they indicated willingness to look at eliminating the existing gaps in this respect.'[79]

The discussions at the latest, joint sessions of the two Committees (of September 1995) on the 'digital agenda,' as mentioned above, were of a general, preliminary nature. However, as much as it touched upon the idea of applying the right of distribution to digital transmissions, it indicated that the chances for a sufficiently broad support for that idea had not improved.

It seems necessary to note that, in the context of the right of distribution discussed above, the notion of 'transmission' is used in a broad sense; probably broader than in the ordinary language where 'to transmit' is a synonym of 'to pass on, to hand on'. The latter meaning refers to an active person or entity who or which transfers, passes on or hands on something to another person or entity whose only role may be to receive that something. In an interactive digital network, the role of a 'receiver' may be much more active; the 'transmitter' may only make the work or object of neighbouring rights *accessible* for *retrieval* by the members of the public who may eventually *cause* the system *to transmit* the work or object of neighbouring rights to them. To avoid possible narrow interpretation of the concept of 'transmission', it may be useful to clarify this.

4.4 RIGHT OF RENTAL

In the Green Paper of the Commission of the European Communities, 'the Commission takes the view that the rental right could be applicable by extension to digital transmissions.'[80] The Commission stresses that '[i]n practical economic terms, electronic rental of works or other protected matter is a competing activity which is essentially the same thing as rental from a shop, so that it seems

78. *See supra* note 10, § 50.

79. *See supra* note 10. § 52.

80. European Commission Green Paper, *supra* note 52, 29.

reasonable to apply the same rights in both cases.' It believes that 'rental' of works or other protected matter, as defined in the Rental Right Directive, 'clearly includes activities such as video on demand and other electronic forms based on point-to-point transmission.'[81]

Article 1(2) of the Rental Right Directive defines 'rental' as follows: 'the making available for use, for a limited period of time and for direct or indirect economic or commercial advantage.' It is interesting to note that the definition does not identify the object of 'making available'. At the same time, the definition of 'rental' in another directive of the European Communities, the Computer Programmes Directive does; under that directive, 'rental' means 'the making available for use, for a limited period of time and for profit-making purposes, of *a computer programme or a copy thereof*' (Article 4(c)- italics added).

It seems that the latter definition follows the ordinary sense of 'rental,' that is, under it, 'rental' is the making available for use (transfer of possession but not property) of tangible objects (in our context, the tangible original or tangible copies of a work or object of neighbouring rights). Therefore, if the proposal of the Commission were accepted, still some clarification would seem necessary, in a new directive or otherwise, concerning the application of the concept of rental for the above-discussed purposes, similar to the one proposed in the United States 'White Paper'.

If the proposal is accepted – it being considered either as a mere clarification or an extension of the concept of 'rental' through legal fiction, which after all is a legitimate legal technique – it may certainly offer a solution within the European Community. The chance of a similar proposal for a sufficiently broad support in the Berne Protocol and 'New Instrument' context would not seem, however, better than that of the above-discussed solution based on a broad interpretation and application of the right of distribution, at least for the time being, or, perhaps, even less, since the opposition to the said solution, as discussed above, is based on the principle that the right of distribution should be limited to the transfer of ownership or possession of *tangible* copies, and since the notion of 'rental' seems to be even more closely connected to *tangible* copies than the notion of 'distribution'.

In this aspect, the proposal of the Commission and the proposal included in the United States White Paper do not seem to be in harmony, since the latter proposal seems to recognize that rental involves the transfer of tangible copies; and, consequently, rental and transmission are presented as alternatives – rather than a more general category and a sub-category of that more general category – in the proposed provision on the right of distribution.

It should be noted that the proposal of the Commission of European Communities includes an underlying idea which refers to the possibility of a more general and more flexible solution to the problem of digital transmissions; namely that it is based on the broad concept of making available a work or object of neighbouring rights (to the public). The original notion of 'rental' actually seems to be narrower than this broad concept (since it seems to only relate to the making available of tangible copies), but as discussed below, this concept might be used as

81. European Commission Green Paper, *supra* note 52, 58.

an element of an umbrella-type regulation, free of any specific legal characterization which may create difficulties at the international level.

4.5 RIGHT OF COMMUNICATION TO THE PUBLIC, RIGHT OF BROADCASTING

It is justified to discuss these two rights together since, at least, under the Berne Convention, communication to the public is a broader concept and broadcasting is a specific form of communication to the public, namely by wireless diffusion of signs, sounds and images. We do not discuss, together with these two rights, a third right – namely the right of public performance, which in certain contexts is frequently referred to together with these two rights. *According to the notion of public performance under the Berne Convention*, this third right is not relevant in the context of digital transmissions, since that notion is limited to performances *in the presence of a public*.

We have underscored the words 'according to the notion (..) under the Berne Convention', because, at the national level, quite differing concepts are used for broadcasting, communication to the public and public performance. There are countries where the concept of public performance is much broader and also covers communication to the public and broadcasting.[82] In other countries the concept of communication to the public is used in a way that it also includes broadcasting.[83] In still other countries, the situation is just the contrary; broadcasting is the general concept and it also covers communication to the public.[84] The list of solutions might be continued in referring to expressions that differ from the ones used in the Berne Convention, but, in this or that way, cover one or more rights provided for in the said Convention as mentioned above.[85]

Our objective now is not to deal with those differing national concepts in detail, since our attention is to be devoted to the international norms. As long as, through those concepts, the existing minimum obligations under the international norms are respected, the use of different language does not create any problems. There is, however, one aspect of these differing national concepts which may have importance if we try to settle the questions of digital transmissions at the international level; namely that, behind these differing concepts, there are differing interests of different groups of owners of rights and users, differing acquired rights and privileges and differing contractual practices. This certainly may make it

82. *See*, e.g., the Law of Intellectual Property Code of France, articles L.122-1 and L.122-2, and the Copyright Act of the United States of America, Section 101.

83. *See*, e.g., the Copyright Act of Colombia, Article 76(d), and the Copyright Law of Venezuela, Article 40.

84. *See*, e.g., The Copyright Decree of Nigeria, Section 39(1).

85. *See*, e.g., the definitions of 'telecommunication' in the Copyright Act of Canada, Section 1, and of 'wire diffusion' and 'wire transmission' in the Copyright Law of Japan, Article 2(ix*bis*) and (xvii).

difficult to opt at the international level for one specific concept and right, to the detriment of others.

Generalized right of communication to the public?

As discussed above, during the discussions by the Berne Protocol Committee and the 'New Instrument' Committee, many delegations favoured a generalized right of communication to the public to be applied for digital transmissions rather than a generalized right of distribution. The first evident problem for the implementation of this idea at the level of the Berne Convention and the Rome Convention is that those Conventions do not provide for an exclusive right of communication to the public in respect of all categories of works and objects of neighbouring rights. Setting aside here the analysis of the more complex situation under the Rome Convention, we only refer to the fact that, although the Berne Convention provides a right of communication to the public in respect of certain works and for certain forms in which works are communicated, namely for cinematographic works (Article 14(1)(ii) and 14*bis*(1)); for performances of musical, dramatic and dramatico-musical works (Article 11(1)(ii)); for recitation of literary works (Article 11*ter*(1)(ii)); and for broadcasting of works (Article 11*bis*(1)(ii) and (iii)), it does not grant the same right, for example, for literary works (except in the form of recitation), including computer programmes (which certainly are never 'recited'), for graphic works, for photographic works and for musical works in sheet music form.

In the Berne Protocol, those gaps of the Convention may, and probably should, be eliminated, and a general communication to the public right may be applicable for digital transmissions. The Government of Australia made a proposal to this effect, and it was supported by other delegations in the Berne Protocol Committee.[86] This, however, would not be sufficient. Certain clarifications would also be needed. First of all, the concept of [communication] 'to the public' should be clarified, and preferably defined, to make it clear that it also extends to on-demand communication, that is, communication to the public takes place irrespective of whether the members of the public may receive the communication in the same place or in separate places, and at the same time or at different times.

Furthermore, the same kind of clarification would be necessary as the one to which we have referred in respect of the right of distribution, namely that 'communication' is used in a broad sense also covering interactive uses where the 'communicator' only makes the work *accessible* for *retrieval* and reception by the members of the public who may eventually *cause* the system *to communicate* the work to them. As far as broadcasting is concerned, if the right of broadcasting is applied to digital transmission by wireless means on the basis of the above-outlined solution, it should be taken into account that no non-voluntary licenses seem justified in the case of on-demand transmissions, and specific provisions might be necessary to eliminate the application of Article 11*bis*(2) in such cases.

While this solution may work in the Berne Protocol, it does not seem to have a reasonable chance for general acceptance in the 'New Instrument' context, at

86. *See supra* note 10, § 313, 316 and 350.

least for the time being. Several countries may have difficulties – probably insurmountable difficulties – to accept a general communication to the public right (and broadcasting right) for performers and producers of phonograms. Although it was quite generally recognized that performers, at least in respect of their performances fixed on phonograms, and producers of phonograms in respect of their phonograms, should have direct control and, thus, exclusive right concerning the on-demand digital transmissions of phonograms, it seems that, for special reasons relating to their legal systems, some countries might not be able to grant such a control and exclusive right through the concept of communication to the public and broadcasting (which could not be easily accepted as general rights in the neighbouring rights context), but rather through the context of distribution (and, because it would be a major contradiction to apply different rights for the same acts in the fields of copyright and neighbouring rights, this, of course, makes it desirable and, in a way inevitable, in those countries, to follow the distribution line also in respect of copyright).

Right of display

The recognition of a right of display in the Berne Protocol may be considered as an alternative to the introduction of a general communication to the public right. The reason may be that the right of communication to the public, in the Convention, is quite closely related to performances (or recitations) of works. A text or a graphic work transmitted to a screen is not communicated in that way; it is rather displayed.

Nevertheless, it seems that this alternative does not deserve being pursued, at least for the time being. The right of display only exists in a small number of countries,[87] and the proposal for the recognition of such a right, as discussed above, did not receive sufficient support during the first series of discussions in the Berne Protocol Committee. Thus, if the idea of a general communication to the public right is accepted, it would seem more appropriate to extend the scope of this right – through a broader interpretation of the concept of communication to the public – to the cases that might be covered by a specific right of display.

Specific digital transmission right

It seems that, at least for the time being, it could not be seriously considered that, in the Berne Protocol and 'New Instrument,' a specific right be included to cover digital transmissions. Such a solution has emerged in legal literature, but it certainly would not receive sufficient support in the Committees dealing with the Berne Protocol and the 'New Instrument.' The governments and legislators dealing with the issues raised by digital technology prefer adopting, and, if necessary, extending the scope of application of, existing concepts and norms, rather than creating new ones. And from the viewpoint of legal policy, this seems to be the right approach.

87. *See*, e.g., the Copyright Act of the United States, sections 101 and 106.

4.6 'UMBRELLA SOLUTION' ALLOWING THE APPLICATION OF DIFFERENT RIGHTS?

As discussed above, the legal regulation of digital transmissions is quite an urgent task at the international level, and, thus, it would be highly desirable to settle this issue in the Berne Protocol and the 'New Instrument' so that those treaties may live up to the justified expectations. The analysis of the various possible options indicates, however, that, so far, there is no emerging consensus, or even any broad agreement, as to which right or rights may be applied in this context.

Two scenarios seem possible. According to the optimistic scenario, considering the two basic concepts, the concept of distribution and the concept of communication to the public, one group will be able to persuade the other to accept its concept. This would be a happy ending. One would be, however, overly optimistic to believe that this may happen relatively easily, and in a relatively short time (or that it may happen at all). The differences in legal approaches, in the specific, legal characterization of the acts involved are so large and the relating interests of the various groups of owners of rights and users to maintain certain acquired positions, contractual practices and the actual balance of interests are so important, that it would be very difficult for many governments to make fundamental compromises.

Therefore, another scenario may also be considered, and the idea of such an alternative scenario in a way already emerged at the September 1995 joint sessions of the Berne Protocol and 'New Instrument' Committees. By this, we refer to the statement of the Delegation of the United States of America, supported by the Delegation of the United Kingdom, which was the following: 'It [is] not the legal characterization which [is] truly important but rather that the acts involved be covered by appropriate exclusive rights.'[88]

Actually, there seems to be fairly broad agreement that the acts involved in the case of a transmission/delivery in a digital network should be covered by exclusive rights, and the views and positions only differ in respect of the legal characterization of the acts. Thus, following the idea of the Delegation of the United States of America, a solution may be to describe the acts to be covered in a neutral way, not including any specific legal characterization, and to leave such characterization and, consequently, the choice of the right or rights to be applied, to national legislation. This could be done, for example, in the following way (this is not a proposal, just an outline of one of the possible solutions; and it only relates to the Berne Protocol, but might also be adapted to the 'New Instrument'):

(a) to provide that authors of literary and artistic works shall have the exclusive right of authorizing the making of their works available in an electronic or similar network, either by wire or by wireless means, to the public (i) to perceive the work on a screen and/or through a loudspeaker, or in any other way, the signs, sound and/or images in which the work is expressed, and/or (ii) to obtain a copy or copies of the work by any means

88. *See* WIPO document BCP/CE/V/I-INR/CE/IV/8, § 20.

and in any form, including the storage of the work, even temporarily, in an electronic or similar storage device;

(b) to provide that, in the application of this provision, a work shall be considered to be made available to the public irrespective of whether the members of the public may have access to the work in the same place or in separate places and at the same time or at different times (this, however, might also be included in a more general provision defining the concept 'to the public');

(c) to provide that it shall be a matter for legislation in the countries party to the Protocol to permit the making available of the works to the public as described under point (a), above, in certain special cases, provided that such an act does not conflict with a normal exploitation of the work and does not unreasonably prejudice the legitimate interests of the author (this again may be included in a provision of broader coverage);

(d) to provide that it shall also be a matter for legislation in the countries party to the Protocol to implement the above-outlined provisions by applying an exclusive right or exclusive rights of authorization to be granted under the Protocol and/or the Berne Convention, or by applying a specific exclusive right to cover the acts or some of the acts described under point (a), or by applying a combination of all these rights (it is to be noted, that for being able to offer all these options, certain 'gaps' in the Convention should be eliminated; for example, a general distribution right should be introduced);

(e) to provide that, where a country party to the Protocol, under the previously mentioned provision, applies the right of distribution provided for in the Protocol and in Articles 14(1)(i) and 14*bis*(1) of the Berne Convention, the act of making a work available to the public as described in point (a), above, shall not be covered by any exhaustion of right that may be provided for in the Protocol or in national legislation;

(f) to include a safeguard clause to the effect that none of the provisions mentioned above shall be interpreted as affecting any obligation under the Protocol and the Berne Convention to grant protection of the rights of authors in their literary and artistic works.

Now that the preparatory work of the Berne Protocol and the 'New Instrument' continues and speeds up, it is hoped that an appropriate solution will be found to the key issues involved in digital transmissions in a way that it will meet with the consensus of the participants in the two Committees as well as in the possible diplomatic conference or conferences which may be convened for the adoption of these new treaties.

The Answer to the Machine is in the Machine

*Charles Clark**

> 'The question surrounding the electronic use of copyright materials is not so much, "How shall we prevent access and use?" as "How shall we monitor access and use?" Generally speaking, intellectual property is made available to the public so that it can be used, and mechanisms which simply prevent use eventually defeat the very reason for which the material was created at all. After all, to publish is to make something available to the public. The real issue is to link identifying, monitoring, control and reward. The ideal is a system which can undertake several different tasks, preferably all at the same time. A system must be able to identify copyright materials, to track usage, to verify users, and to record usage and appropriate compensation. In addition, the system should provide security for the integrity of the copyrighted material (freedom from tampering) and some level of confidentiality or privacy for the user. It might also provide the user with a price list showing various costs for different uses and individual materials along the model of a retail establishment.'

The above quotation[1] sets the scene for much active research in the field known broadly as Electronic Copyright Management Systems (ECMS). There is intensive work being invested by an impressively large number of researchers and institutions mainly in the United States,[2] but also in the European Union and in Japan. The Association of Scientific Technical and Medical Publishers (STM) recently and very helpfully made available an inventory of such initiatives, prepared by Douglas Armati. No less than twenty American, six European and five Japanese projects are in hand for the management of literary works.

Closed Circuit Systems

The anxieties of STM publishers, faced with potential mass piracy on digital networks and highways, will, it is suggested, incline them to seek first some security in *closed circuit* systems, for which there is likely shortly to be the relevant 'architecture'. Publishers will not wish to make the intellectual property of

---

* Legal adviser, International Publishers Copyright Council (IPCC).

1. *The Publisher in the Electronic World*, Report from International Publishers Copyright Council, Turin, May 1994, 35.
2. Cf. Association of American Publishers, *Enabling Technologies*, Final Report, Washington, D.C., Summer, 1995.

themselves and their authors available to *open access* until 'identifying, monitoring, control and compensation' models are much nearer secure reality.

One example of a closed circuit system is being pioneered and tested in the United Kingdom by a consortium of users, publishers and technologists under the name INFOBIKE (so called because the basic system architecture resembles a stylized bicycle - one wheel being Bibliographic Databases, and the other wheel being Document Servers). The projects mission statement is 'to make available, and prove, in a real environment, an "electronic document" finding, ordering, browsing and delivery service'. The consortium members include Blackwell Science and Academic Press who provide the learned journals contents for the project; ICL who will develop the document server system; the Universities of Kent, Keele & Staffordshire; and the Consortium of Academic Libraries in Manchester (CALIM). Last and perhaps most important are the participation and the project leadership of the Bath University Information and Data Services (BIDS).

The overall objective is to provide for services (to quote the consortium's proposal) 'which will allow users to have browsing and reading access to a large range of journals in electronic form, for which their institutions have paid licence fees. This (the Bibliographic Database wheel) will be backed up by an electronic document delivery facility (the Document Servers wheel), charged on a usage basis. Such services must be established taking account of the legitimate interests of users, libraries, publishers and authors. One of the factors which is critical to the introduction of such a service will be pricing models that are acceptable to all the parties.'

Similar pilot schemes are in hand in the Netherlands. Publishers may well in the next few years become reasonably comfortable with this kind of closed circuit system, which has features of both electronic subscription fees and 'pay as you use' transactional fees. The IPCC (International Publishers Copyright Council) has been specifically charged with the task of monitoring such systems as they develop.

Open Access Systems

The longer term future, however, must involve the publishers in *open access* systems. The first and foremost solution, on which all other solutions depend, will then be to find an *identifying* system. The World Intellectual Property Organisation (WIPO) recently called together a Working Group, including lawyers, software experts and standards officers, to examine this key issue. Its full title is Consultation Forum for NGOs on the Protection and Management of Copyright and Neighbouring Rights in Digital Systems. One critical choice will be between 'intelligent' and 'dumb' identifiers. An intelligent identifier would encompass all the information relevant to identifying the copyright work, its various rightsholders, the terms on which the work can be licensed for various uses, etc. A dumb identifier would simply identify the work, and refer to a repository of relevant further information. One advantage of dumb rather than intelligent identifiers is that information which changes (just as each year works pass out of copyright into the public domain or, indeed, have their copyright extended or revived) can be kept securely up to date in the repository.

A dumb identifier strongly suggests a role for collecting societies which are well used to handling and updating work-specific information. Development of the Copyright Licensing Agency's Rapid Clearance System (CLARCS) in the UK, which calls up from its database work-specific information for licensing purposes, is, for example, likely to lean towards such a 'repository' function.

It is rather ironic that the book trade, thought of often as a 'steam-age' trade, has actually pioneered unique identifiers, first with ISBNs, then with ISSNs, over 25 years ago, and now with journal article identifiers (SICI).[3] Whether and how that system can be adapted must currently be an open question. It must, certainly, continue in existence for trading purposes even if universally compatible codes or one universal code for all categories of copyright works become realistic.

The CISAC Common Information System

Exciting work is now in hand by CISAC in creating a Common Information System (CIS), which may become capable of application to all categories of copyright works.[4] The latest available plan from CISAC sets out the following Principles:

'The CIS program rests on four underlying "principles of copyright information management" for the protection of copyright within the international network in the digital age. These will be incorporated into the 'Principles and Standard Protocol' to which all participants in the CIS plan will in due course be expected to subscribe. The four principles are:

1. *The Principle of Authority*
   The proper source of information about a creator and his works is the creator.
2. *The Principle of Responsibility*
   Each creator or his authorised agent is responsible for the establishment of information about himself and his works within the network.
3. *The Principle of Identification*
   Each creator and agent, each work and each agreement governing the ownership of works must be uniquely numbered and described to agreed international standards.
4. *The Principle of Access*
   Information about the identity of creators, works and the current assignments of rights in works should be made available within the networks by means

3. *ISBN*: International Standard Book Number; *ISSN*: International Standard Serial Number; *SICI*: Serial Item and Contribution Identifier.
4. *See* Dominique Yon, 'Towards an international system for identifying works in the digital transmission chain'. CISAC presentation at hearing European Commission (DG XV), Brussels, 8-9 January 1996.

and at a level of detail compatible with the identify of the interested party requesting the information.

Application of principles

Any organisation wishing to play a full part in the Common Information System must respect these four principles. The net result of the four principles should be that anyone can identify the current rights owner of a copyright work in a given territory for the purposes of licensing, reporting and royalty payment.

In applying these principles, especially the principle of access, a number of other considerations must also be respected:

- The provisions of data protection legislation.
- The internal security of each organisations computer systems.
- The confidentiality of the specific terms and provisions of copyright agreements.
- The costs to the data provider, which may be met by service charges where appropriate.

It is likely that an international project will soon emerge to co-ordinate, in particular, the American and European initiatives. One critical choice in this ongoing exploration will be the level of work which it is sought to identify. Technical experts state that a sentence of a book or learned journal article, or a bar of music, can be identified. It may be that identification needs to start only at the threshold beyond which intellectual property value is measured by fees.

Allied to that issue is one raised recently by Daniel Gervais, the Assistant General Secretary of CISAC, which he described as *the problem of the smallest protected unit*:[5]

> 'The question of the smallest work concerns the definition of the notion of work and, more precisely, how small can a creation be and still embody a sufficiently high degree of originality. (..) In the literary field, a single word is not protected, but there are cases where a single sentence has been said to be protected. There is no universal answer to the question.'

Gervais then quotes from a presentation by Dr Thomas Dreier at the WIPO Harvard Symposium in Spring 1993:

> '[I]f digital technology and networking thus have a tendency to replace the "author" with mere contributors, the dissolution of what constitutes a "work" (..) seems to work quite to the contrary, i.e. in favour of the contributors' status as authors. The reason for this is the fact that, if single parts of the entirety that was traditionally considered a work - eventually even any combination of data to which a meaning is attached - are regarded as independent "works", it would consequently be possible for independent "authorship" to attach to any of these minimal combinations.'[6]

---

5. Daniel Gervais, paper presented at Knowright Conference, Vienna, August 1995.
6. Th. Dreier, 'Copyright Digitized: Philosophical Impacts and Practical Implications for Informatiion Exchange in Digital Networks', in: *WIPO Worldwide Symposium on the Impact of*

The CITED Project

In Europe, the European Union's CITED project (Copyright in Transmitted Electronic Data) was concluded in 1994 with meetings held throughout Europe to describe the model which the CITED team developed with funding from the ESPRIT research programme. In an article in *New Society* Andy Lawrence gave a short and very clear overview of the CITED model:[7]

> 'These proposals went further than merely specifying ways of encrypting information so that only authorised key holders can grab an electronic document from the Internet and convert it into a usable form. CITED tackled the tricky problem of what happens after the material has been decoded. If a computer file containing music, or the page of a journal is sitting on the hard disc of a computer that is hooked up to a local area network, with basic encryption systems there is nothing to stop the authorised user from redistributing, or even printing those files.
>
> The model that the pan-European team has come up with is built around a tamper-proof software module which acts rather like indestructible tachometers installed on long-distance coaches and lorries, recording everything that happens to the copyrighted or commercially valuable material. As with the Cerberus approach, the basic idea is that the valuable material is linked to a specific piece of software. This software is required to gain access to the material, and it can only be converted into its usable form by someone in possession of the right key or password.
>
> The difference with the CITED approach is that, when the authorised user requests a piece of software or some pages of a report or journal, he or she will have to key in a password. From then on, each time a program is run or a print of a page is made, the associated software module sends a message back to the secure database stored on the computer. The database can then track every activity carried out by the organisation's software modules, so providing an audit trail which show whether pages are being printed or copied electronically. Eventually, it may be possible to forward this information to rights societies to help them determine how much artists, authors and publishers should be paid.'

CITED is now being applied in various successor projects, e.g. COPICAT, funded by the European Union. Particular attention should be paid to IMPRIMATUR, a new and very ambitious EU-funded project whose overall aim is to provide a 'new settlement' for the digital era.

These indications of current work suggest that sooner or later the answer to the machine will indeed be found in the machine. Two consequent issues will then loom large. The first is whether the information society can wait for a further 20 years while owners of competing patented systems slug it out in the marketplace.

Digital Technology on Copyright and Neighboring Rights, Harvard University, 31 March-2 April, 1993, WIPO Publication No. 723 (E), Geneva, 1993, 187, at 192.

7. Andy Lawrence, *New Society*, February 1995.

Technical compatibility, possibly through the International Standards Organisation (ISO), must come soon onto the agenda.

Reinforcement of Technical Protection

The second consequent issue is the need for controlling legislation to reinforce technical protection. A draft article, for possible inclusion in the Protocol to the Berne Convention, is offered here:

> Contracting Parties shall by civil and criminal measures prohibit the importation, the manufacture, the possession in the course of business, the distribution, the transmission, the sale, the lease, the use of any device, product, computer program or component incorporated into a device, product or computer program; and/or the offer or performance of any service or other act, the effect of which is to avoid, to bypass, to deactivate, to modify, to disable, to circumvent in any way without authority, any process, treatment, mechanism or system which prevents or restricts the unauthorised exercise of any rights incorporated in the Berne Convention or in this Protocol.

There is precedent for such a provision in article 7 (1)(c) of the European Directive on the Legal Protection of Computer Programs. Further support is provided by specific statutory language in the U.S. White Paper regarding 'Circumvention of Copyright Protection Systems' and 'Integrity of Copyright Management Information'.[8] It is, however, recognised that there will need to be provision for acceptable exemptions. Two examples, come to mind: one for certain products of the consumer electronic industry; and one for the law-enforcement agencies.

Finally, as the U.S. pioneers quickly acknowledged, the National Information Infrastructure (NII) has rapidly become the Global Information Infrastructure (GII). In that global perspective, there is an increasing mismatch between the traditional concept of the nation-state as the engine of economic and social management, including intellectual property, and the reality of the rise of transnational activity. The Internet is a vastly challenging transnational phenomenon, operating in over 75 countries, reaching over 25 million people who access the Internet via over two million PCs, with no concern for 'nation state' interests whatever. Nor will other information delivery systems have any such concern, e.g. university distance learning networks. And we see now very large firms operating across the world, sometimes with a purely technical relationship, merely that of registration as a business activity, with the traditional nation state.

We approach, therefore, in the words of Eric Hobsbawn in his book,[9] 'a state of economic activities for which state territories and state frontiers are not the basic framework but merely complicating factors'. Yet our copyright system, as the

---

8. Report (White Paper) of the Working Group on Intellectual Property Rights, *Intellectual Property and the National Information Infrastructure*, Washington D.C., 1995, Appendix I, 6-7.

9. Eric Hobsbawn, *Age of Extremes. The Short 20th Century, 1914-1991*, New York, 1995.

central pillar of national treatment in the Berne Convention makes clear, is founded on the nation state. Can publishers maintain the territoriality of copyright in an environment of unstoppable transnational/transborder flow of information over the digital highways?

One way forward is being pioneered by the music business in an alliance of tracking systems and collective administration. Godfrey Rust,[10] the Database Controller of the Mechanical Copyright Protection Society (MCPS), offers the following instructive example of how the development of codes[11] can lock in to the development of collective administration:

> 'A French songwriter writes a song, which, some months later, is recorded in the USA. Afterwards the recording is used in Australia. The composer already has a unique CAE (Compositeur, Auteur, Editeur) number, which identifies him as author and owner. His new song is given an ISWC, an International Standard Work Code, by his publisher or, if he has none, by his society. In the USA, when applying for its licence, the record company tells the Fox Agency of the recording's international standard recording code, the ISRC. The agency identifies the song through the French database, and links the recording code to the work code. In Australia the recording is played somewhere, perhaps on a smart-card music-on-demand system on a superhighway. The ISRC is automatically tracked and reported to the Australian performing rights society, APRA. Through the network, thanks to the earlier work of Fox and SACEM, APRA automatically retrieves the work code and the CAE number. In due time they attach the appropriate payment, which goes through the French society to the composer's account.'

Such a practical alliance of identifier codes with collective administration may become one central strategy for maintaining reward for uses of copyright works in the digital environments, as envisaged in the pioneering Common Information System whose basic principles are set out above.

In short conclusion, the aim of this article has been to draw attention to the scale of work now proceeding to find appropriate *record and reward* systems, and to suggest the need first to find *closed circuit* solutions if rightsholders are to find the confidence which will be needed *in a world of open access*. The answer to the machine may turn out to be not only in the machine, but the machine will certainly be an important part of the answer.

---

10. Godfrey Rust, 'Distribution in the Digital Age', *Copyright World*, No. 46, December 1994/January 1995, 34, at 36.
11. Note the plural 'codes': the ISBN code identifies only the book which contains the authors' work (or authors' works) and the publisher of the book; it does not identify the work itself (or the works themselves).

Collective Administration of Electronic Rights: A Realistic Option?

*Ferdinand Melichar**

Collecting societies should collectively administer only *secondary* and *further* rights, not *primary* rights. This principle has prevailed until today. It is not the rights in the printed text of a literary work, for example, which are collectively administered, but the reprographic reproduction of that once printed and published text.[1] This was already the case with the foundation of the first collecting society in the world. When in 1851 composers and music publishers formed SACEM, it was clear that the object of the collective administration should not be the printing of sheet music, but rather the public performance of their musical works, made possible by the sheet music.

An important exception to the principle that collecting societies do not administer primary rights is to be found in the licensing of music records. Even in states which do not provide for legal or compulsory licences on the basis of Article 13 of the Berne Convention, the rights as to the production of phonograms, the *mechanical* rights, are as a rule administered by collecting societies.[2] Although this is an important counter-example, it should not lead to the conclusion that collecting societies may only administer secondary rights.

In the future the possibilities of electronic/digital technology will render the distinction between primary and secondary uses blurred. Scientific journals are already being produced and distributed initially in electronic form, and then only as a second step is a paper copy of the journal or of its individual articles produced, for example through online subscriptions. Similarly, one can imagine that there are musical works which are initially stored in a digital jukebox, to which customers have online access. The customers can then, if necessary, make a hard copy on tape or other media.[3] According to the traditional view, the (first) paper copy or (first) tape recording represents a secondary use – a paradoxical result which shows that in the digital future the distinction between primary and secondary uses will no longer be meaningful.

---

* Managing Director of VG WORT; Attorney at law; and Lecturer, University of Munich.

1. *Cf.* F. Melichar, *Die Wahrnehmung von Urheberrechten durch Verwertungsgesellschaften*, Munich, 1983, 5.
2. WIPO, *Collective Administration of Copyright and Neighbouring Rights*, Geneva, 1990, 20.
3. J. Becker and Th. Dreier (ed.), *Urheberrecht und digitale Technologie*, Baden-Baden, 1994, 46.

Pragmatic Solutions

On the basis of theoretical criteria, we should no longer attempt to answer the question whether a particular right should be administered collectively or individually. Rather we should seek a purely pragmatic answer. Regarding each type of use, we should consider the following:

1. Can the individual rightholder exercise an exclusive right, i.e. prohibit this particular use, and does he want to do so?
2. Can the individual rightholder license this specific use, and does he want to do so?

If neither of these questions can be answered in the affirmative, we have an appropriate case for collective administration. Obviously, the answering of these questions does not depend solely on legal provisions; rather it depends above all on factual circumstances. To give you an example from Italy, how could an individual rightholder really prevent private copying on tape, even though such copying was prohibited by the Italian Copyright Law until 1993?[4]

Another important criterion with respect to these questions is whether the individual rightholder really exercises his rights in practice. Here it needs to be borne in mind that individual rights need to be exercised as quickly as possible on the appearance of new forms of use – otherwise there is a danger that the well-known "normative power of the factual situation" will apply, as the following example shows.

In Germany, several specialized *information* centres were established during the financial crisis of the post-war years.[5] As many libraries could not afford to collect all publications in various relevant areas, one library was selected in each case to assemble, for the benefit of the whole of Germany, a comprehensive collection of works concerning a particular scientific field. Over the last 15 years or so, such information centres have also provided document delivery services charging high fees to the customers. The publishers, who were the rightholders in this case, watched this development without taking action, but did not transfer their rights to a collecting society. Only in 1994 did they decide on a test case and brought action against the Fachinformationsbibliothek Technik (TIB) in Hannover alleging infringement of their reproduction and distribution rights. The Landgericht Munich, as court of first instance, rejected this claim.[6] The publishers may appeal, but their chances of winning would certainly be much better if they had decided either to prohibit or to licence this new type of use as soon as it appeared.

In order to answer the question whether the collective administration of electronic rights is a realistic option one should not draw a theoretical distinction between primary and secondary uses. Rather, one should inquire in relation to each type of use whether the individual rightholders can and do prohibit or licence that use. If these questions cannot be answered affirmatively, then collective administration is the only alternative.

---

4. G. Jarach, *Manuale del Diritto d'Autore*, Milan, 1983, 106.
5. Bundesvereinigung Deutscher Bibliothekverbände, *Bibliotheken '93*, Berlin/Göttingen, 1994, 55.
6. LG München I, Judgement of 18 May 1995 (7 0 18987/94), unpublished.

Practical Examples

I would like to demonstrate my proposal by referring to two examples, both far removed from the information highway.

Inhouse electronic use

More and more industrial enterprises are storing their specialized libraries in a central electronic database by means of scanning. The advantage compared with the traditional library is that employees do not have to visit the library but can obtain the desired information on their desk-screens and, if they so wish, make a paper copy of it. Even if such in-house use is regarded by the national copyright law as a restricted act, I do not believe that such a prohibition can be enforced in practice (any more than the prohibition of private audio-copying in Italy in the previous example). The only remaining possibility is to at least licence such in-house use. To do so on an individual basis would, however, impose too much of a burden on the rightholders and industrial enterprises alike. This leaves, in my opinion, collective administration of the rights as the only way of meeting the requirements of both rightholders and users.

Electronic press digests

In almost every newspaper there is a section in which short excerpts from leading articles and commentaries from other newspapers are reproduced. Since the advent of improved and cheaper copying machines in the Seventies, organisations have increasingly produced press digests. Today, there is scarcely a large industrial firm, a political party or an administrative authority, which does not produce for its employees and members a current press clipping containing the most important and interesting articles and commentaries from the daily press. In many countries collecting societies receive remuneration for the copying and compilation of such press digests. This may be through voluntary licences, as in the United States or France, or through legal licences based on article 10*bis* (1) of the Berne Convention, as with article 49 of the German Copyright Law.

A recent development, especially among companies, has been to scan such press digests into a central database, rather than to assemble them in paper form, thereby enabling all employees, as in the previous example, to access the digest on their screens and make print-outs if they so wish.[7] It is hardly practicable to forbid these 'electronic press digests', even if they do not fall under a legal licence. The only alternative is to licence them, and as with paper press digests, this can only be achieved through collecting societies.

In order to demonstrate which criteria are needed to answer the central question of this article, I have so far deliberately concentrated, not on the information superhighway, with all its visions of the future, but on actual practice. An honest answer to the key questions I have asked – *whether the individual rightholders can/wish to prohibit/licence these uses* – is sufficient to determine the

7. Melichar, *supra* note 1, at 86, 91.

position in all cases. Collective administration should only be introduced if it is *necessary*, but should that not be the case then the rightholders must not delay in enabling the collecting societies to put it into practice.

Political Considerations

In answering the question posed by my title, it should not be forgotten that political considerations increasingly are playing an important role. Consumer protection, a concept which is often misunderstood, is an increasingly important factor in the considerations of national and international legislators. Freedom of information is raised as a principle, in relation not only to 'information', but to copyright-protected material as well. Further, copyright law, conferring exclusive rights, is regarded by many as suspect from the standpoint of anti-trust law. Finally, the problem of data protection also plays a part.

The effects of such system-hostile influences can be seen almost daily on the national and international scene. One need only consider, for example, the European directive on satellite and cable TV, in which cable retransmission across national borders was made subject to compulsory administration by collecting societies.[8] One also finds such tendencies in the recent Green Paper of the European Commission.[9] On the question of licensing of multimedia products, the Commission comes to the following conclusion:

> The Commission takes the view that the emergence of digital technology is likely to change the shape of rights management in some respects. Centralized schemes for the administration of rights, which would be voluntary in character, would be a appropriate response to the information society. It would be a matter for interested parties themselves to set up such schemes.[10]

On reading these lines the famous Goethe quotation comes to mind: 'Und bist Du nicht willig, so braucht'ich Gewalt' (And if you aren't willing, I will need to use force). Clearly, for individual administration of rights to be a viable option, it is not sufficient that the relevant (new and characteristic) types of use can be legally and practically prohibited by individual copyright holders. The implementation of the prohibition must also be politically acceptable; otherwise there is the risk of compulsory legal provisions being imposed.

---

8. Directive 93/83/EEC of 27 September 1993, O.J.E.C. No. L248 of 6 October 1993, 15.
9. Commission of the European Communities, *Green Paper. Copyright and Related Rights in the Information Society*, Brussels, 19 July 1995, COM (95) 382 final.
10. *Supra* note 9, at 78.

Central Administration

Despite the need for collective administration in the case of some electronic uses, as shown by the circumstances described above, and the strength of the call by, for example, the users of databases world-wide for a one-stop shop, the rightholders, particularly the publishers, are quite openly reluctant to entrust collecting societies with the administration of the rights for digital uses. The system of individual administration of rights through publishers on the one side, and the collective administration of rights through collective societies on the other side, have so far appeared irreconcilable. Digitization should, however, be the occasion and chance to change this apparently fixed dual system.

At the risk of stating the obvious, it must be recalled that collecting societies were originally established in order to deal with specific uses of works on an individual basis. Earlier I mentioned the example of SACEM. Musicians who want a licence for their public performance today still have to provide detailed 'programmes' including the title and author of the musical work they have played. The collecting society grants these licences on an individual basis. It would, in this case, be better to speak of 'central' rather than 'collective' administration (significantly SACEM originally called itself *agence centrale*[11]).

Such individual administration first proved impracticable in relation to the public performance of phonograms or radio broadcasts. Since it is not possible to check in which public house or restaurant, which radio broadcasts or phonograms are played at what time, the distribution schemes of the collective societies are based on the 'objective possibility of use', since every broadcast, every phonogram, *can* be communicated to the public.[12] This is a helpful criterion which was later especially preserved in relation to the remuneration from private copying and reprography. It is in this context that the term 'collective administration' is correctly applied.

Now digital technology does not only make possible the use of copyright protected works on a previously unthought-of scale; it offers at the same time the possibility of keeping track of every single use. Already, by means of scanning all sorts of administrative details – author, title, source, volume – can be registered. The same is true for the browsing of texts from a database. I can and will not, in the present context, go into the technical details, but I am sure that the electronic footprint will make this possible. The enormous quantity of registered data will be no problem for computerized systems of collecting societies The collecting societies can thereby now return to their original task – the *central* administration of *individually* registered and billed uses.

In contrast with the uniform tariff system in the administration of rights in private copying or reprography, the following principles must be observed in such central administration:

11. Lemoine, *La Société des Auteurs, Compositeurs et Editeurs de Musique*, Paris, 1950, 16.
12. Steinmetz, *ÖBI*, Vienna, 1972, 56.

1. The tariff structure must be as flexible as possible. Electronic technology can easily handle differential tariffs, for example different tariffs for different categories of works or products.
2. Distribution must be individual, taking into account every registered use. Efficient systems should distribute both author and publisher shares direct to the rightholders. This is, in any event, in accordance with the Continental European 'droit d'auteur' tradition. I am convinced that only if authors and publishers work together will it be possible to control and licence effectively the digital uses of their works.
3. An additional reason for this last principle is that the *droit moral*, which belongs exclusively to the author according to Article 6bis of the Berne Convention, is especially important in relation to digital uses.

If these three principles are strictly adhered to, then at least no ideological obstacles will stand in the way of a central administration of the electronic uses of copyright protected works. After these considerations I believe that it is obvious that the central administration of electronic rights is a realistic option.

Copyright and Related Rights in the Information Society

*Paul Vandoren**

1. Introduction

1.1 THE EUROPEAN UNION'S APPROACH

The European approach to the concept of the 'Information Society' was initiated by the European Commission's 'White Paper on Growth, Competitiveness, Employment: The Challenges and Ways forward into the 21st Century'.[1] In that document the Commission for the first time underlined the need to 'combine our efforts in Europe and make a greater use of synergy in order to achieve as soon as possible objectives aimed at building efficient European information infrastructure'.[2]

Following the proposals of this White Paper, a task force on 'Europe and the Information Society', chaired by former Commission Vice-President Bangemann, presented a report to the Corfu European Council in June 1994, pointing out that 'technological progress now enables us to process, store, retrieve and communicate information in whatever form it may take – oral, written or visual – unconstrained by distance, time and volume'.[3] With regard to the impact of the Information Society on intellectual property rights, the group stressed 'that intellectual property protection must rise to the new challenges of globalization and multimedia and must continue to have a high priority at both European and international levels'.[4] In the same context, the Bangemann group called for the protection of intellectual property to continue to be a high priority and stated that its level of protection must be adequate.

---

* Head of Unit DG XV/E/4, European Commission. The views expressed are personal and do not necessarily represent those of the European Commission.

1. Commission of the European Communities, *White Paper on Growth, Competitiveness, Employment: The Challenges and Ways forward into the 21st Century*, COM(93) 700 final, Brussels, 5 December 1993.
2. *Supra* note 1, 115.
3. Commission of the European Communities, *Europe and the global information society*, Recommendations to the European Council, Brussels, 26 May 1994, 4.
4. *Supra* note 3, 17.

Subsequently, the European Commission issued a Communication on the subject titled *Europe's way to the Information Society. An Action Plan.*[5] This action plan sets out the Commission's ambitious programme for Europe's entry into the Information Society, opening the way for more specific initiatives on key areas like intellectual property. As regards the latter, it calls for examination of all measures in the field of copyright and neighbouring rights, whether adopted or still under examination, to see whether they respond to the new technological challenges and to examine if additional measures are required. These political orientations were fully endorsed by the Industry Council of September 1994.

It is in this context that the Commission has recently adopted a *Green Paper on Copyright and related rights in the Information Society.*[6] which will stimulate the debate with interested parties on the challenges at stake. In this paper I would like to bring to your attention what the trends are of our reflection. As a starting point for this exercise, the written submissions in response to a questionnaire on 'Intellectual property in the Information Society' and the observations made by interested parties[7] at a preliminary hearing in Brussels on July 7-8, 1994 were used.

1.2 THE INTERNAL MARKET CONTEXT

A response by the European Union in a key area such as intellectual property is crucial in the era of the Information Society. Without a critical mass of services to use these networks, the significant infrastructure investment required for the information highways will not be forthcoming. But many of the new services and products will be viable only if an adequate level of protection is granted throughout the European Union. It is obvious that the future of communications networks is such that these new services will not and should not be stopped at national frontiers.

So, we attach much importance to this new phase of the consultation process to be launched with our Green Paper. The replies should enable the Commission:

- to get an even clearer picture of the implications of the new services which will be available in the Information Society;
- to assess more accurately whether the subsisting differences in protection granted by the Member States are of a nature to constitute a barrier to trade in goods and services in the Internal Market and whether there is a need for legislative action by proposing new directives or amendments to existing directives;
- and, last not least, to assess the possible need for new or amended international rules on authors' rights and neighbouring rights.

---

5. Communication from the Commission to the Council and the European Parliament and to the Economic and Social Committee and the Committee of Regions of 19 July 1994, COM(94) 347 final.
6. Commission of the European Communities, *Green Paper. Copyright and Related Rights in the Information Society*, Brussels, 19 July 1995, COM (95) 382 final.
7. *Replies from Interested Parties on 'Copyright and neighbouring rights in the Information Society'*, European Commission (DG XV), Brussels, 1995.

When undertaking this exercise, the Commission takes account of the economic, social and cultural aspects of the Information Society.

1.3 THE HEARING OF JULY 1994: NO NEED FOR RADICAL CHANGES

As mentioned before, the European Commission's first phase of the consultation process on the copyright and related rights aspects of the Information Society started with the hearing in July 1994.

As a preliminary conclusion, it can be said that the hearing confirmed the first impression of the Commission services that the new technological environment does not ask for radical changes of the existing regulatory framework. On the contrary, a prudent approach is required, not least due to the fact that the establishment of the Information Society is an evolutionary and dynamic process which is far from being completed. Indeed, it is difficult for legislators to draft new rules with regard to products and services which change continuously or have not even been put on the market.

This, however, does not mean that we think that there is no need for a regulatory framework. On the contrary, the digital environment implies a mass digitization of works and other protected material and a dramatic increase in various forms of their exploitation. This process is more difficult to control than in the past. The need to agree on comparable standards of intellectual property protection has, therefore, substantially risen. However, it appears at present that there is no need for intellectual property rules which are technologically specific. Many interested parties have indicated that national, Community and international intellectual property right provisions could be adapted to adequately cover the new acts of transmission.

2. The Legal Framework in the European Union

I would like to point out that, in the European Union, we already have a basic legal framework in place which will serve as a good basis to respond to the technological challenges at stake, thanks to the adoption of four directives in the field of copyright and neighbouring rights:

- Council Directive 91/250 on the legal protection of computer programmes;[8]
- Council Directive 92/100 on rental and lending rights and certain rights related to copyright in the field of intellectual property;[9]
- Council Directive 93/83 on the coordination of certain rules concerning copyright and rights related to copyright applicable to satellite broadcasting and cable retransmission;[10]

---

8. OJ No. L 122 of 17 May 1991, 42.
9. OJ No. L 346 of 27 November 92, 61.
10. OJ No. L 248 of 6 October 1993, 15.

- Council Directive 93/98 harmonizing the term of protection of copyright and certain related rights.[11]

2.1 THE LEGAL PROTECTION OF DATABASES IN THE EUROPEAN UNION

The above legal framework is likely to be completed in the near future with a Council Directive on the legal protection of databases. The latter proposal[12] is critically important in the context of the Information Society as databases will be at the very heart of most of the new services. It is not exaggerated to say that this Directive will place the Community far ahead of its partners.

As most services will be provided from an electronic database available on-line or off-line (CD-ROM, CD-i, etc.), the protection of databases takes on added importance. Databases will also have a major impact on the creation of new multimedia products. It is therefore essential that a clear and well-defined level of protection for database exists so as to ensure an attractive environment for investment while safeguarding users' interests.

Being aware of this need, the European Commission already proposed a directive relating to the legal protection of electronic databases in 1992, the aim of which was to provide a harmonized and stable legal regime protecting databases created within the European Union and, above all, to create a new right protecting the investor against unauthorized extraction and reutilization of the content of his database.

Such a new right is crucial, as the development of databases requires the investment of considerable human, technical and financial resources whilst, at the same time, such databases can be copied at a fraction of the cost needed to develop them independently. Hence, unauthorized access to a database and removal of its content constitute acts which can have the gravest economic and technical consequences.

2.2 THE EUROPEAN DATABASE DIRECTIVE

The forthcoming Directive provides for legal protection of databases in any form, i.e. electronic and paper-based databases. In addition, the Directive will not only deal with compilations of data and other material, but also with a variety of collections of works. The two major objectives of the Directive are to harmonize copyright law applicable to the structure of databases and to create a new right which protects the investor against unauthorized extraction and/or reutilization of the whole or a substantial part of the database.

---

11. OJ No. L 290 of 24 November 1993, 9.

12. Proposal for a Council Directive on the Legal protection of Databases, COM(92) 24 final – 393, OJ No C 156 of 23 June 1992, 4; Amended proposal for a Council Directive on the Legal Protection of Databases, COM(93) 464 final – SYN 393, OJ No C 308 of 15 November 1993, 1.

The main feature of the Directive is undoubtedly the creation of this exclusive new economic right, which constitutes an important legal innovation. This *sui generis* right will be granted to the manufacturer of a database to ensure protection of any substantial investment in obtaining, verifying or presenting the contents of a database, irrespective of whether the database is in itself innovative. The substantial character of the investment is considered from a qualitative or quantitative point of view. The protection is granted independently of the eligibility of the database for protection by copyright. It does not extend to the contents of a database and is without prejudice to any copyright or other right subsisting in the content.

This *sui generis* right is important as it will restrict, for a period of 15 years, unauthorized extraction and reutilization of the entirety or a substantial part of the database. It refers equally to users going beyond lawful use by extracting substantial parts from a database and to competitors committing acts that are prejudicial to the legitimate interests of the database manufacturer.

It should be noted that the *sui generis* right does not comprise non-substantial parts of a database. Therefore, the maker of a database, which is made available to the public, may not prevent a legitimate user of the base from extracting and reutilizing non-substantial parts for any purpose whatsoever.

Member States will have the option to provide for a restricted number of exceptions to the *sui generis* right, enabling the legitimate users of a database, which is made available to the public, to extract and/or reutilize a substantial part of the contents without the authorization of the maker. The exceptions cover the following cases:

- extraction for private purposes of the contents of a non-electronic database;
- extraction for the purposes of illustration for teaching or scientific research;
- extraction and/or reutilization for the purposes of public security or the proper performance of an administrative or judicial procedure.

The draft instrument ensures the protection of the basic rights of the legitimate user, thus rendering contractual provisions to the contrary null and void. Nevertheless, legitimate users may not perform acts which unreasonably prejudice the legitimate interests of the maker of the database or of holders of a copyright or related right in respect of the content of the base. It creates a delicate balance between the interests of database manufacturers, their competitors, third party rightholders, and society at large. As the information market is global, it is paramount that the EU initiative be followed, as soon as possible, by a global solution along similar lines.

In general, we will now have to examine whether this degree of harmonization is sufficient or whether it is necessary to go further, and if so, how far. This might prove to be necessary, as I already indicated, to avoid that the development of new services be hampered by fragmented markets, as these services will require an exploitation on a larger scale than within national boundaries in order to be viable.

3. The Green Paper: Issues Deserving Priority Attention

Let me briefly outline the nine key issues to be addressed in the Green Paper, requiring priority attention in the exercise at stake. The Green Paper consists of two chapters. In its first Chapter, the reasons for its need are explained, the issues at stake identified and a short description of the existing legal framework in the European Union given. In addition, a number of preliminary questions are raised. In the second Chapter, a rather detailed study is carried out of the possible implications of new technologies for the systems of copyright and related rights, discussing nine issues:

- two general topics:
  - the determination of the applicable law
  - the exhaustion principle;
- several specific rights:
  - reproduction right
  - communication to the public
  - digital transmission right
  - digital broadcasting right;
- the issue of moral rights;
- two issues regarding the exploitation of rights:
  - the acquisition/administration of rights
  - technical systems of identification and protection.

3.1 DETERMINATION OF THE APPLICABLE LAW

Traditionally, the intellectual property law of the country in which protection is sought, is applied.[13] Due to the international dimension of the Information Society, this solution may no longer be adequate, as it may imply that several national laws will be applied to one single act of transmission. This could unduly hamper the flow of works and services on their journey on the network and imply inappropriate legal uncertainty.[14]

The paramount question is therefore: does the transnational dimension of the Information Society necessitate the harmonization of the applicable law which shall govern the entire transmission of the works and other protected material?

13. Covering such points as the rights granted, exceptions, and the law of contract.

14. To a certain extent the principle of contractual freedom will help to find appropriate solutions, as it allows parties to a contract to determine the law applicable, apart from public order legislation. However, given the fact that in certain Community Member States in particular, there has been more and more precise regulation on certain forms of contracts (such as publishing contracts and audio-visual production) which parties must take account of, the principle of contractual freedom to decide on the applicable law does not seem to solve the issue at stake.

Application of the country-of-origin principle?

From the Internal Market perspective, it appears to be indispensable to tackle this question. In fact, it is imperative that a service provider is not left in doubt as to the copyright and related rights which will apply to transborder business. This, however, is hardly guaranteed in a situation of cumulative application of national laws to one single act of transmission.

In determining what law is to apply there are two fundamental factors which must be taken into account:

- the protection of rightholders must remain intact, and
- it must be possible to supply the service with maximum economic efficiency.

Good arguments have been put forward suggesting that the applicable law ought to be the law of the Member State from which the service originates (the principle of the country-of-origin). However, if this were to be made the solution, *a conditio sine qua non* would be to first harmonize the relevant laws of the Member States as regards the protection of digital transmission acts, the level of the rights to be granted and the categories of rightholders to be vested the rights. Otherwise we might face deflections of trade and loss of protection for rightholders.

Council Directive 93/83/EEC on cable and satellite broadcasting provides for a rule in this respect as regards satellite broadcasting. The situation of digital point-to-point transmissions, with which we are confronted now, seems to be comparable to the situation of cable and satellite broadcasting. In fact, making a service available in one Member State may have consequences in various others; for example, an on-line video-on-demand service in one Member State might in practice be accessible from other Member States too.

As regards transmissions coming into the Community from outside, absent a high level of international harmonization, it might prove necessary to consider other mechanisms, or at least safeguard clauses to ensure the protection of rights of authors or holders of related rights. In any case and without doubt, the question of the applicable law is one of the issues where a global solution seems to be desirable, as it is a global issue. However, this will be possible only if there is an agreement on the substantive law on copyright and related rights which ensures a high level of protection and sufficient measure of harmonization. There is certainly no such agreement at present but we are willing to work on it, particularly in the context of the negotiations under way in the World Intellectual Property Organisation to which I will refer later.[15]

15. The Council of Europe's Convention relating to questions of copyright law and neighbouring rights in the framework of transfrontier broadcasting by satellite of May 11, 1994 sets an important precedent here, because in order to allow the application of the law of the country on whose territory the broadcast originates it provides that the Berne Convention (Paris Act 1971) and the Rome Convention of 1961 are to apply.

3.2 EXHAUSTION OF RIGHTS AND PARALLEL IMPORTS

The second general issue addresses the principle of exhaustion. This principle constitutes a restriction to the right of distribution. This right is exhausted once copies of a work have been brought into circulation by or under license of the copyright owner. This principle can be applied within different territories, i.e. nationally, regionally or internationally. The principle of 'Community exhaustion', which has been developed by the European Court of Justice in respect of intra-community distribution of goods protected by intellectual property rights, is a fundamental element of primary Community law as it allows the reconciliation of the principles of the free circulation of goods and the territorial feature of intellectual property rights.

Future role in the digital network environment

The hearing in July 1994 has already made clear that interested parties feel that it should be ensured that the rights are not exhausted by the information superhighway. The question of whether and to what extent the 'exhaustion principle' should apply in the digital network environment is closely linked to the specific rights which will apply to the acts of digital transmission, whether we consider them to be within the scope of the 'communication to the public' rights or within the scope of the rights related to 'distribution'.

Within the Community, it is clear that the principle of community exhaustion does not apply to the provision of services. As a result, the principle of exhaustion should not be applied to acts protected by copyright such as broadcasting, rental or lending. That has already been recognized by the Court of Justice in two decisions in cases concerning film projection and the right of public performance of musical works.[16]

In principle, it would seem that the impact of the exhaustion principle on the new digital environment will be rather limited, as the prevailing mode of exploitation will probably be by means of on-demand programme delivery services.

Let me now turn to the specific rights, which, in my view, constitute the most important issues.

3.3 DIGITAL REPRODUCTION

The digital network age has made it indispensable to reassess the traditional reproduction right and the legitimate exceptions to it. In fact, this need has not evolved overnight, but gradually, with the technological developments in the field of photocopiers, as well as music and film recording equipment, allowing for good quality copies of printed, audio and audio-visual works and/or other protected

16. Concerning film projection *see* Case 62/79, *Coditel v. Ciné-Vog Films*, (1980) ECR 881, and Case 262/81, *Coditel v. Ciné-Vog Films*, (1982) ECR 3381. Concerning rental rights *see* Case 156/86, *Warner Brothers and Metronome Video v. Christiansen*, (1988) ECR 2605.

material at moderate prices. Thus, copying, for a long time now, has become a mass phenomenon which prejudices the legitimate economic interests of rightholders. To respond to this development, a large number of countries, in fact the majority of our Member States, have introduced particular legal regimes on reprography and/or on private copying.

The digitization has multiplied the need for action, as works and other protected material, once converted into electronic digital form and delivered on the information highway, are even more vulnerable to exploitation by copying, not least as digitization allows for reproduction without any loss of quality.

Reviewing the scope of the reproduction right

An important question will be whether the digitization of a work or other protected subject matter should qualify as a restricted act of reproduction, necessitating the prior authorization of the rightholder. In view of the broad formulations of the reproduction right in the relevant international conventions,[17] the answer is likely to be in the affirmative. Similar questions arise in the context of the subsequent journey of that work on the network. For instance, do the (temporary) loading of the work in a computer memory and its subsequent downloading qualify as acts of reproduction?

In order for the Information Society to work smoothly, it is important that these questions are tackled at the widest level possible. Within the European Union, appropriate solutions already exist with regard to some aspects of the reproduction right: as regards authors' rights, the Computer Programmes Directive provides for the protection of software, ensuring an exclusive author's right to do or to authorize 'permanent or temporary reproduction (..) by any means and in any form'.[18] The reproduction right provided for computer programmes is very strong as the reproduction of this type of works is particularly likely to conflict with the normal exploitation of the work to the prejudice of the legitimate interest of the author (a strong right is also likely to be adopted in the context of the protection of databases).

With regard to related rights, the Rental Rights Directive sets out an exclusive reproduction right for the benefit of performers, phonogram producers, producers of the first fixations of films and broadcasting organizations.[19] The scope of this reproduction right is not as clearly stated as in the case of computer programmes.

In view of all these considerations and in order to make the Internal Market function properly, we will have to fill the remaining gaps to ensure, for instance, that the conversion of a work or other protected material in digital forms also enjoys the same protection Union-wide. Otherwise, it may happen that a Member State will refuse to allow for the transmission of protected works or goods coming, for instance, from a Member State in which the digitization does not require the authorization of the rightholder.

---

17. *See* e.g. Article 9 Berne Convention; Articles 10 and 13 Rome Convention; Article 14 TRIPs.
18. Article 4(a) of Council Directive 91/250.
19. Article 7 of Council Directive 92/100.

Reviewing exceptions to the right

A distinct issue will be to reconsider existing exceptions to the reproduction right, as for instance provided for in Article 9(2) of the Berne Convention. In view of the new digital environment, some exceptions may no longer prove to be appropriate. At present, the legal regimes on 'private copying' existing in the various Member States differ substantially. It is a matter of time before this diversity results in severe problems from the point of view of the Internal Market. For instance, it will not be possible to impose the installation of technical devices in Member States where private copying is authorized, whereas such devices may be made obligatory in other Member States. This will result in barriers to trade with regard to the relevant equipment involved.

For these reasons, answers to these issues have to be found, at least at the Community level. We will have to decide:

- whether private copying, so far not yet harmonized, shall be covered by the exclusive right of reproduction;
- whether at least one copy should be admissible; or
- whether private copying should be admissible as such, with or without compensation.

3.4 COMMUNICATION TO THE PUBLIC

As important will be to closely examine the notion of 'public' as contained in the right of 'communication to the public'. In fact, so far as this latter right is concerned, the concept of 'public' is the key to the current discussion. However, there is no precise definition of the concept. The WIPO Glossary defines 'communication to the public' as follows:

'Making a work, performance, phonogram or broadcast perceptible in any appropriate manner to persons in general, that is, not restricted to specific individuals belonging to a private group. This notion is broader than publication and also covers, among others, forms of use such as public performance, broadcasting, communication to the public by wire, or direct communication to the public of the reception of a broadcast'.[20]

On the basis of this definition we can provisionally distinguish private use, which is in effect tolerated, and thus not as a rule covered by the right to authorize or prohibit, from uses which are indeed covered by exclusive rights.[21] Private use need not necessarily be confined to cases where a person makes use of a work in his home using equipment which is not linked to a network. However, where are the limits of this private use?

---

20. WIPO, *Glossary of terms of the law of copyright and neighbouring rights*, Geneva, 1980, ISBN 92-805-0016-3.
21. The same does not apply to private copying, which is covered by the reproduction right. Private copying is therefore prohibited in certain Member States, even if it is carried out for purely personal purposes.

What about on-line communications providing access by several individuals within a company? What about video conferencing?

Community law has not so far settled the question of the definition of 'communication to the public'. As the Information Society advances, it appears indispensable to consider whether the permissible exceptions to the general Community rules will have to be tightened up, and this will involve defining 'communication to the public' in a uniform fashion.

The answers to these questions will have much impact on the attractiveness of the future information highway as such. If we do not find the right balance between the legitimate interests of rightholders in a fair exploitation of their works and other protected material and the interest of consumers in freedom of access to 'everything of interest', the viability of the Information Society may be at stake.

3.5 DIGITAL TRANSMISSION RIGHT

Compared to analogue methods, the technical scope of digital transmission is so great, and the quality so high, that the question of the right applicable to digital transmission is one of the central questions of intellectual property law in the Information Society. Which right do rightholders dispose of with regard to digital transmission of their works or of other protected material? In fact, the impact of making works and related subject matter available in digital form has led some categories of rightholders to plead in favour of introducing a new exclusive right to authorize or to forbid the digital transmission of works or other protected material, as they fear that their market may escape any sort of control. We will have to study the issue carefully.

The point of departure for such an analysis should be to distinguish between, on the one hand, point-to-point transmissions and, on the other hand, point-to-multipoint transmissions. As services transmitted point-to-point differ substantially from current point-to multipoint broadcasting, since the consumer can access and interact with them, it seems appropriate to apply a specific legal regime to digital point-to-point transmissions.

From that point of view 'digital point-to-point transmission' would include transmission from a personal computer, or other digital unit belonging to a private person, or from a database, to one or more personal computers or other digital units belonging to private persons or firms. Thus a video-on-demand system enabling consumers to ask for cinematographic works of their choice to be sent to them electronically, would be covered.

Once the concept of 'public' has been clarified, the crucial points will be:

- How should these categories of acts be classified and defined?
- How they should they be treated – exclusive rights, equitable remuneration, or complete freedom?
- Which categories of rightholders will be granted the rights that would eventually be recognized?

Need for an exclusive digital transmission right?

The exclusive right of communication to the public provided for by the Berne and Rome Conventions does not necessarily include transmission to a limited number of people. Also, Community law, as it stands, does not explicitly provide for a general exclusive right as regards point-to-point transmissions. It may, however, be held that digital point-to-point transmissions, such as video-on-demand, qualify as 'rental' as defined for the purposes of Council Directive 92/100/EEC on rental rights[22]

In fact, the Rental Right Directive defines 'rental' very broadly as 'making available for use, for a limited period of time and for direct or indirect economic or commercial advantage'.[23] 'Rental' of works or other protected matter, as defined in the directive, especially by opposition to public performance and broadcasting (cf. the corresponding recital), thus should include activities such as video-on-demand and other electronic forms of delivery based on point-to-point transmission.

Also, in practical economic terms electronic rental of works or other protected matter is a competing activity which is essentially the same thing as rental from a shop, so that it seems reasonable to apply the same rights in both cases. This interpretation implies that rightholders today, at the Community level, already dispose of an exclusive rental right for electronic delivery. It would nonetheless be desirable for the sake of clarity and legal certainty that this should be spelled out in legislation, where necessary.

We will have to await whether the consultation process will confirm our first evaluation, thus to treat digital transmission as a part of the rental right. Whatever solution we will agree on – and we should not be dogmatic – we will have to make sure that the relevant rightholders dispose of a strong right. Otherwise, we face the risk that they will be hesitant to agree on the exploitation of their works and other protected material on the network. This would be counterproductive, as the viability of the Information Society fundamentally depends on the existence of a multitude of differentiated services being offered.

3.6 DIGITAL BROADCASTING

Another important issue addressed in the Green Paper concerns digital broadcasting. Without doubt, digital broadcasting will substantially change the landscape in broadcasting programmes. Thanks to digital technology, consumers may prefer to make copies of their favourite music received through broadcasting instead of buying CD's, as the quality of their recording will be the same as on CD's. The problem is aggravated by compression techniques which allow far more

22. A specific rental right is also provided for in Article 4(c) of Council Directive 91/250/EEC on the legal protection of computer programmes.
23. Article 1(2), Directive 92/100/EEC. The very broad character of the definition is underscored in a recital which states that it is desirable to exclude from 'rental' certain forms of making available 'as for instance making available phonograms or film (..) for the purpose of public performance or broadcasting'.

programmes to be broadcast. The large number of channels will permit a high degree of consumer choice over what to hear/watch and when to do so. This seems to be very similar to providing 'services on demand', in particular if broadcasters were to broadcast whole records or films in succession. The consumer would only have to check at what time the material of his choice was to be broadcast; he could then copy it in full, free of charge.

It has thus been argued that broadcasting, which in the past was considered a secondary use of a work, has now acquired importance as a primary form of exploitation, and that its treatment in law should change in consequence. In particular neighbouring rightholders who, at present – at the international level[24] as well as at the Community level[25] – dispose only of a right to an equitable remuneration, strongly favour an exclusive right to authorize and prevent digital broadcasting. We will have to carefully study in how far these developments take place and require action.[26] A distinction might be needed between traditional forms of broadcasting, even if of digital quality, and specific forms of multichannel digital broadcasting. It would be premature, at this stage, to say that measures covering all types of broadcasting are indispensable.

Should the consultation process, however, lead to the conclusion that the risk of massive copying may necessitate stronger rights for holders of related rights, action would need to be taken at the Community level, at least as far as transfrontier broadcasting is concerned, to ensure coherence within the Internal Market.

3.7 MORAL RIGHTS

Last, not least we ask interested parties on their view on the new risks for moral rights. Modifications and adaptations of existing works and protected services have never been as easy as they are today in the digital environment, due to the new technologies. This trend will continue. We may see the day where almost anybody could change the colours of a film or replace the heads of artists and, then, send the film back on the network. Whilst these technological innovations are applauded by certain sectors, it is not a surprise that they are seen with some unease by others – authors and artists. We may thus face a situation in which rightholders will make more use of their moral rights, which, at the Community level, have not as yet been harmonized.[27]

---

24. *See* e.g. Article 12 Rome Convention.

25. Article 4 of Council Directive 93/83/EEC on cable and satellite broadcasting.

26. In this context other initiatives must be taken into account as well, notably those in the context of 'private copying' or as regards technical protection devices which may be introduced in the listeners' receiver.

27. As concluded at a hearing on moral rights, organized by the European Commission in 1992, the situation may change in view of new technologies. At this hearing it appeared that moral rights are rarely relied upon with a view to prohibit the exploitation of a work. This can be explained by the fact that in many sectors in which moral rights are a sensitive issue, pragmatic arrangements are made.

We will thus have to study carefully whether the disparities of the legislation of Member States on 'moral rights' are still acceptable, even in the new digital environment, or whether Community action is now required.

3.8 ACQUISITION AND ADMINISTRATION OF RIGHTS

The Information Society will offer a great number of new opportunities to exploit and to enjoy works and other protected material. This new and almost unlimited offer of and demand for works and related subject matter will require that the administration of rights, which presently varies to a great extent, adapts to the new technological environment. This is crucial, notably so that the creation of multimedia works, which can contain at the same time music, text, photographs, films, etc., will not be hampered by cumbersome acquisitions of rights.

In fact, in the present situation producers of so-called 'multimedia' products who want to use pre-existing works, have to obtain the authorization of a great number of authors and holders of related rights. To obtain these licences, they will in some cases have to approach the rightholder himself; in other cases they will have to turn to collecting societies. All in all, it will not be exaggerated to say that 'producers' of such 'multimedia' may have to spend much time and money to receive all necessary authorizations. In addition, the absence of one authorization may mean, as a consequence, that the entire multimedia work cannot be put on the market.

For new digital products to be economically viable, it will thus be crucial that their 'producers' are in a position to easily identify the rightholder of the work or related matters with a view to negotiating balanced conditions of authorization. This will necessitate, amongst others, a rationalization of the administration of rights and a restructuring of information necessary for such operations.

Creation of 'one-stop shops'?

It is thus reasonable to suppose that certain new alliances would be a major step forward for collecting societies, which are currently organized by category of work or class of rightholders (e.g. authors, performers, etc.). To allow centralized management or administration of rights over all works, performances and other protected matter incorporated into multimedia works, the collecting societies and other rights managers ought to be encouraged to set up joint bodies allowing a simplification of rights management. Uniting the available information would be an appropriate way to ensure the right environment for creativity in the multimedia age, since it would increase the transparency and efficiency of the current system. Increasing transparency in such a way can only benefit the interested commercial parties, the rightholders just as much as the users.

Should parties decide not only to centralize the identification of individual rightholders but also certain management aspects, it will be important to ensure that this should not exclude the possibility of going back to more individualized management. Individual contracts between the different parties must in any case remain possible, as must individualized licences; in such a case each rightholder would determine the price to be paid to him for the rights. The parties' freedom of contract must be respected.

The transparency and effectiveness of the systems of management are most important in order to ensure the healthy development of the Information Society. Obviously, both the agreements establishing such links and the actual administration of the rights will have to comply with the competition rules of the EC Treaty. The competition rules are fundamental. On the other hand, I would see no reason why they should be in contradiction with the idea of centralized schemes as such.

At the hearing of July, 1994 the interested parties expressed some sympathy for solutions going in the direction of so called 'one-stop shops'. It was, however, stressed that any such initiative should come from the professionals themselves and should take place on a voluntary basis. We will see what the consultation will bring.

3.9 TECHNICAL SYSTEMS OF IDENTIFICATION AND PROTECTION

The digitization of works and other protected material implies at the same time a major opportunity and a big risk for rightholders. Digital technology and its permanently growing capacities with regard to the treatment of data will allow for better protection of works and services by means of, amongst others, systematic identification of works and protected material on the basis of codes,[28] or a systematic tattooing of works and other protected material,[29] which promises to substantially improve the administration of rights. Also, some initiatives may result in technical protection devices installed in the equipment as such. Systems of the SCMS type (Serial Copyright Management System), which technically limit possibilities of excessive private copying, are important in this regard.

The international conventions do not yet deal with these aspects. However, the subject matter is under discussion in the framework of the Berne Protocol and the New Instrument. Many countries in the European Union consider technical identification and protection devices to be of the utmost importance, as is already reflected in the Computer Programme Directive.[30] Moreover, the Commission is drafting a Green Paper on encryption of broadcasting services.

Furthermore, I should mention the CITED project (*Copyright in Transmitted Electronic Documents*), which is financed by the European Commission in the

28. Publications in the field of literature already contain an ISDN number which permits identification. Other codes, such as the ISCR with regard to phonograms, go even further, listing rightholders and the licensing conditions. Similar codes can be created for other fields of creativity.

29. *See*, for instance, the *Cyphertech* project, which will allow for an automatic administration of rights.

30. Pursuant to article 7(a) of the Computer Programme Directive, Member States shall provide in their national legislation for appropriate remedies against persons who put in circulation or hold in possession, for commercial purposes, any means the sole intended purpose of which is to facilitate the unauthorized removal or circumvention of any technical device which may have been applied to protect a computer programme.

context of the ESPRIT program. CITED takes account of the needs of the 'information industry' in the large sense. It will help to protect works and other material when stored and distributed in digital form. In addition to the creation of such a 'protection scheme', it shall also facilitate the 'management' of all relevant information. With the CITED programme, we have tried to find a generic solution to the problems at stake, and thus a solution which could be applicable to the different sectors. In addition, CITED defines the measures necessary to fight piracy. CITED will now be tested in pilot projects.

In the context of the European Commission's hearing of July 1994, the usefulness or even the need to provide for technical devices on identification and protection devices was confirmed, although a considerable part of the audience pleaded in favour of voluntary schemes.

The parties involved (rightholders, producers of equipment, distributors of works and services, as well as network operators) will have to agree on such devices, because it is important to avoid conflicting approaches. Once such systems of protection and/or identification exist and are accepted by all, the Community will have to carefully study, in the light of the principle of subsidiarity and its standardization policy, if a need for a harmonized introduction of such systems exists. This would be the case, if some Member States were to impose protection devices in the relevant equipment, while forbidding the sale of non-protected materials.

Selling Wine without Bottles. The Economy of Mind on the Global Net

*John Perry Barlow**

> If nature has made any one thing less susceptible than all others of exclusive property, it is the action of the thinking power called an idea, which an individual may exclusively possess as long as he keeps it to himself; but the moment it is divulged, it forces itself into the possession of everyone, and the receiver cannot dispossess himself of it. Its peculiar character, too, is that no one possesses the less, because every other possesses the whole of it. He who receives an idea from me, receives instruction himself without lessening mine; as he who lights his taper at mine, receives light without darkening me. That ideas should freely spread from one to another over the globe, for the moral and mutual instruction of man, and improvement of his condition, seems to have been peculiarly and benevolently designed by nature, when she made them, like fire, expansible over all space, without lessening their density at any point, and like the air in which we breathe, move, and have our physical being, incapable of confinement or exclusive appropriation. Inventions then cannot, in nature, be a subject of property.
>
> *Thomas Jefferson*

Throughout the time I've been groping around Cyberspace, there has remained unsolved an immense conundrum that seems to be at the root of nearly every legal, ethical, governmental, and social vexation to be found in the Virtual World. I refer to the problem of digitized property. The riddle is this: if our property can be infinitely reproduced and instantaneously distributed all over the planet without cost, without our knowledge, without its even leaving our possession, how can we protect it? How are we going to get paid for the work we do with our minds? And, if we can't get paid, what will assure the continued creation and distribution of such work?

Since we don't have a solution to what is a profoundly new kind of challenge, and are apparently unable to delay the galloping digitization of everything not obstinately physical, we are sailing into the future on a sinking ship. This vessel, the accumulated canon of copyright and patent law, was developed to convey

---

* Retired cattle rancher, lyricist for the Grateful Dead, and co-founder of the Electronic Frontier Foundation. This article was previously published in (1994) *Wired* 2.03. The thoughts in it have not been mine alone but have assembled themselves in a field of interaction that has existed between myself and numerous others, to whom I am grateful. They particularly include: Pamela Samuelson, Kevin Kelly, Mitch Kapor, Mike Godwin, Stewart Brand, Mike Holderness, Miriam Barlow, Danny Hillis, Trip Hawkins, and Alvin Toffler.

forms and methods of expression entirely different from the vaporous cargo it is now being asked to carry. It is leaking as much from within as without.

Legal efforts to keep the old boat floating are taking three forms: a frenzy of deck chair rearrangement, stern warnings to the passengers that if she goes down, they will face harsh criminal penalties, and serene, glassy-eyed denial.

Intellectual property law cannot be patched, retrofitted, or expanded to contain the gasses of digitized expression any more than real estate law might be revised to cover the allocation of broadcasting spectrum. (Which, in fact, rather resembles what is being attempted here.) We will need to develop an entirely new set of methods as befits this entirely new set of circumstances.

Most of the people who actually create soft property – the programmers, hackers, and Net surfers – already know this. Unfortunately, neither the companies they work for nor the lawyers these companies hire have enough direct experience with immaterial goods to understand why they are so problematic. They are proceeding as though the old laws can somehow be made to work, either by grotesque expansion or by force. They are wrong.

1. Vanishing Bottles

The source of this conundrum is as simple as its solution is complex. Digital technology is detaching information from the physical plane, where property law of all sorts has always found definition. Throughout the history of copyrights and patents, the proprietary assertions of thinkers have been focused not on their ideas but on the expression of those ideas. The ideas themselves, as well as facts about the phenomena of the world, were considered to be the collective property of humanity. One could claim franchise, in the case of copyright, on the precise turn of phrase used to convey a particular idea or the order in which facts were presented.

The point at which this franchise was imposed was that moment when the 'word became flesh' by departing the mind of its originator and entering some physical object, whether book or widget. The subsequent arrival of other commercial media besides books didn't alter the legal importance of this moment. Law protected expression and, with few (and recent) exceptions, to express was to make physical.

Protecting physical expression had the force of convenience on its side. Copyright worked well because, Gutenberg notwithstanding, it was hard to make a book. Furthermore, books froze their contents into a condition that was as challenging to alter as it was to reproduce. Counterfeiting or distributing counterfeit volumes were obvious and visible activities, easy enough to catch somebody in the act of doing. Finally, unlike unbounded words or images, books had material surfaces to which one could attach copyright notices, publisher's marques, and price tags.

Mental to physical conversion was even more central to patent. A patent, until recently, was either a description of the form into which materials were to be rendered in the service of some purpose or a description of the process by which rendition occurred. In either case, the conceptual heart of patent was the material result. If no purposeful object could be rendered due to some material limitation, the patent was rejected. Neither a Klein bottle nor a shovel made of silk could be patented. It had to be a thing and the thing had to work.

Thus, the rights of invention and authorship adhered to activities in the physical world. One didn't get paid for ideas but for the ability to deliver them into reality. For all practical purposes, the value was in the conveyance and not the thought conveyed. In other words, the bottle was protected, not the wine.

Now, as information enters Cyberspace, the native home of Mind, these bottles are vanishing. With the advent of digitization, it is now possible to replace all previous information storage forms with one meta-bottle: complex – and highly liquid – patterns of ones and zeros. Even the physical/digital bottles to which we've become accustomed, floppy disks, CD-ROM's, and other discrete, shrink-wrappable bit-packages, will disappear as all computers jack in to the global Net. While the Internet may never include every single CPU on the planet, it is more than doubling every year and can be expected to become the principal medium of information conveyance if, eventually, the only one.

Once that has happened, all the goods of the Information Age – all of expressions once contained in books or film strips or records or newsletters – will exist either as pure thought or something very much like thought: voltage conditions darting around the Net at the speed of light, in conditions which one might behold in effect, as glowing pixels or transmitted sounds, but never touch or claim to 'own' in the old sense of the word.

Some might argue that information will still require some physical manifestation, such as its magnetic existence on the titanic hard disks of distant servers, but these are bottles that have no macroscopically discrete or personally meaningful form. Some will also argue that we have been dealing with unbottled expression since the advent of radio, and they would be right. But for most of the history of broadcast, there was no convenient way to capture soft goods from the electromagnetic ether and reproduce them in anything like the quality available in commercial packages. Only recently has this changed and little has been done legally or technically to address the change.

Generally, the issue of consumer payment for broadcast products was irrelevant. The consumers themselves were the product. Broadcast media were supported either by selling the attention of their audience to advertisers, using government to assess payment through taxes, or the whining mendicancy of annual donor drives.

All of broadcast support models are flawed. Support either by advertisers or government has almost invariably tainted the purity of the goods delivered. Besides, direct marketing is gradually killing the advertiser support model anyway. Broadcast media gave us another payment method for a virtual product in the royalties which broadcasters pay songwriters through such organizations as ASCAP and BMI. But, as a member of ASCAP, I can assure you this is not a model that we should emulate. The monitoring methods are wildly approximate. There is no parallel system of accounting in the revenue stream. It doesn't really work. Honest.

In any case, without our old methods of physically defining the expression of ideas, and in the absence of successful new models for non-physical transaction, we simply don't know how to assure reliable payment for mental works. To make matters worse, this comes at a time when the human mind is replacing sunlight and mineral deposits as the principal source of new wealth.

Furthermore, the increasing difficulty of enforcing existing copyright and patent laws is already placing in peril the ultimate source of intellectual property, the free exchange of ideas. That is, when the primary articles of commerce in a society look so much like speech as to be indistinguishable from it, and when the traditional methods of protecting their ownership have become ineffectual, attempting to fix the problem with broader and more vigorous enforcement will inevitably threaten freedom of speech. The greatest constraint on your future liberties may come not from government but from corporate legal departments labouring to protect by force what can no longer be protected by practical efficiency or general social consent.

Furthermore, when Jefferson and his fellow creatures of The Enlightenment designed the system that became American copyright law, their primary objective was assuring the widespread distribution of thought, not profit. Profit was the fuel that would carry ideas into the libraries and minds of their new republic. Libraries would purchase books, thus rewarding the authors for their work in assembling ideas, which otherwise 'incapable of confinement' would then become freely available to the public. But what is the role of libraries if there are no books? How does society now pay for the distribution of ideas if not by charging for the ideas themselves?

Additionally complicating the matter is the fact that along with the physical bottles in which intellectual property protection has resided, digital technology is also erasing the legal jurisdictions of the physical world, and replacing them with the unbounded and perhaps permanently lawless seas of Cyberspace. In Cyberspace, there are not only no national or local boundaries to contain the scene of a crime and determine the method of its prosecution, there are no clear cultural agreements on what a crime might be. Unresolved and basic differences between European and Asian cultural assumptions about intellectual property can only be exacerbated in a region where many transactions are taking place in both hemispheres and yet, somehow, in neither.

Even in the most local of digital conditions, jurisdiction and responsibility are hard to assess. A group of music publishers filed suit against Compuserve for it having allowed its users to upload musical compositions into areas where other users might get them. But since Compuserve cannot practically exercise much control over the flood of bits that pass between its subscribers, it probably shouldn't be held responsible for unlawfully 'publishing' these works.

Notions of property, value, ownership, and the nature of wealth itself are changing more fundamentally than at any time since the Sumerians first poked cuneiform into wet clay and called it stored grain. Only a very few people are aware of the enormity of this shift and fewer of them are lawyers or public officials. Those who do see these changes must prepare responses for the legal and social confusion that will erupt as efforts to protect new forms of property with old methods become more obviously futile, and, as a consequence, more adamant.

2. From Swords to Writs to Bits

Humanity now seems bent on creating a world economy primarily based on goods that take no material form. In doing so, we may be eliminating any predictable connection between creators and a fair reward for the utility or pleasure others may find in their works. Without that connection, and without a fundamental change in consciousness to accommodate its loss, we are building our future on furore, litigation, and institutionalized evasion of payment except in response to raw force. We may return to the Bad Old Days of property.

Throughout the darker parts of human history, the possession and distribution of property was a largely military matter. 'Ownership' was assured those with the nastiest tools, whether fists or armies, and the most resolute will to use them. Property was the divine right of thugs. By the turn of the First Millennium AD, the emergence of merchant classes and landed gentry forced the development of ethical understandings for the resolution of property disputes. In the late Middle Ages, enlightened rulers like England's Henry II began to codify this unwritten 'common law' into recorded canons. These laws were local, but this didn't matter much as they were primarily directed at real estate, a form of property that is local by definition. And which, as the name implied, was very real.

This continued to be the case as long as the origin of wealth was agricultural, but with the dawning of the Industrial Revolution, humanity began to focus as much on means as ends. Tools acquired a new social value and, thanks to their own development, it became possible to duplicate and distribute them in quantity. To encourage their invention, copyright and patent law were developed in most western countries. These laws were devoted to the delicate task of getting mental creations into the world where they could be used – and enter the minds of others – while assuring their inventors compensation for the value of their use. And, as previously stated, the systems of both law and practice that grew up around that task were based on physical expression.

Since it is now possible to convey ideas from one mind to another without ever making them physical, we are now claiming to own ideas themselves and not merely their expression. And since it is likewise now possible to create useful tools that never take physical form, we have taken to patenting abstractions, sequences of virtual events, and mathematical formulae – the most *un-real* estate imaginable. In certain areas, this leaves rights of ownership in such an ambiguous condition that once again property adheres to those who can muster the largest armies. The only difference is that this time the armies consist of lawyers.

Threatening their opponents with the endless Purgatory of litigation, over which some might prefer death itself, they assert claim to any thought that might have entered another cranium within the collective body of the corporations they serve. They act as though these ideas appeared in splendid detachment from all previous human thought. And they pretend that thinking about a product is somehow as good as manufacturing, distributing, and selling it. What was previously considered a common human resource, distributed among the minds and libraries of the world, as well as the phenomena of nature herself, is now being fenced and deeded. It is as though a new class of enterprise had arisen which claimed to own air and water.

Dancing on the grave of copyright

What is to be done? While there is a certain grim fun to be had in it, dancing on the grave of copyright and patent will solve little, especially when so few are willing to admit that the occupant of this grave is even deceased and are trying to up by force what can no longer be upheld by popular consent.

The legalists, desperate over their slipping grip, are vigorously trying to extend it. Indeed, the United States and other proponents of GATT are making are making adherence to our moribund systems of intellectual property protection a condition of membership in the marketplace of nations. For example, China will be denied Most Favoured nation trading status unless they agree to uphold a set of culturally alien principles that are no longer even sensibly applicable in their country of origin.

In a more perfect world, we'd be wise to declare a moratorium on litigation, legislation, and international treaties in this area until we had a clearer sense of the terms and conditions of enterprise in Cyberspace. Ideally, laws ratify already developed social consensus. They are less the Social Contract itself than a series of memoranda expressing a collective intent that has emerged out of many millions of human interactions.

Humans have not inhabited Cyberspace long enough or in sufficient diversity to have developed a Social Contract that conforms to the strange new conditions of that world. Laws developed prior to consensus usually serve the already established few who can get them passed and not society as a whole.

To the extent that either law or established social practice exists in this area, they are already in dangerous disagreement. The laws regarding unlicensed reproduction of commercial software are clear and stern... and rarely observed. Software piracy laws are so practically unenforceable and breaking them has become so socially acceptable that only a thin minority appears compelled, either by fear or conscience, to obey them. I sometimes give speeches on this subject, and I always ask how many people in the audience can honestly claim to have no unauthorized software on their hard disks. I've never seen more than ten percent of the hands go up.

Whenever there is such profound divergence between the law and social practice, it is not society that adapts. And, against the swift tide of custom, the Software Publishers' current practice of hanging a few visible scapegoats is so obviously capricious as to only further diminish respect for the law.

Part of the widespread popular disregard for commercial software copyrights stems from a legislative failure to understand the conditions into which it was inserted. To assume that systems of law based in the physical world will serve in an environment that is as fundamentally different as Cyberspace is a folly for which everyone doing business in the future will pay. As I will discuss in the next segment, unbounded intellectual property is very different from physical property and can no longer be protected as though these differences did not exist. For example, if we continue to assume that value is based on scarcity, as it is with regard to physical objects, we will create laws that are precisely contrary to the nature of information, which may, in many cases, increase in value with distribution.

The large, legally risk-averse institutions most likely to play by the old rules will suffer for their compliance. The more lawyers, guns, and money they invest in either protecting their rights or subverting those of their opponents, the more commercial competition will resemble the Kwakiutl Potlatch Ceremony, in which adversaries competed by destroying their own possessions. Their ability to produce new technology will simply grind to a halt as every move they make drives them deeper into a tar pit of courtroom warfare.

Faith in law will not be an effective strategy for high tech companies. Law adapts by continuous increments and at a pace second only to geology in its stateliness. Technology advances in the lunging jerks, like the punctuation of biological evolution grotesquely accelerated. Real world conditions will continue to change at a blinding pace, and the law will get further behind, more profoundly confused. This mismatch is permanent.

Promising economies based on purely digital products will either be born in a state of paralysis, as appears to be the case with multimedia, or continue in a brave and willful refusal by their owners to play the ownership game at all. In the United States one can already see a parallel economy developing, mostly among small fast moving enterprises who protect their ideas by getting into the marketplace quicker then their larger competitors who base their protection on fear and litigation. Perhaps those who are part of the problem will simply quarantine themselves in court while those who are part of the solution will create a new society based, at first, on piracy and freebooting. It may be that when the current system of intellectual property law has collapsed, as seems inevitable, that no new legal structure will arise in its place.

But something will happen. After all, people do business. When a currency becomes meaningless, business is done in barter. When societies develop outside the law, they develop their own unwritten codes, practices, and ethical systems. While technology may undo law, technology offers methods for restoring creative rights.

3. A Taxonomy of Information

It seems to me that the most productive thing to do now is to look hard into the true nature of what we're trying to protect. How much do we really know about information and its natural behaviours? What are the essential characteristics of unbounded creation? How does it differ from previous forms of property? How many of our assumptions about it have actually been about its containers rather than their mysterious contents? What are its different species and how does each of them lend itself to control? What technologies will be useful in creating new virtual bottles to replace the old physical ones?

Of course, information is, by its nature, intangible and hard to define. Like other such deep phenomena as light or matter, it is a natural host to paradox. And as it is most helpful to understand light as being both a particle and a wave, an understanding of information may emerge in the abstract congruence of its several different properties that might be described by the following three statements:

- Information is an activity.
- Information is a life form.
- Information is a relationship.

In the following section, I will examine each of these.

3.1 INFORMATION IS AN ACTIVITY

Information is a verb, not a noun.

Freed of its containers, information is obviously not a thing. In fact, it is something that happens in the field of interaction between minds or objects or other pieces of information.

Gregory Bateson, expanding on the information theory of Claude Shannon, said, 'Information is a difference which makes a difference'. The making of that difference is an activity within a relationship. Information is an action that occupies time rather than a state of being which occupies physical space, as is the case with hard goods. It is the pitch, not the baseball, the dance, not the dancer.

Information is experienced, not possessed

Even when it has been encapsulated in some static form like a book or a hard disk, information is still something that happens to you as you mentally decompress it from its storage code. But, whether it's running at gigabits per second or words per minute, the actual decoding is a process that must be performed by and upon a mind, a process that must take place in time.

There was a cartoon in the Bulletin of Atomic Scientists a few years ago which illustrated this point beautifully. In the drawing, a holdup man trains his gun on the sort of bespectacled fellow you'd figure might have a lot of information stored in his head. 'Quick,' orders the bandit, 'Give me all your ideas.'

Information has to move

Sharks are said to die of suffocation if they stop swimming, and the same is nearly true of information. Information that isn't moving ceases to exist as anything but potential...at least until it is allowed to move again. For this reason, the practice of information hoarding, common in bureaucracies, is an especially wrong-headed artefact of physically based value systems.

Information is conveyed by propagation, not distribution

The way in which information spreads is also very different from the distribution of physical goods. It moves more like something from nature than from a factory. It can concatenate like falling dominoes or grow in the usual fractal lattice, like frost spreading on a window, but it cannot be shipped around like widgets, except to the extent that it can be contained in them. It doesn't simply move on. It leaves a trail of itself everywhere it's been.

The central economic distinction between information and physical property is the ability of information to be transferred without leaving the possession of the original owner. If I sell you my horse, I can't ride him after that. If I sell you what I know, we both know it.

3.2 INFORMATION IS A LIFE FORM

Information wants to be free

Stewart Brand is generally credited with this elegant statement of the obvious, recognizing both the natural desire of secrets to be told and the fact that they might be capable of possessing something like a 'desire' in the first place. English Biologist and Philosopher Richard Dawkins proposed the idea of 'memes', self-replicating, patterns of information that propagate themselves across the ecologies of mind, saying they were like life forms.

I believe they are life forms in every respect but a basis in the carbon atom. They self-reproduce, they interact with their surroundings and adapt to them, they mutate, they persist. Like any other life form they evolve to fill the possibility spaces of their local environments, which are, in this case, the surrounding belief systems and cultures of their hosts, namely, us. Indeed, the sociobiologists like Dawkins make a plausible case that carbon-based life forms are information as well, that, as the chicken is an egg's way of making another egg, the entire biological spectacle is just the DNA molecule's means of copying out more information strings exactly like itself.

Information replicates into the cracks of possibility

Like DNA helices, ideas are relentless expansionists, always seeking new opportunities for lebensraum. And, as in carbon-based nature, the more robust organisms are extremely adept at finding new places to live. Thus, just as the common housefly has insinuated itself into practically every ecosystem on the planet, so has the meme of 'life after death' found a niche in most minds, or psycho-ecologies.

The more universally resonant an idea or image or song, the more minds it will enter and remain within. Trying to stop the spread of a really robust piece of information is about as easy as keeping killer bees South of the Border. The stuff just leaks.

Information wants to change

If ideas and other interactive patterns of information are, indeed, life forms, they can be expected to evolve constantly into forms that will be more perfectly adapted to their surroundings. And, as we see, they are doing this all the time. But for a long time, our static media, whether carvings in stone, ink on paper, or dye on celluloid, have strongly resisted the evolutionary impulse, exalting as a consequence the author's ability to determine the finished product. But, as in an oral tradition, digitized information has no 'final cut'.

Digital information, unconstrained by packaging, is a continuing process more like the metamorphosing tales of prehistory than anything that will fit in shrink wrap. From the Neolithic to Gutenberg, information was passed on, mouth to ear, changing with every re-telling (or re-singing). The stories that once shaped our sense of the world didn't have authoritative versions. They adapted to each culture in which they found themselves being told.

Because there was never a moment when the story was frozen in print, the so-called 'moral' right of storytellers to keep the tale their own was neither protected nor recognized. The story simply passed through each of them on its way to the next, where it would assume a different form. As we return to continuous information, we can expect the importance of authorship to diminish. Creative people may have to renew their acquaintance with humility.

But our system of copyright makes no accommodation whatever for expressions that don't at some point become 'fixed' nor for cultural expressions which lack a specific author or inventor. Jazz improvisations, stand-up comedy routines, mime performances, developing monologues, and unrecorded broadcast transmissions all lack the Constitutional requirement of fixation as a 'writing'. Without being fixed by a point of publication the liquid works of the future will all look more like these continuously adapting and changing forms and will therefore exist beyond the reach of copyright.

Copyright expert Pamela Samuelson tells of having attended a conference convened around the fact that Western countries may legally appropriate the music, designs, and biomedical lore of aboriginal people without compensation to their tribe of origin since that tribe is not an 'author' or 'inventor'. But soon most information will be generated collaboratively by the cyber-tribal hunter-gatherers of Cyberspace. Our arrogant legal dismissal of the rights of 'primitives' will be back to haunt us soon.

Information is perishable

With the exception of the rare classic, most information is like farm produce. Its quality degrades rapidly both over time and in distance from the source of production. But even here, value is highly subjective and conditional. Yesterday's papers are quite valuable to the historian. In fact, the older they are, the more valuable they become. On the other hand, a commodities broker might consider news of an event that is more than an hour old to have lost any relevance.

3.3 INFORMATION IS A RELATIONSHIP

Meaning has value and is unique to each case

In most cases, we assign value to information based on its meaningfulness. The place where information dwells, the holy moment where transmission becomes reception, is a region that has many shifting characteristics and flavours depending on the relationship of sender and receiver, the depth of their interactivity. Each such relationship is unique. Even in cases where the sender is a broadcast medium, and no response is returned, the receiver is hardly passive. Receiving information is often as creative an act as generating it.

The value of what is sent depends entirely on the extent to which each individual receiver has the receptors – shared terminology, attention, interest, language, paradigm – necessary to render what is received meaningful. Understanding is a critical element increasingly overlooked in the effort to turn information into a commodity. Data may be any set of facts, useful or not, intelligible or inscrutable, germane or irrelevant. Computers can crank out new data all night long without human help, and the results may be offered for sale as information. They may or may not actually be so. Only a human being can recognize the meaning that separates information from data.

In fact, information, in the economic sense of the word, consists of data that have been passed through a particular human mind and found meaningful within that mental context. One fella's information is all just data to someone else. If you're an anthropologist, my detailed charts of Tasa day kinship patterns might be critical information to you. If you're a banker from Hong Kong, they might barely seem to be data.

Familiarity has more value than scarcity

With physical goods, there is a direct correlation between scarcity and value. Gold is more valuable than wheat, even though you can't eat it . While this is not always the case, the situation with information is usually precisely the reverse. Most soft goods increase in value as they become more common. Familiarity is an important asset in the world of information. It may often be the case that the best thing you can do to raise the demand for your product is to give it away.

While this has not always worked with shareware, it could be argued that there is a connection between the extent to which commercial software is pirated and the amount that gets sold. Broadly pirated software, such as Lotus 1-2-3 or WordPerfect, becomes a standard and benefits from the Law of Increasing Returns based on familiarity.

Regarding my own soft product, rock and roll songs, there is no question that the band I write them for, the Grateful Dead, has increased its popularity enormously by giving them away. We have been letting people tape our concerts since the early seventies, but instead of reducing the demand for our product, we are now the largest concert draw in America, a fact that is at least in part attributable to the popularity generated by those tapes.

True, I don't get any royalties on the millions of copies of my songs that have been extracted from concerts, but I see no reason to complain. The fact is, no one but the Grateful Dead can perform a Grateful Dead song, so if you want the experience and not its thin projection, you have to buy a ticket from us. In other words, our intellectual property protection derives from our being the only real-time source of it.

Exclusivity has value

The problem with a model that turns the physical scarcity/value ratio on its head is that sometimes the value of information is very much based on its scarcity. Exclusive possession of certain facts makes them more useful. If everyone knows about conditions that might drive a stock price up, the information is valueless.

But again, the critical factor is usually time. It doesn't matter if this kind of information eventually becomes ubiquitous. What matters is being among the first who possess it and act on it. While potent secrets usually don't stay secret, they may remain so long enough to advance the cause of their original holders.

Point of view and authority have value

In a world of floating realities and contradictory maps, rewards will accrue to those commentators whose maps seem to fit their territory snugly, based on their ability to yield predictable results for those who use them. In aesthetic information, whether poetry or rock 'n' roll, people are willing to buy the new product of an artist, sight-unseen, based on their having been delivered a pleasurable experience by previous work.

Reality is an edit. People are willing to pay for the authority of those editors whose filtering point of view seems to fit best. And again, point of view is an asset that cannot be stolen or duplicated. No one but Esther Dyson sees the world as she does and the handsome fee she charges for her newsletter is actually for the privilege of looking at the world through her unique eyes.

Time replaces space

In the physical world, value depends heavily on possession, or proximity in space. One owns that material that falls inside certain dimensional boundaries and the ability to act directly, exclusively, and as one wishes upon what falls inside those boundaries is the principal right of ownership. And of course there is the relationship between value and scarcity, a limitation in space.

In the virtual world, proximity in time is a value determinant. An informational product is generally more valuable the closer the purchaser can place himself to the moment of its expression, a limitation in time. Many kinds of information degrade rapidly with either time or reproduction. Relevance fades as the territory they map changes. Noise is introduced and bandwidth lost with passage away from the point where the information is first produced.

Thus, listening to a Grateful Dead tape is hardly the same experience as attending a Grateful Dead concert. The closer one can get to the head waters of an informational stream, the better his chances of finding an accurate picture of reality in it. In an era of easy reproduction, the informational abstractions of popular experiences will propagate out from their source moments to reach anyone who's interested. But it's easy enough to restrict the real experience of the desirable event, whether knock-out punch or guitar lick, to those willing to pay for being there.

The protection of execution

In the hick town I come from, they don't give you much credit for just having ideas. You are judged by what you can make of them. As things continue to speed up, I think we see that execution is the best protection for those designs that become physical products. Or, as Steve Jobs once put it, 'Real artistship'. The big winner is usually the one who gets to the market first (and with enough organizational force to keep the lead).

But, as we become fixated upon information commerce, many of us seem to think that originality alone is sufficient to convey value, deserving , with the right legal assurances, of a steady wage. In fact, the best way to protect intellectual property is to act on it. It's not enough to invent and patent, one has to innovate as well. Someone claims to have patented the microprocessor before Intel. Maybe so. If he'd actually started shipping microprocessors before Intel, his claim would seem far less spurious.

Information as its own reward

It is now a commonplace to say that money is information. With the exception of Kruger rands, crumpled cab-fare, and the contents of those suit-cases which drug lords are reputed to carry, most of the money in the informatized world is in ones and zeros. The global money supply sloshes around the Net, as fluid as weather. It is also obvious, as I have discussed, that information has become as fundamental to the creation of modern wealth as land and sunlight once were. What is less obvious is the extent to which information is acquiring intrinsic value, not as a means to acquisition but as the object to be acquired. I suppose this has always been less explicitly the case. In politics and academia, potency and information have always been closely related.

However, as we increasingly buy information with money, we begin to see that buying information with other information is simple economic exchange without the necessity of converting the product into and out of currency. This is somewhat challenging for those who like clean accounting, since, information theory aside, informational exchange rates are too squishy to quantify to the decimal point. Nevertheless, most of what a middle class American purchases has little to do with survival. We buy beauty, prestige, experience, education, and all the obscure pleasures of owning. Many of these things cannot only be expressed in non-material terms, they can be acquired by non-material means.

And then there are the inexplicable pleasures of information itself, the joys of learning, knowing, and teaching. The strange good feeling of information coming into and out of oneself. Playing with ideas is a recreation which people must be willing to pay a lot for, given the market for books and elective seminars. We'd likely spend even more money for such pleasures if there weren't so many opportunities to pay for ideas with other ideas.

This explains much of the collective 'volunteer' work that fills the archives, news groups, and databases of the Internet. Its denizens are not working for nothing, as is widely believed. Rather they are getting paid in something besides money. It is an economy that consists almost entirely of information. This may become the dominant form of human trade, and if we persist in modelling economics on a strictly monetary basis, we may be gravely misled.

4. Getting Paid in Cyberspace

How all the foregoing relates to solutions to the crisis in intellectual property is something I've barely started to wrap my mind around. It's fairly paradigm-warping to look at information through fresh eyes, to see how very little it is like pig iron or pork bellies, to imagine the tottering travesties of case law we will stack up if we go on treating it legally as though it were. As I've said, I believe these towers of outmoded boilerplate will be a smoking heap sometime in the next decade and we mind miners will have no choice but to cast our lot with new systems that work.

I'm not really so gloomy about our prospects as readers of this jeremiad so far might conclude. Solutions will emerge. Nature abhors a vacuum and so does commerce. Indeed, one of the aspects of the electronic frontier that I have always found most appealing – and the reason Mitch Kapor and I used that phrase in naming our foundation – is the degree to which it resembles the 19th Century American West in its natural preference for social devices which emerge from its conditions rather than those which are imposed from the outside. Until the West was fully settled and 'civilized' in this century, order was established according to an unwritten Code of the West that had the fluidity of etiquette rather than the rigidity of law. Ethics were more important than rules. Understandings were preferred over laws, which were, in any event, largely unenforceable.

I believe that law, as we understand it, was developed to protect the interests that arose in the two economic 'waves' which Alvin Toffler accurately identified in The Third Wave. The First Wave was agriculturally based and required law to order ownership of the principal source of production, land. In the Second Wave, manufacturing became the economic mainspring, and the structure of modern law grew around the centralized institutions that needed protection for their reserves of capital, manpower, and hardware. Both of these economic systems required stability. Their laws were designed to resist change and to assure some equability of distribution within a fairly static social framework. The possibility spaces had to be constrained to preserve the predictability necessary to either land stewardship or capital formation.

In the Third Wave we have now entered, information to a large extent replaces land, capital, and hardware, and as I have detailed in the preceding section, information is most at home in a much more fluid and adaptable environment. The

Third Wave is likely to bring a fundamental shift in the purposes and methods of law that will affect far more than simply those statutes that govern intellectual property.

The 'terrain' itself – the architecture of the Net – may come to serve many of the purposes that could only be maintained in the past by legal imposition. For example, it may be unnecessary to constitutionally assure freedom of expression in an environment that, in the words of my fellow EFF co-founder John Gilmore, 'treats censorship as a malfunction' and re-routes proscribed ideas around it. Similar natural balancing mechanisms may arise to smooth over the social discontinuities that previously required legal intercession to set right. On the Net, these differences are more likely to be spanned by a continuous spectrum that connects as much as it separates.

And, despite their fierce grip on the old legal structure, companies which trade in information are likely to find that in their increasing inability to deal sensibly with technological issues, the courts will not produce results that are predictable enough to be supportive of long-term enterprise. Every litigation becomes like a game of Russian roulette, depending on the depth of the presiding judge's clue-impairment.

Uncodified or adaptive 'law,' while as 'fast, loose, and out of control' as other emergent forms, is probably more likely to yield something like justice at this point. In fact, one can already see in development new practices to suit the conditions of virtual commerce. The life forms of information are evolving methods to protect their continued reproduction. For example, while all the tiny print on a commercial diskette envelope punctiliously requires much of those who would open it, there are, as I say, few who read those provisos, let alone follow them to the letter. And yet, the software business remains a very healthy sector of the American economy.

Why is this? Because people seem to eventually buy the software they really use. Once a program becomes central to your work, you want the latest version of it, the best support, the actual manuals, all privileges that are attached to ownership. Such practical considerations will, in the absence of working law, become more and more important in getting paid for what might easily be obtained for nothing.

I do think that some software is being purchased in the service of ethics or the abstract awareness that the failure to buy it will result in its not being produced any longer, but I'm going to leave those motivators aside. While I believe that the failure of law will almost certainly result in a compensating re-emergence of ethics as the ordering template of society, this is a belief I don't have room to support here. Instead, I think that, as in the case cited above, compensation for soft products will be driven primarily by practical considerations, all of them consistent with the true properties of digital information, where the value lies in it, and how it can be both manipulated and protected by technology.

While the conundrum remains a conundrum, I can begin to see the directions from which solutions may emerge, based in part on broadening those practical solutions that are already in practice.

5. Relationship and its Tools

I believe one idea is central to understanding liquid commerce: information economics, in the absence of objects, will be based more on relationship than possession.

One existing model for the future conveyance of intellectual property is real time performance, a medium currently used only in theater, music, lectures, stand-up comedy and pedagogy. I believe the concept of performance will expand to include most of the information economy, from multi-casted soap operas to stock analysis. In these instances, commercial exchange will be more like ticket sales to a continuous show than the purchase of discrete bundles of that which is being shown.

The other model, of course, is service. The entire professional class – doctors, lawyers, consultants, architects, etc. – are already being paid directly for their intellectual property. Who needs copyright when you're on a retainer? In fact, this model was applied to much of what is now copyrighted until the late 18th Century. Before the industrialization of creation, writers, composers, artists, and the like produced their products in the private service of patrons. Without objects to distribute in a mass market, creative people will return to a condition somewhat like this, except that they will serve many patrons, rather than one.

We can already see the emergence of companies that base their existence on supporting and enhancing the soft property they create rather than selling it by the shrink-wrapped piece or embedding it in widgets. Trip Hawkins' new company for creating and licensing multimedia tools, 3DO, is an example of what I'm talking about. 3DO doesn't intend to produce any commercial software or consumer devices. Instead, they will act as a kind of private standards setting body, mediating among software and device creators who will be their licensees. They will provide a point of commonalty for relationships between a broad spectrum of entities.

In any case, whether you think of yourself as a service provider or a performer, the future protection of your intellectual property will depend on your ability to control your relationship to the market – a relationship that will most likely live and grow over time. The value of that relationship will reside in the quality of performance, the uniqueness of your point of view, the validity of your expertise, its relevance to your market, and, underlying everything, the ability of that market to access your creative services swiftly, conveniently, and interactively.

6. Interaction and Protection

Direct interaction will provide a lot of intellectual property protection in the future, and, indeed, it already has. No one knows how many software pirates have bought legitimate copies of a program after calling its publisher for technical support and being asked for some proof of purchase, but I would guess the number is very high. The same kind of controls will be applicable to 'question and answer' relationships between authorities (or artists) and those who seek their expertise. Newsletters, magazines, and books will be supplemented by the ability of their subscribers to ask direct questions of authors.

Interactivity will be a billable commodity even without authorship. As people move into the Net and increasingly get their information directly from its point of production, unfiltered by centralized media, they will attempt to develop the same interactive ability to probe reality which only experience has provided them in the past. Live access to these distant 'eyes and ears' will be much easier to cordon than access to static bundles of stored but easily reproducible information.

In most cases, control will be based on restricting access to the freshest, highest bandwidth information. It will be a matter of defining the ticket, the venue, the performer, and the identity of the ticket holder, definitions that I believe will take their forms from technology, not law. In most cases, the defining technology will be cryptography.

7. Crypto Bottling

Cryptography, as I've said perhaps too many times, is the 'material' from which the walls, boundaries – and bottles – of Cyberspace will be fashioned. Of course there are problems with cryptography or any other purely technical method of property protection. It has always appeared to me that the more security you hide your goods behind, the more likely you are to turn your sanctuary into a target. Having come from a place where people leave their keys in their cars and don't even have keys to their houses, I remain convinced that the best obstacle to crime is a society with its ethics intact.

While I admit that this is not the kind of society most of us live in, I also believe that a social over-reliance on protection by barricades rather than conscience will eventually wither the latter by turning intrusion and theft into a sport, rather than a crime. This is already occurring in the digital domain as is evident in the activities of computer crackers.

Furthermore, I would argue that initial efforts to protect digital copyright by copy protection contributed to the current condition in which most otherwise ethical computer users seem morally untroubled by their possession of pirated software. Instead of cultivating among the newly computerized a sense of respect for the work of their fellows, early reliance on copy protection led to the subliminal notion that cracking into a software package somehow 'earned' one the right to use it. Limited not by conscience but by technical skill, many soon felt free to do whatever they could get away with. This will continue to be a potential liability of the encryption of digitized commerce.

Furthermore, it's cautionary to remember that copy protection was rejected by the market in most areas. Many of the upcoming efforts to use cryptography-based protection schemes will probably suffer the same fate. People are not going to tolerate much which makes computers harder to use than they already are without any benefit to the user.

Nevertheless, encryption has already demonstrated a certain blunt utility. New subscriptions to various commercial satellite TV services sky-rocketed recently after their deployment of more robust encryption of their feeds. This, despite a booming backwoods trade in black decoder chips conducted by folks who'd look more at home running moonshine than cracking code.

Another obvious problem with encryption as a global solution is that once something has been unscrambled by a legitimate licensee, it may be openly available to massive reproduction. In some instances, reproduction following decryption may not be a problem. Many soft products degrade sharply in value with time. It may be that the only real interest in some such products will be among those who have purchased the keys to immediacy.

Furthermore, as software becomes more modular and distribution moves online, it will begin to metamorphose in direct interaction with its user base. Discontinuous upgrades will smooth into a constant process of incremental improvement and adaptation, some of it man-made and some of it arising through genetic algorithms. Pirated copies of software may be come too static to have much value to anyone.

Even in cases such as images, where the information is expected to remain fixed, the unencrypted file could still be interwoven with code which could continue to protect it by a wide variety of means. In most of the schemes I can project, the file would be 'alive' with permanently embedded software that could 'sense' the surrounding conditions and interact with them, For example, it might contain code that could detect the process of duplication and cause it to self-destruct.

Other methods might give the file the ability to 'phone home' through the Net to its original owner. The continued integrity of some files might require periodic 'feeding' with digital cash from their host, which they would then relay back to their authors. Of course, files that possess the independent ability to communicate upstream sound uncomfortably like the Morris Internet Worm. 'Live' files do have a certain viral quality. And serious privacy issues would arise if everyone's computer were packed with digital spies.

The point is that cryptography will enable a lot of protection technologies that will develop rapidly in the obsessive competition that has always existed between lock-makers and lock-breakers. But cryptography will not be used simply for making locks. It is also at the heart of both digital signatures and the aforementioned digital cash, both of which I believe will be central to the future protection of intellectual property.

I believe that the generally acknowledged failure of the shareware model in software had less to do with dishonesty than with the simple inconvenience of paying for shareware. If the payment process can be automated, as digital cash and signature will make possible, I believe that soft product creators will reap a much higher return from the bread they cast upon the waters of Cyberspace.

Moreover, they will be spared much of the overhead that presently adheres to the marketing, manufacture, sales, and distribution of information products, whether those products are computer programs, books, CD's, or motion pictures. This will reduce prices and further increase the likelihood of non-compulsory payment.

But, of course, there is a fundamental problem with a system that requires, through technology, payment for every access to a particular expression. It defeats the original Jeffersonian purpose of seeing that ideas were available to everyone, regardless of their economic station. I am not comfortable with a model that will restrict inquiry to the wealthy.

8. An Economy of Verbs

The future forms and protections of intellectual property are densely obscured from the entrance to the Virtual Age. Nevertheless, I can make (or reiterate) a few flat statements that I earnestly believe won't look too silly in fifty years:

- In the absence of the old containers, almost everything we think we know about intellectual property is wrong. We are going to have to unlearn it. We are going to have to look at information as though we'd never seen the stuff before.
- The protections that we will develop will rely far more on ethics and technology than on law.
- Encryption will be the technical basis for most intellectual property protection. (And should, for this and other reasons, be made more widely available.)
- The economy of the future will be based on relationship rather than possession. It will be continuous rather than sequential.
- And finally, in the years to come, most human exchange will be virtual rather than physical, consisting not of stuff but the stuff of which dreams are made. Our future business will be conducted in a world made more of verbs than nouns.

Putting Cars on the 'Information Superhighway': Authors, Exploiters and Copyright in Cyberspace

*Jane C. Ginsburg**

1. Introduction

The advent of the 'Information Superhighway' has sparked much speculation about the roles of authorship, of readership, and of literary property in the vast system of interlinked computer networks that has come to be known as 'cyberspace'.[1] Through computers linked to a digital network, users can access and add to vast quantities of material. At least in theory, every computer user can become his or her own publisher, and every terminal can become a library, bookstore, or audio and video jukebox.

The prospect of pervasive audience access to and ability to copy and further disseminate works of authorship challenges the traditional roles not only of information providers – be they publishers, motion picture producers or record producers[2] – but of the individuals who create the works. On the one hand, authors

---

* Jane C. Ginsburg is Morton L. Janklow professor of Literary and Artistic Property Law, Columbia University School of Law. This article originally appeared in the Columbia Law Review, Vol. 95 (November 1995). Many thanks for substantive suggestions to Professor Shira Perlmutter, Professor Marci Hamilton and to Steven Shaber, Columbia Law School class of 1996; thanks for research to Justine Harris, Columbia Law School class of 1996.

1. *See*, e.g., I. Trotter Hardy, 'The Proper Legal Regime for "Cyberspace",' 55 *U. Pitt. L. Rev.* 1994, at 993; Jessica Litman, 'The Exclusive Right to Read,' 13 *Cardozo Arts & Ent. L.J.* 1994, at 29; David J. Loundy, 'E-Law: Legal Issues Affecting Computer Information Systems and Systems Operator Liability,' 3 *Alb. L.J. Sci. & Tech.* 1993, at 79; Raymond T. Nimmer & Patricia A. Krauthaus, 'Copyright on the Information Superhighway: Requiem for a Middleweight,' 6 *Stan. L. & Pol'y Rev.* 1994, at 25. On the creation of works in digital media, see, e.g., Pamela Samuelson, 'Some New Kinds of Authorship Made Possible by Computers and Some Intellectual Property Questions They Raise,' 53 *U. Pitt. L. Rev.* 1992, at 685; Robert D. Sprague, 'Multimedia: The Convergence of New Technologies and Traditional Copyright Issues,' 71 *Denv. U. L. Rev.* 1994, at 635; Jennifer D. Choe, Note, 'Interactive Multimedia: A New Technology Tests the Limits of Copyright Law,' 46 *Rutgers L. Rev.* 1994, at 929.

2. A variety of local and international conferences have recently focused on the rights and liabilities of information providers, publishers and producers in the digital era. *See*, e.g., WIPO Worldwide Symposium on the Future of Copyright and Neighboring Rights (on file with the author) [hereinafter *WIPO Louvre*] (symposium held June 1-3, 1995 at the Louvre); WIPO Worldwide Symposium on the Impact of Digital Technology on Copyright and Neighboring Rights, March 19, 1993 (on file with the author) [hereinafter *WIPO Harvard]* (symposium held March 31 –

will be able to disseminate their works directly to the entire world of online users. On the other hand, this kind of dissemination ensures neither payment nor the security that users will not copy, alter, or further circulate the author's work. Does the 'Information Superhighway' put the author in the driver's seat, or will the author become, as Garrison Keillor has warned, 'the deer in the headlights' of a vast traffic the author cannot control?[3]

While circulation in cyberspace may place works of authorship at the risk of uncontrolled copying or adaptation, the works have first to be made available for digital exploitation. As a result, Mort Janklow, a leading literary agent, offers a more hopeful prediction than Keillor's. The entrepreneurs of cyberspace still depend on the participation of authors: as Janklow puts it, 'they've got the highway, but I've got the cars.'[4] That is, one can build the highway, but it does not follow that the cars will choose to come. Unless they can become author-friendly, digital media may remain just that: media, without content. Today's travellers on the infohighway are largely (although by no means exclusively) the bicycles and tricycles of e-mail exchanges, and the tractor trailers of enormous data compilations. If all kinds of works of authorship, particularly those of intense creativity and imagination, are to embark willingly on the cyber-road, then authors require some assurance that the journey will not turn into a hijacking.

But if cyberspace threatens authors' ability to control the exploitation of their works, it also offers them new opportunities for creation. By facilitating communication among creators and enhancing their ability to disseminate the fruits of their labours, cyberspace may promote new modes of authorship, particularly of a collaborative kind. Today's casual e-mail exchanges may become tomorrow's multimedia productions, as many widely scattered contributors together elaborate works combining words, images, and/or music. This article therefore analyses the copyright law consequences of creation as well as of exploitation of works in cyberspace. Moreover, because cyberspace knows no national borders, the evaluation of both topics necessarily takes into account foreign as well as domestic U.S copyright law.

This article will address three broad problems: first, who owns the copyright in works created on the infohighway?; second, what rights do the copyright owners of these works – as well as of pre-existing works posted in cyberspace – enjoy?; and third, how may they enforce their rights? Because the law in this area is far from settled, the analysis cannot be purely descriptive; the conclusions offered here are often proposals derived from my analysis of the available elements of positive copyright law. Finally, two premises underlie this analysis. First, in applying or adapting copyright law to issues of copyright ownership and exploitation in cyberspace, I am claiming that copyright law properly does apply, or can successfully be adapted, to digital creation and communication of works of

---

April 2, 1993 at Harvard University); Seminar, Business and Legal Aspects of the Internet and Online Services (September 14-15, 1995).

3. Remarks at panel discussion, Session III, Conference on Intellectual Property Rights and the Arts: The Impact of New Technologies 43 (Dec. 13, 1994) (transcript on file with the Columbia Law Review) (sponsored by The New York International Festival of the Arts).

4. Interview with Morton L. Janklow, Columbia Law School (Oct. 25, 1994).

authorship. Thus, I do not believe that the digital format of the works, or their networked dissemination, radically undermines the bases of copyright laws conceived in an analog world.[5]

Second, in articulating and examining the issues from the point of view of authors and copyright owners, I am claiming that fostering authorship remains a primary goal of copyright law, whatever the medium in which works are created and disseminated. It is true that cyberspace vastly enhances the power of users of works: it not only makes works available to individual users more easily and in greater volume than in the hard copy world, but also communicates them in an easily manipulated format that users can instantly recopy, adapt, or forward to other users. Nonetheless, the perspective of user rights, albeit important, should remain secondary. Without authors, there are no works to use.[6] Copyright law has maintained the balance between encouraging authorship and enlightening the public; as the Copyright Clause of the Constitution declares, the 'Progress of Science' is 'promote[d]' by 'securing for limited Times to Authors (..) the exclusive Right to their (..) Writings.'[7]

2. Who Owns the Copyright in the 'Cars'?

Some of the problems posed by electronic networks concern communication and protection of previously created works. These works present no problems of copyright ownership specific to cyberspace: traditional copyright principles can identify their authors or initial copyright owners.[8] For example, the author of a hard copy photograph that has been scanned and uploaded to a network does not cease being the work's sole author simply because the work's format or mode of communication has changed.[9] Cyberspace can raise novel copyright ownership questions, however, with respect to works wholly or partially created on electronic

5. For the opposite proposition, *see*, e.g., Nimmer & Krauthaus, *supra* note 1, at 32 (arguing that existing scope and nature of copyright protection are poorly attuned to new milieu of information highway). *See also* Thomas Dreier, 'Copyright Digitized: Philosophical Impacts and Practical Implications for Information Exchange in Digital Networks,' *in* WIPO Harvard, *supra* note 2, at SDT/15, 27 (exploring strains put on traditional copyright concepts when digital media provide the "dissolution" of the work of authorship).

6. Cf. *Harper & Row, Publishers v. Nation Enters.*, 471 U.S. 539, 559 1985 (quoting Lionel S. Sobel, 'Copyright and the First Amendment: A Gathering Storm?,' 19 *Copyright L. Symp. (ASCAP)* 43, 78 (1971)) ('If every volume that was in the public interest could be pirated away by a competing publisher, (..) the public [soon] would have nothing worth reading').

7. U.S. Const. art I, § 8, cl. 8.

8. *See*, e.g., Jane C. Ginsburg, 'Domestic and International Copyright Issues Implicated in the Compilation of a Multimedia Product,' 25 *Seton Hall L. Rev.* 1995, 101, 105, 113-16 (outlining traditional copyright principles and describing how they can be applied to problems posed by electronic networks).

9. Moreover, the person effecting the scanning would not be considered the 'author' of the digital version, since she would have vested no independent creativity in scanning the photo. *See*, e.g., *L. Batlin & Son v. Snyder*, 536 F.2d 486, 491 (2d Cir.), cert. denied, 429 U.S. 857 (1976) (simply transforming the medium in which a work is expressed – in that case converting a cast iron 'Uncle Sam' bank to a plastic version – is not an act of authorship).

networks. Participants in bulletin boards and 'chat lines',[10] or users of electronic mail, can together create works of authorship through multiple online exchanges. The number and location of the participants can be as vast as the number of bulletin board or chat line subscribers, or even more broadly, as the number of persons with access to e-mail.

Consider the following hypothetical. Suppose that an author writes the beginning of a short story, which she posts on an electronic bulletin board, inviting any and all participants to compose endings for the tale.[11] In due course, hundreds of writers respond. The initiating author would now like to publish her beginning, as joined to her assembling and editing of her favourite fifty conclusions. Moreover, she hopes to do so free of any copyright claims of the fifty selected contributors. Who owns what rights under copyright in the story and its components?

2.1 JOINT WORKS

Classifying this work affords a starting point for determining its copyright ownership. The collaborative nature of the work might make the Copyright Act's 'joint work' category the most apt for the story with all its endings.[12] The Copyright Act defines a 'joint work' as 'a work prepared by two or more authors with the intention that their contributions be merged into inseparable or interdependent parts of a unitary whole.'[13] Our compendium of endings seems to fit that standard: those who responded to the initiating author's invitation surely intended to merge their endings to her beginning, as did she intend to combine her beginning with their endings.

One might object that the completed stories should not be considered joint works unless the participants collaborated together in space or time, or unless each participant knew whom the others were. But even before the infohighway, joint works did not necessarily imply temporal and spatial proximity. For example, in the 'old' days, a composer might have written a melody, hoping and intending that, at some later date, a lyricist would come along and supply the words. In this

---

10. Electronic 'chatting' is described as 'involv[ing] messaging between nodes on a network. When your computer connects with a host on a LAN, the host sends a login prompt to which your computer responds so that the connection can be made.' Tom Fahey, *Net.Speak: The Internet Dictionary* 35 (1994).

11. The hypothetical is inspired by an old-technology event: in 1876, Mark Twain wrote a story titled 'A Murder, A Mystery and A Marriage.' He proposed to the Atlantic Monthly 'that a number of other famous writers of the period (..) be enlisted, each to write his own final chapter for the work, so that for the mystery set up in the first few chapters, each author would compose a solution, in addition to, or in competition with Twain's own denouement. In other words, as planned by Twain, there was to be a common plot for the story, with a number of different endings.' *Chamberlain v. Feldman*, 89 N.E.2d 863, 863-64 (N.Y. 1949) (concerning rights in Twain's manuscript, his project never having come to fruition).

12. *See* 17 U.S.C. § 101 (1988). The work would most likely not be considered a 'work made for hire,' *see infra* note 26.

13. 17 U.S.C. § 101.

instance, although the authors did not work together toward their goal (indeed, the authors may never have met or corresponded), both sought to create a work that would combine words and music.[14] While the 1976 Copyright Act emphasizes the intent of the authors at the time their respective contributions were made,[15] it does not require that that intent be simultaneously expressed. The legislative history of the Act in the House and Senate Reports envisions two situations giving rise to a joint work: (1) 'the authors collaborated with each other', or (2) 'each of the authors prepared his contribution with the knowledge and intention [sic] that it would be merged with the contributions of other authors as "inseparable or interdependent parts of a unitary whole".'[16] While collaboration implies simultaneity of intent, the House Report's other example, of contributions created with the intent that they be merged, arguably accommodates the hypothetical composer awaiting a lyricist, as well as our initiating author and her cyber-collaborators.

However, the legislative history suggests that, while the co-authors need not actually meet and work together, they must not only intend, but must also be aware of each other's contributions. For there to be not only an 'intention at the time the writing is done' to combine the parts,[17] but also the knowledge (or at least the reasonable expectation) that the contributions will be merged, it would seem that each contributor's intent must be fairly contemporaneous.[18] Even so, our initiating author may satisfy the statutory criteria of joint authorship. When she posts the opening of her story on the electronic bulletin board, she does not know who will come along to complete it, but she can be reasonably certain that someone (or many someones) will respond. Moreover, to enhance her knowledge of the contributions she intends to merge with her own, she can at all times monitor the progress of her invitation, and thus watch the collaboration unfold. As a result, even though their contributions are serial rather than simultaneous, all the contributors (including the initiator) know, before each begins, that their efforts will form 'inseparable or interdependent parts of a unitary whole.'

As the co-owner of a 'joint' work, the initiating author would be entitled, under U.S. law, to exploit the work on a nonexclusive basis without obtaining her

---

14. Or suppose the composer had no intent regarding the pairing of her tune with words, but a lyricist nonetheless joined a text to the tune. The lyricist certainly intended to create a work that was 'joint' in the sense that he bound the words and music together. The Second Circuit, in a much criticized decision under the 1909 Act, held that the intent of the subsequent author sufficed to qualify the combined work as 'joint.' *Shapiro, Bernstein & Co. v. Jerry Vogel Music Co.*, 221 F.2d 569, 570 (2d Cir.), rev'd on other grounds, 223 F.2d 252 (2d Cir. 1955) (the *12th Street Rag* case). The primary basis for the criticism of this decision, however, is the lack of the first author's intent to create a joint work, rather than the belatedness of the second author's contribution.

15. *See* S. Rep. No. 473, 94th Cong., 1st Sess. 103-04 (1975); H.R. Rep. No. 1476, 94th Cong., 2d Sess. 120 (1976).

16. S. Rep. No. 473, *supra* note 15, at 103; H.R. Rep. No. 1476, *supra* note 15, at 120.

17. S. Rep. No. 473, *supra* note 15, at 103; H.R. Rep. No. 1476, *supra* note 15, at 120.

18. *See*, e.g., S. Rep. No. 473, *supra* note 15, at 103 ('although a novelist, playwright, or songwriter may write a work with the hope or expectation that it will be used in a motion picture, this clearly is a case of separate or independent authorship rather than one where the basic intention behind the writing of the work was for motion picture use.').

co-authors' permission.[19] However, she could not grant third parties *exclusive* rights without the co-authors' permission. Moreover, absent a contract to the contrary, any nonexclusive exploitation in which the initiating author engages gives rise to a duty to account to her co-authors.[20] Accounting for profits among fifty co-authors could prove cumbersome – and relatively unprofitable.[21] Moreover, under some foreign copyright laws, joint authors may not individually exploit the joint work, even on a nonexclusive basis, without obtaining all the co-authors' accord.[22] Thus, the rights afforded to the co-authors under copyright's joint works regime are significantly constrained, both in the U.S. and abroad. But these limited rights reflect only the basic framework: the initiating author may alter that arrangement by contract. Our next inquiry therefore addresses cyberspace assignments of copyright, and the extent to which they comply with copyright law requirements.

2.2 TRANSFERS OF EXCLUSIVE RIGHTS UNDER COPYRIGHT

To enjoy maximum freedom to dispose of the collection of stories, our initiating author would like to obtain assignments of all of the contributors' copyright interests. (This would be true whether the contributors were considered co-authors of each story, co-authors of the whole collection, or individual authors of their distinct story endings.) To this end, suppose she includes the following notice when she posts the beginning of her story and her invitation to others to finish the tale:

> By contributing material to the completion of the story, you thereby assign to me all your right, title, and interest, in and to any copyright in your contribution, for the full term of copyright, and any renewals and extensions thereof. The territory covered by this agreement shall be the whole world. The laws of the United States and of the State of New York shall govern this agreement.

Is the notice – which is a sort of cyberspace analog to the 'shrinkwrap license' of software distribution fame[23] – effective to transfer the contributors' copyrights?

---

19. *See*, e.g., *Werbungs und Commerz Union Austalt v. LeShufy*, 6 U.S.P.Q.2d (BNA) 1153, 1154 (S.D.N.Y. 1987) (citing M. Nimmer, *Copyright* § 6.10, 1987).

20. *See*, e.g., *Oddo v. Ries*, 743 F.2d 630 (9th Cir. 1984); *Jerry Vogel Music Co. v. Miller Music*, 74 N.Y.S.2d 425, 427-28 (App. Div. 1947), aff'd, 87 N.E.2d 681, 681 (N.Y. 1949).

21. Moreover, the other joint authors may, in the absence of an agreement to the contrary, exploit the initiating author's contribution.

22. *See*, e.g., Law No. 57-298 on Literary and Artistic Property, art. 10 (as amended up to July 3, 1985) (Fr.), reprinted in 2 Copyright Laws and Treaties of the World, France: Item 1, at 2 (UNESCO Supp. 1992) [hereinafter *Copyright Laws of the World*]; Law No. 22/1987 on Intellectual Property art. 7; Law on the Protection of Copyright, art. 9(1) (Saudi Arabia); Law No. 633 for the Protection of Copyright and Other Rights Connected With the Exercise Thereof, art. 10 (Italy); Law Amending the Federal Law of Copyright, arts. 12-13 (Mex.).

23. A 'shrinkwrap license' is an adhesion contract that purports to take effect when the consumer opens the package and retains the goods. In the computer software area, shrinkwrap licenses typically claim to have transferred possession, but not ownership, of a copy of a computer

The U.S. Copyright Act provides that authors may transfer their rights under copyright in whole or in part, but that a grant of exclusive rights must be made in an 'instrument or conveyance of a note or memorandum of the transfer' 'in writing and signed by the owner of the rights conveyed'.[24] While the notice may be a writing sufficient to meet the Copyright Act's formal requirements, where is the signature? In the absence of authority recognizing online assents as equivalent to signed writings,[25] our initiating author may not be able to rely on the medium of cyberspace to secure the necessary contracts. Rather, she may have to resort to paper mailings (or faxes) to and from her contributors.[26]

On the other hand, the notice may suffice to transfer *non*exclusive rights in the contributions. The Copyright Act does not require nonexclusive grants to be in writing; rather, they may be made orally, or inferred from the parties' conduct.[27] Thus, suppose the initiating author posts a notice stating her intention to compile and publish the results of her invitation, and further providing that their

---

program to the purchaser, subject to a variety of conditions concerning permissible copying or adaptation of the work. *See*, e.g., cc:Mail Program License Agreement (on file with the Columbia Law Review) ('Opening this package and/or using this program indicates your acceptance of the terms and conditions stated below (..) cc:Mail, Inc. grants you a non-exclusive license to use this software product (..)'). For legal commentary on copyright and shrinkwrap licenses, *see*, e.g., David L. Hayes, 'Shrinkwrap License Agreements: New Light on a Vexing Problem,' 15 *Hastings Comm. & Ent. L.J.* 1993, 653; David W. Maher, 'The Shrink-Wrap License: Old Problems in a New Wrapper,' 34 *J. Copyr. Soc.* 1987, 292; Richard H. Stern, 'Shrink-Wrap Licenses of Mass Marketed Software: Enforceable Contracts or Whistling in the Dark?,' 11 *Rutgers Computer & Tech. L.J.* 1985, 51; *see* also *Step-Saver Data Systems v. Wyse Technology*, 939 F.2d 91 (3d Cir. 1991) (analyzing acceptance of shrinkwrap license terms under UCC § 2-207).

24. 17 U.S.C. § 204(a).

25. *Cf.* David R. Johnson & Kevin A. Marks, 'Mapping Electronic Data Communications Onto Existing Legal Metaphors: Should We Let Our Conscience (and Our Contracts) Be Our Guide?,' 38 *Vill. L. Rev.* 1993, 487, 491 (posing, but not answering the question of what should constitute a signature in cyberspace). *See* generally Bernard D. Reams, Jr. & L.J. Kutten, *Electronic Contracting Law* 162-64, 1994 ('Until the legislature takes action, electronic signatures, passwords and algorithms may not meet the signature requirements of courts of law.'); Benjamin Wright, *The Law of Electronic Commerce EDI, FAX and E-Mail: Technology, Proof, and Liability*, at § 16.4.4.2, 1991, Part V 'Electronic Contract Issues' (in discussing application of UCC § 2-201 signing requirement to electronic transactions).

26. For the same reason, the initiating author may not succeed in characterizing the collection as a 'work made for hire,' of which the initiating author would be the 'employer' and initial holder of all rights under copyright. While the collection of stories would be a compilation or a collective work, to which a specially ordered or commissioned contribution can be a work made for hire, the Copyright Act further requires that there be a writing, signed by both the initiator and the contributor, stating that the contribution will be considered a work made for hire. *See* 17 U.S.C. § 101 (1988). Moreover, the writing should be executed before the work is undertaken. See *Schiller & Schmidt, Inc. v. Nordisco Corp.*, 969 F.2d 410, 412 (7th Cir. 1992). But see *Playboy v. Dumas*, 53 F.3d 549, 559 (2d Cir. 1995) ('The writing requirement of § 101(2) can be met by a writing executed after the work is created, if the writing confirms a prior agreement, either explicit or implicit made before the creation of the work.'). Finally, any purported transfer of exclusive rights or of authorship status may be ineffective, or at least insecure, as to contributors under the age of capacity to contract – as many participants in cyberspace communications are likely to be.

27. *See*, e.g., *Effects Assoc. v. Cohen*, 908 F.2d 555 (9th Cir. 1990), cert. denied, 498 U.S. 1103 (1991).

participation in the story constitutes permission to publish, without payment to the contributors, their contributions as part of the collected results. In that case, a nonexclusive license from the contributors can reasonably be inferred. Moreover, the license, stated to be royalty-free, would absolve the initiating author of any duty to account to the contributors. In this respect, the nonexclusive license solves some of the problems inherent in the basic joint works regime.[28]

2.3 COPYRIGHT OWNERSHIP OF A COMPILATION

Having concluded that the initiating author can at least assert nonexclusive rights in the contributions, and therefore may insulate herself from infringement claims of the contributors,[29] we should inquire whether the initiating author also enjoys any exclusive rights of her own. While she is not a copyright owner of the various endings taken individually,[30] she is the author and thus the copyright owner of her beginning, and moreover, of her assembly of the beginning with the endings. That is, assuming she has engaged in a minimally original selection and arrangement of the contributed endings, the resulting collection enjoys its own copyright as a 'compilation.'[31] The owner of the copyright in a compilation holds exclusive rights in the reproduction and public display (among other rights) of the work, as edited by its compiler.[32] The compilation copyright does not extend to the compiled elements, but only to their collective presentation.[33] This means that the initiating author may protect her collection against total or substantial copying, but would have no claim against a third-party who excerpted one or a few endings.

The above analysis, while made under U.S. copyright law, would be essentially the same under many foreign copyright laws. As a general matter, the initiator and compiler of a 'collective work', such as a newspaper or an

28. Both the joint works and the nonexclusive license regimes avoid another potential impediment to dissemination of the collection, the 1976 Act termination right. Under § 203(b), a grant of exclusive rights made after 1977 may be terminated by the grantor (or her statutory successors) thirty-five years after the grant was made. If the grant is terminated, the grantee may no longer exploit the work in its original form (although she may continue to exploit derivative works prepared under the authority of the grant). By contrast, there is no termination right of a nonexclusive grant, nor may co-authors terminate each others' rights. *See* 17 U.S.C. §§ 203(a), 304(c) (1988 & Supp. V 1993).

29. This conclusion also depends on the validity in foreign jurisdictions of the notice's choice of law provision. If, under foreign law, the notice was not recognized as a contract, or if the choice of law clause was rejected, then it would be necessary to inquire whether, under the law of that jurisdiction, the notice, or the participants' conduct, gave rise to or permitted an inference of a nonexclusive royalty-free license.

30. The statute defines a copyright owner as an owner of any exclusive right under copyright. *See* 17 U.S.C. § 101 (1988).

31. *See id.* § 101, 103; *Feist Publications v. Rural Tel. Serv.*, 499 U.S. 340 (1991); *see also* Council of the European Communities, Common Position on Directive on the Legal Protection of Databases (July 7, 1995), O.J. No C 288 of 30 October 1995, 14, art. 3.1 (standard of originality required for protection of databases by draft European Union database directive).

32. *See* 17 U.S.C. §§ 103, 106 (1988).

33. *See id.* § 103(b); *Feist*, 499 U.S. at 348-49.

encyclopaedia, enjoys exclusive rights in the work in its collective presentation, but is not the initial copyright owner of the various contributions making up the work.[34]

So, our initiating author is a copyright owner, but is her legal ownership of certain exclusive rights in the compilation at all meaningful in a networked environment? For that matter, is *any* author's or other proprietor's copyright ownership – whether of new works created on digital networks, or of pre-existing works posted to a network – meaningful? Will authors and copyright owners be happy surfers in cyberspace, or will they 'wipe out' in the 'third wave information age'? To address this question, we will review the exclusive rights comprehended in a copyright, and their application to electronic network communications. Finally, if our initiating author's copyright still has content, how can it be enforced, and against whom? This question prompts inquiry into the copyright liability of the bulletin board service or online operator that carried the infringing material.

3. Rights Under Copyright in Cyberspace

Copyright is often referred to as a 'bundle of rights'.[35] It includes the exclusive rights to reproduce the work in copies, to prepare derivative works based on the copyrighted work, to distribute copies of the work, and to perform or display the work publicly.[36] All of these rights can come into play in a networked environment. Moreover, in principle, the rights copyright confers will be the same whatever the format of the work, whether originally created in hard copy or in digital format, including, as in the case of our initiating author, works created in whole or in part on digital networks.[37] As a result, the following discussion applies

34. *See*, e.g., Law No. 57-298 on Literary and Artistic Property, art. 9 (as amended up to July 3, 1985) (Fr.), reprinted in 1 *Copyright Laws of the World, supra* note 22, France: Item 1, at 2; Law on the Protection of Copyright, art. 9(2) (Saudi Arabia), reprinted in 3 Copyright Laws of the World, *supra* note 22, Saudi Arabia: Item 1, at 3; Law No. 633 for the Protection of Copyright and Other Rights Connected with the Exercise Thereof, arts. 3, 7 (as amended up to July 29, 1981) (Italy), reprinted in 2 *Copyright Laws of the World, supra* note 22, Italy: Item 1, at 2; Law Amending the Federal Law of Copyright of December 29, 1956, arts. 12-13 (as amended up to December 30, 1981) (Mex.), reprinted in 2 *Copyright Laws of the World, supra* note 22, Mexico: Item 1, at 2-3; Law No. 22/1987 on Intellectual Property art. 8 (Spain), reprinted in *3 Copyright Laws of the World, supra* note 22, Spain: Item 1, at 4.

35. *See*, e.g., H.R. Rep. No. 1476, 94th Congress, 2d Sess. 61 (1976); *Stewart v. Abend*, 495 U.S. 207, 220 (1990).

36. *See* 17 U.S.C. § 106 (1988); *see also*, e.g., Law No. 57-298 on Literary and Artistic property, art. 26-28 (as amended up to July 3, 1985) (Fr.), reprinted in 1 *Copyright Laws of the World, supra* note 22, France: Item 1, at 4; An Act Dealing With Copyright and Related Rights, sect. IV.3. (as amended up to March 7, 1990) (Germany), reprinted in 2 *Copyright Laws of the World, supra* note 22, Germany: Item 1, at 3; Copyright Law of 1970, art. 79, 80 (as amended up to June 28, 1989) (Japan), reprinted in 2 *Copyright Laws of the World, supra* note 22, Japan: Item 1, at 20; Law No. 22/1987 on Intellectual Property, Chap. III, Sec. 2 (Spain), reprinted in *3 Copyright Laws of the World, supra* note 22, Spain: Item 1, at 5-7.

37. Section 102(a) of the Copyright Act, one of the 1976 revisions, poses the principle of the indifference of the medium (whether 'now known or later developed') in which the work is expressed. 17 U.S.C. § 102(a); *see also* H.R. Rep. No. 1476, *supra* note 35, at 52: 'it makes no

not only to our initiating author, but to authors of all kinds of works, however originally elaborated, whose works are made available on digital networks.[38]

3.1 REPRODUCTION RIGHT

Copies of a work are made not only when the online user stores a work to a hard or floppy disk, or prints it out, but also when a temporary copy is received in the memory of her computer.[39] Thus, simply accessing a work online implicates the reproduction right, even if the user does not make a more permanent copy on a hard or floppy disk.

Does this mean that every reader of online material is by definition a copyright infringer?[40] Not necessarily, since the access may have been permitted, depending on the circumstances under which the reader obtained the material. Much material distributed over the Internet is made available for free (or on a

---

difference what the form, manner or medium of fixation may be – whether it is in words, numbers, notes, sounds, pictures or any other graphic or symbolic indicia, whether embodied in a physical object in written, printed, photographic, sculptural, punched, magnetic, or any other stable form, and whether it is capable of perception directly or by means of any machine or device now known or later developed.'

38. The one exception is sound recordings; these works do not currently enjoy the full scope of copyright protection, since there is no exclusive public performance right in a sound recording, and the reproduction and derivative works rights are limited to acts of copying, not imitating, the actual recorded sounds. *See* 17 U.S.C. § 114 (1988). Legislation is currently pending to recognize a public performance right in digital transmissions of sound recordings. *See* S. 227, 104th Cong. 1st Sess. (1995).

39. Electronic distribution entails the making of 'copies' within the meaning of the 1976 Copyright Act, at least as amended in 1980, when Congress adopted the recommendations of the Commission on New Technological Uses (CONTU). Under the CONTU approach, a 'copy' is made when a computer program (or by extension, any work expressed digitally) is received into the computer's temporary memory. *See* Report of the Commission on New Technological Uses, quoted in Robert A. Gorman & Jane C. Ginsburg, *Copyright for the Nineties* 692-94 (4th ed. 1993). This approach is the premise for § 117 of the U.S. Copyright Act, and has been followed in the European Union. *See* Council Directive 91/250, art. 4(a), 1991 O.J. (L 122) 42. U.S. courts have also applied this principle. *See*, e.g., *MAI Sys. Corp. v. Peak Computer, Inc.*, 991 F.2d 511, 517-18 (9th Cir. 1993), cert. dismissed, 114 S. Ct. 671 (1994); *Advanced Computer Servs. v. MAI Sys. Corp.*, 845 F. Supp. 356, 362-64 (E.D. Va. 1994) (unauthorized loading of a program into computer's temporary memory held to create an infringing copy); *Telerate Sys. Inc. v. Caro,* 689 F. Supp. 221, 231 (S.D.N.Y. 1988) (unauthorized remote access to database: receipt of data in unauthorized user's computer held to create a copy). Thus, to receive an electronic distribution is to make a copy, even if no further, more permanent, copy follows. *See* generally, *Information Infrastructure Task Force, Intellectual Property and the National Information Infrastructure,* Report of the Working Group on Intellectual Property Rights 64-66 (1995) [hereafter *NII White Paper*]. However, several commentators have questioned or even strongly criticised the proposition that receipt in a computer's random access memory entails making a 'copy.' *See*, e.g., David Post, 'New Wine, Old Bottles: The Case of the Evanescent Copy,' *Am. Lawyer*, May, 1995, at 103, 103-04 (questioning); Litman, *supra* note 1, at 40-43 (criticizing); Pamela Samuelson, 'Legally Speaking: The NII Intellectual Property Report,' *Communications of the ACM*, December 1994, at 21, 22-23 (criticizing).

40. *See* generally Litman, *supra* note 1, at 40 (criticizing the NII White Paper, *supra* note 39, on the ground that it would confer on copyright owners the 'exclusive right to read').

share-ware basis[41]); accessing, and even storing it can come within the scope of the creator's implicit or explicit license to the readers. Material distributed by commercial online services such as CompuServe, America Online, and Prodigy, may carry charges; the services' subscriber agreements or other notices generally specify the conditions of access and permissible copying. By contrast, material acquired by 'hacking' into an online service and accessing without permission would be obtained in violation of the copyright law (as well, potentially, as of other laws[42]).

One might object that even if mere accessing of electronic documents is 'copying', it is, at least initially, done by private individuals for their personal enjoyment. Many if not most users who access online documents simply to view them do not seek to compete with the copyright owner by commercializing or engaging in further reproduction and dissemination of the document. Indeed, whether the 'copy' resides temporarily in a computer, or is created or stored in a more permanent medium, including in hard copy, pursuit of individual copyists seems both unfeasible and distasteful. One might therefore expect copyright law to exclude from the copyright owner's control purely personal, noncommercial copying.

While the U.S. has not traditionally included a general 'private copying' exception of this kind,[43] many European countries have.[44] However, the entire concept of 'private copying' makes little sense in a world where the work is predominantly marketed directly to the end user. Much copying in cyberspace will be 'private', because intermediaries, such as traditional publishers (and booksellers and librarians) who reproduce, package and distribute copies to end users, will no longer be necessary.[45] As a result, the market for, or 'normal exploitation of', the work will by and large be the private copying market.[46]

---

41. Share-ware is defined as: A form of software distribution that makes copyrighted programs freely available on a trial basis; if you like the program and use it, you are expected to register your copy and send a small fee to the program creator. Once your copy is registered, you might receive a more complete manual, technical support, access to the programmer's bulletin board or information about upgrades. You can download share-ware from many bulletin boards including CompuServe and it is often available from your local user group. Peter Dyson, *The PC User's 'essential accessible' Pocket Dictionary* 468 (1994).

42. *See* Computer Fraud and Abuse Act, 18 U.S.C. § 1030 (1988); Electronic Communications Privacy Act, 18 U.S.C. § 2510 (1988). Hackers have also been prosecuted under wirefraud statutes, and under provisions regarding the interstate transport of stolen goods, 18 U.S.C. § 2314 (1988). *See*, e.g., *U.S. v. Riggs*, 739 F. Supp. 414 (N.D. Ill. 1990). *See* generally Robert L. Dunne, 'Deterring Unauthorized Access to Computers: Controlling Behavior in Cyberspace Through a Contract Law Paradigm,' 35 *Jurimetrics J.* 1994, at 1.

43. *See*, e.g., A. Latman, *Fair Use of Copyrighted Works* (1958), reprinted in Study No. 14 for the Senate Committee on the Judiciary, Copyright Law Revision, Studies Prepared for the Subcommittee on Patents, Trademarks, and Copyrights, 86th Cong., 2d Sess. 1 (1960); *Sony Corp. of America v. Universal City* Studios, 464 U.S. 417, 465-66 (1984) (Blackmun, J., dissenting).

44. *See* Latman, *supra* note 43, at 24-29 (study prepared for U.S. Copyright Office concerning fair use in U.S. related doctrines abroad). *See* generally Gillian Davies, *Private Copying of Sound and Audio-visual Recordings* (1984) (study of many countries' laws regarding private copying).

45. Thus, there has been much speculation that certain kinds of publishing, particularly of academic journals, will be supplanted by direct communications of scientific articles over the Internet. *See*,

The supplanting of traditional distribution of copyrighted materials by private copying represents the end point on a continuum that has been evolving since the introduction of the photocopier and the audiotape recorder in the 1960s. These technologies first undermined, and then eradicated, the premise underlying private copying exemptions: that private copying would be laborious and economically insignificant.[47] In Europe, the diffusion of these technologies has led legislators to limit the exemption, or, in some cases, to eliminate it altogether.[48]

By contrast, in a U.S. controversy concerning the dissemination of technologies facilitating private copying, the Supreme Court employed both implied license and economic insignificance justifications to create a limited private copying exception. In the *Betamax* case, the Court considered whether 'time-shifting' – videotaping TV programs for deferred viewing and subsequent erasure – by individual VCR owners constituted copyright infringement. The Court held that because the public had been 'invited to witness [the programs in their] entirety free of charge', copying them for time-shifting purposes was a 'fair use' of

---

e.g., Andrew M. Odlyzko, 'Tragic Loss or Good Riddance? The Impending Demise of Traditional Scholarly Journals,' 42 *Notices of the Am. Mathematical Soc'y* 1995, at 49 (arguing that the growth in size of scholarly literature combined with the growth of electronic technology will result in the disappearance of traditional scholarly journals and their replacement by online versions). Thanks to my colleague Gerry Neuman for giving me this article. *See also* Eugene Volokh, 'Cheap Speech and What It Will Do,' 104 *Yale L.J.* 1995, 1805, 1807 ('Control over what is said and heard will shift from intermediaries (..) to speakers and listeners themselves.').

46. *Cf.* Berne Convention for the Protection of Literary and Artistic Works, Sept. 9, 1886, as revised at Paris on July 24, 1971 and amended in 1979, art. 9.2, S. Treaty Doc. No. 99-27, 99th Cong., 2d Sess. 43 (1986) [hereinafter *Berne Convention*] (member countries may 'permit the reproduction of [literary and artistic] works in certain special cases, provided that such reproduction does not conflict with a normal exploitation of the work').

47. *See*, e.g., Copyright Law of 1941, art. 68 (as amended up to July 29, 1981) (Italy), reprinted in 2 *Copyright Laws of the World*, *supra* note 22, Italy: Item 1 at 10 ('The reproduction of single works or of portions of works for the personal use of readers, when made by hand or by a means of reproduction unsuitable for circulating or diffusing the work in public, shall be free.').

48. When the copies generated by these new means of reproduction began to compete with purchases of copies of the works, European legislators permitted private individuals to make copies, but imposed a variety of private copying levies on the machinery and/or media of reproduction, and provided for distribution of the levies to the authors, producers and performers of the musical and audiovisual works captured by audio and video tape recorders. *See*, e.g., An Act Dealing with Copyright and Related Rights, art. 68 (as amended up to March 7, 1990) (Germany), reprinted in 2 *Copyright Laws of the World*, *supra* note 22, Germany: Item 1 at 10-11; Law No. 57-298 on Literary and Artistic Property, art. 40, 41 (as amended up to July 3, 1985) (Fr.), reprinted in 1 *Copyright Laws of the World*, *supra* note 22, France: Item 1 at 7; Law No. 22/1987 on Intellectual Property, art. 25 (Spain), reprinted in 3 *Copyright Laws of the World*, *supra* note 22, Spain: Item 1 at 5-7; Royal Decree No. 287, of March 21, 1989, (Spain), reprinted in 3 *Copyright Laws of the World*, *supra* note 22, Spain: Item 2E at 1 (regulating 'Compensatory Remuneration' for the reproduction for personal use of books, phonograms and videograms by means of non-typographical technical apparatus). Finally, in the case of computer programs, the European Commission's 1991 Directive to harmonize the copyright laws of the European Union's member countries precludes private copying, except for the making of a back-up copy by 'a person having the right to use the computer program (..) insofar as it is necessary for that use.' Council Directive 91/250 of 14 May 1991 on the Legal Protection of Computer Programs, art. 5.2, 1991 O.J. (L 122) 42, 44. Presumably, if the software copyright owner includes a back-up disk in the software package sold, then the user has no right to make her own back up disk.

the copyrighted works.[49] Particularly significant to the Court's analysis was its perception that time-shifting was not likely to have a negative impact on existing or potential markets for the copied work.

Applying the 'Betamax' criteria to online documents, if the document is made freely available for copying in the first place, it is not necessary to inquire whether private copying was fair use: fair use excuses prima facie infringements,[50] and where the copying was permitted, there is not even prima facie infringement. However, if the document is available only through a commercial online service, then the public is not 'invited to [view it] (..) free of charge', and copying it, even temporarily (as in time-shifting) has a much weaker claim to being fair use. This is especially true if, as anticipated, private copying adversely affects the 'potential market for or value of the copyrighted work'.[51]

While the market impact justification for exempting private copying from the scope of an author's exclusive rights may be out of place in cyberspace, a different justification may still apply – impracticality of enforcement. Because the issue of enforcement of rights in cyberspace extends beyond the problem of private copying, however, we will defer that inquiry until we have examined the application of other exclusive rights in cyberspace.

3.2 PUBLIC PERFORMANCE AND DISPLAY RIGHTS

Disseminating works over electronic networks also calls into play the copyright owner's public performance and display rights. The Copyright Act defines a public performance or display to include the following conduct:

> 'to transmit or otherwise communicate a performance or display of the work (..) to the public, by means of any device or process, whether the members of the public capable of receiving the performance or display receive it in the same place or in separate places and at the same time or at different times.'[52]

Thus, if an online reader of our initiating author's collection of variously-ended stories were to forward the collection to a mailing list of mystery lovers, the transmission could be both a public display, and a reproduction. A reproduction would occur in the temporary memories of the recipients (as well, potentially, as in the memories of their e-mail servers[53]). The forwarding to the mailing list would be

49. *Sony Corp. of America v. Universal City Studios, Inc.*, 464 U.S. 417, 449 (1984).

50. *See*, e.g., *Campbell v. Acuff-Rose*, 114 S.Ct. 1164, 1177 (1994) ('fair use is an affirmative defense.'). *See* generally William F. Patry, *The Fair Use Privilege in Copyright Law* 385-402 (1985) (study of history, policy, and implementation of the fair use defense).

51. 17 U.S.C. § 107(4) (1988).

52. 17 U.S.C. § 101. The Act also provides: 'To "transmit" a performance or display is to communicate it by any device or process whereby images or sounds are received beyond the place from which they are sent.' Id.

53. A 'server' is 'a specialized network device of software that provides a service to other devices. The most common services on a LAN are printer servers, file servers and mail servers.' Tom Fahey, *Net. Speak: The Internet Dictionary* 164 (1994). A 'mail server' is 'an application that distributes email items in response to requests.' *Id.* at 119.

a public display by means of transmission if its recipients constituted 'the public'. The Copyright Act does not define 'the public', but it does provide that a work is performed or displayed 'publicly' if it is performed or displayed 'at any place where a substantial number of persons outside a normal circle of a family and its social acquaintances is gathered.'[54] One might therefore inquire if the mailing list comprises 'a substantial number of persons outside of a normal circle of family and its social acquaintances'. Some might contend that in the 'global village' of cyberspace, the entire community of network users – or if not all users, then at least the users of a given bulletin board service – would be considered 'a normal circle of a family and its social acquaintances'. However, even acknowledging that cyberspace can promote a kind of friendship and perhaps even familial feeling among correspondents who do not otherwise know each other, the potential 'circle' of networked acquaintances is too capacious to fit the statutory definition or intent.[55]

Is simply posting a work on a network, without directly sending it to members of the public, also a 'public performance or display'? Once the work is posted, members of the public with access to that network are 'capable of receiving the performance or display (..) in separate places and at the same time or at different times'. While the users will not receive the performance or display until they call the work up, the text of the Copyright Act provides for disjunction in times of receiving the program. Case law involving more rudimentary technologies illustrates the point. In *On Command Video Corp. v. Columbia Pictures Industries*,[56] a federal district court held that a hotel video system through which guests could electronically order the transmission of videocassette motion pictures to the televisions in their rooms 'publicly performed' the movies, even though no film would be sent to more than one room's television at a time. The video service had contended that the serial (rather than simultaneous) nature of the transmissions removed them from the category of public performances. However, the court applied the Copyright Act's definition to hold that the transmissions were made 'to the public' (the hotel's clientele was 'the public') in different places (different rooms) at different times.

There is one difference between transmitting a work via a hotel video system and posting a work in cyberspace. At the hotel, each time a guest ordered a film, the hotel's system sent it directly to the guest; in our hypothetical, the person who posts the material leaves it to the network to send the material on. Thus, the public performance would be directly attributable to the network operator (or bulletin board service) rather than to the individual poster.[57] Nonetheless, one may argue from this decision that placing the material in a system that makes it possible for 'the public' to receive it by deferred transmissions also 'publicly performs or displays' the work, or at least is a contributory infringement of the public

54. *See* 17 U.S.C. § 101.

55. *Cf*. H.R. Rep. No. 1476, *supra* note 15, at 64 ('One of the purposes of the definition [of public performance] was to make clear that (..) performances in "semipublic" places such as clubs, lodges, factories, schools are "public performances" subject to copyright control').

56. 777 F. Supp. 787 (N.D. Cal. 1991).

57. *See*, e.g., *Playboy Enter. v. Frena*, 839 F. Supp. 1552 (M.D. Fla. 1993).

performance or display right.[58] Arguably, the text of the Copyright Act does assume that the performance or display will in fact be received by the members of the public: in the definition of public performance the members of the public 'capable of receiving' the performance do 'receive' it. But the key element would seem to be making the performance available for receipt. For example, even if no viewers tuned in to a particular television broadcast, the unpopular transmission should still be considered a public performance. Similarly, while it is possible (even if unlikely), that no end user would choose to access a work posted on a network, the result should be no different.[59]

3.3 DISTRIBUTION RIGHT

The Copyright Act also grants the author the exclusive right 'to distribute copies (..) of the work to the public by sale or the transfer of ownership (..).'[60] Disseminating a work on a digital network may not only constitute a public performance or display by means of transmission,[61] it might also be considered a distribution of copies, since the network servers and all those who access the work on the network receive 'copies' of the work in their computers.[62] However, while a distributor of 'hard' copies must part with the physical object embodying the copy, a distributor of digital copies may cause new copies to be made in the servers' and recipients' computers, all the while retaining her own copy. As a result, there may be no 'transfer of ownership' of the distributor's copy, and the distribution right, as currently defined, may not be implicated.

The possible lack of fit between the statutory distribution right and digital dissemination may not significantly undermine the author's copyright, so long as digital transmissions can be deemed public performances or displays. Nonetheless, there may be a practical reason to distinguish between digital performances or displays and digital distribution of copies: the author may license (or retain) rights separately. If the only exclusive right pertaining to digital transmissions was the public performance/display right, then the holder of that right could block the holder of the reproduction right from disseminating copies of the work over digital networks.

The Information Infrastructure Task Force, appointed by President Clinton in 1993, has recently issued a report recommending amendment of the Copyright Act to specify an exclusive right to 'distribute copies (..) to the public (..) by transmission'.[63] The Task Force would also supplement the definition of 'transmit'

58. *See*, e.g., *Sega Enter. v. MAPHIA*, 857 F. Supp. 679 (N.D. Cal. 1994). On contributory infringement, *see* discussion *infra* text accompanying notes 77-82.

59. *Cf.* 17 U.S.C. § 101 (Supp. V 1993) (defining 'publication' as including the 'offering to distribute copies or phonorecords to a group of persons for purposes of further distribution, public performance, or public display').

60. 17 U.S.C. §s 106(3) (1988).

61. *See* discussion *supra* text accompanying notes 50-57.

62. *See* discussion *supra* text accompanying note 39.

63. NII White Paper, *supra* note 39, at 213-20, Appendix 1 at 2.

by adding: 'To transmit a reproduction is to distribute it by any device or process whereby a copy or phonorecord of the work is fixed beyond the place from which it was sent.'[64] This definition thus accommodates the distributor's retention of her copy. The Task Force stresses, however, that 'The proposed amendment does not create a new right. It is an express recognition that, as a result of technological developments, the distribution right can be exercised by means of transmission – just as the reproduction, public performance and public display rights may be.'[65]

To the extent that the proposed right of digital distribution simply transposes to computer networks the traditional right to distribute (physical) copies of the work, the White Paper is correct that the right is not 'new'. While the traditional right's subject matter focus on material copies makes little sense in the digital environment, the activity targeted (dissemination) and its result (consumers receiving copies) remain the same. Nonetheless, the proposed right of digital distribution by means of transmission underscores something that is new: because digital communication de-materializes copies, the same act can be analyzed as either (or both) a reproduction or a public performance or display. For example, an act which the user may perceive as a public performance, such as a digital broadcast of a popular song, is also a transmission of copies to the listeners' computers. An act which the user may perceive as reproduction, such as ordering the delivery of a document to her computer's screen and memory, is also a public display by means of transmission. The traditional reproduction/public performance distinction thus becomes increasingly elusive.[66] In the short term, recognizing a right of digital distribution of copies may assist grantees of the reproduction right in resisting the claims of competing of the public performance right. In the long run, however, in the digital world it may make most sense to recharacterize the rights of reproduction, distribution, and public performance or display as facets of a general right of communication of works to the public.[67]

3.4 DERIVATIVE WORKS RIGHT

There is another right in the bundle – the right to prepare derivative works[68] – that might also be at issue in a variety of online circumstances. The Copyright Act defines a derivative work as encompassing any 'form in which a work may be

---

64. *Id.* This definition could apply to transmissions by fax as well. While sending a fax to one person or to a restricted group would not be a transmission of copies 'to the public,' a mass faxing would be.

65. *Id.* at 213-14.

66. The prior version of the NII White Paper, the 'Green Paper,' attempted to maintain the distinction by dividing digital transmissions into those that were primarily public performances, and those that were primarily reproductions. *See Intellectual Property and the National Information Infrastructure*, Preliminary Draft of the Report of the Working Group on Intellectual Property Rights (1994). This attempt provoked widespread criticism, *see* Litman, *supra* note 1, and the NII White Paper abandoned the distinction.

67. *Cf.* Council Directive 93/83, *O.J.* No L 248 of 27 September 1993, 15, art. 1 (2) (right of communication to the public covers public performances, transmissions, and lending of copies).

68. *See* 17 U.S.C. § 106(2) (1988).

recast, transformed or adapted'.[69] The derivative works right thus covers all kinds of adaptations of the work of authorship, including but not limited to sequels, spin-offs, dramatizations and translations. For example, our initiating author would control translation and sequel rights in the collection of variously-ended stories, at least with respect to the beginning of the story. If she is not the holder of exclusive rights in the story endings, she would lack authority either to license or to bring an infringement action against adaptations of that material. On the other hand, adaptations of her contributions to the collection, for example, of her selection, arrangement and editing of the endings, would come within the scope of her derivative works right. Thus, if a third party made a motion picture – or in cyberspace, posted a digital video – based on a sequence of stories drawn from the collection, our initiating author would allege violations of her exclusive rights to prepare derivative works based on the beginning of the story, and based on the sequence (selection and arrangement) set forth in the collection.[70] Similarly, a sound recording of a reading of the stories, possibly together with music or other sound effects, is also a derivative work,[71] and would come within our initiating author's copyright monopoly.

What if third-party entrepreneurs, rather than recording a reading of the stories, which reproduces the literary work onto the audio format, produced a sound recording omitting the stories' words, but supplying appropriate musical and other sound effects, timed to complement the user's own reading of the stories? Or what of illustrations produced to complement the stories? While ventures of these kinds are improbable in an analog world – who would buy a book, separately purchase illustrations, and collate the two? – they may be quite feasible in a digital environment. The user can easily integrate the text and the images and/or the sounds, thus creating her own multimedia 'derivative work' of which the entrepreneurs will have supplied the components, without directly producing the derivative work. One may imagine the development of a substantial market for peripheral works annexed to, or to be used together with, the primary copyrighted work. Does this market come within the copyright owner's control?

Where the third-party work 'goes with' but does not itself reproduce or alter the copyrighted work, no rights under copyright are implicated, despite the economic dependence of the peripheral work on the primary work.[72] In our hypothetical, however, the user puts the two (or more) works together to create a

---

69. 17 U.S.C. § 101.

70. *See* discussion *supra* text accompanying notes 29-34.

71. *See* 17 U.S.C. § 101 (1988).

72. *See*, e.g., H.R. Rep. No. 1476, *supra* note 15, at 62 ('To constitute a violation of section 106(2), the infringing work must incorporate a portion of the copyrighted work in some form; for example, a detailed commentary on a work or a programmatic musical composition inspired by a novel would not normally constitute infringements under this clause.') But see *Worlds of Wonder, Inc. v. Vector Intercontinental, Inc.*, 653 F. Supp. 135 (N.D. Ohio 1986) (independently produced audiotapes to be played inside 'Teddy Ruxpin' dolls held to violate derivative works right in the dolls); *Worlds of Wonder, Inc. v. Veritel Learning Sys.*, 658 F. Supp. 351 (N.D. Tex. 1986) (same); but cf. *Addison-Wesley Publishing Co. v. Brown*, 223 F. Supp. 219 (E.D.N.Y. 1963) (answer key to questions in high school physics textbook held to infringe copyright in the textbook).

new derivative work. The case law addressing this kind of situation is not plentiful, but it is divided. The two relevant cases both involved additions to video games. In one case, the Seventh Circuit held that the sale of a 'Promblaster' circuit board designed to enable the consumer to speed up the action of plaintiff's games yielded unauthorized adaptations of the games and thus violated the derivative works right.[73] However, the Ninth Circuit held that the sale of 'Game Genie' video game 'enhancers' that altered the action of Nintendo video game characters did not create unauthorized derivative works.[74] The Ninth Circuit's holding turned on its determination that the altered game had no 'form' because the Game Genie could not itself produce an audiovisual display: the display resulted from the interaction of the Game Genie and the Nintendo video game cartridge.[75] This formalistic conclusion is probably erroneous: in determining if the altered presentation is a derivative work, it should not matter whether the presentation resides in a particular piece of hardware. The point is that the interaction of the machines produces a variation of the game.[76] Under the Ninth Circuit approach, disseminating peripherals for users to combine with copyrighted works would not infringe, while the result under the Seventh Circuit's analysis portends less well for third-party entrepreneurs.

There is another approach to the problem of peripheral works designed to permit the end user to create her own unauthorized derivative work. Dissemination of the peripheral works could be contributory infringement: 'One who, with knowledge of the infringing activity, induces, causes, or materially contributes to the infringing conduct of another, may be held liable as a 'contributory infringer'.[77] Is the end user's creation of an unauthorized derivative work 'infringing conduct'? Under the analysis set out earlier,[78] just as 'private' copying should not (or should no longer) escape characterization as infringement merely because the copyist is an end user, so 'private' adaptations should not enjoy automatic exemptions from liability.

One might object that this analysis is inconsistent with the Supreme Court's determination in the 'Betamax' case.[79] There, the Court held that the dissemination of a product (video recording equipment) that can be used for infringing purposes is not contributory infringement if the product is also 'widely used for legitimate, unobjectionable purposes. Indeed, it need merely be capable of substantial non-infringing uses'.[80] In that case, the 'substantial non-infringing use' was 'time-

73. See *Midway Mfg. Co. v. Artic Int'l.*, 704 F.2d 1009 (7th Cir.), cert. denied, 464 U.S. 823 (1983).

74. See *Lewis Galoob Toys v. Nintendo of Am.*, 964 F.2d 965 (9th Cir. 1992), cert. denied, 113 S. Ct. 1582 (1993).

75. *Id.* at 968.

76. *Cf.* H.R. Rep. No. 1476, *supra* note 72, at 62 (derivative works right is 'broader than' the reproduction right 'in the sense that reproduction requires fixation in copies or phonorecords, whereas the preparation of a derivative work, such as a ballet, pantomime, or improvised performance, may be an infringement even though nothing is ever fixed in tangible form').

77. *Gershwin Publishing Corp. v. Columbia Artists Mgmt.*, 443 F.2d 1159, 1162 (2d Cir. 1971); *see* also *Demetriades v. Kaufman*, 690 F. Supp. 289 (S.D.N.Y. 1988).

78. *See* discussion *supra* text accompanying notes 43-51.

79. *Sony Corp. of Am. v. Universal City Studios*, 464 U.S. 417 (1984).

80. *Id.* at 442.

shifting' of 'free' broadcast television programs.[81] The majority opinion did not explicitly address whether 'librarying' the copy would also be fair use, but the emphasis of its analysis was on the temporary nature of the copy.[82]

Here we are positing that the peripheral work has no substantial use other than in connection with the targeted copyrighted work. Whether that use is non-infringing may turn on two factual questions. First, was access to the copyrighted work 'free', or did the author or proprietor impose conditions of payment and/or limitations on usage as part of the work's dissemination? Second, analogizing to the 'time-shifting'/'librarying' distinction, is the user making a one time derivative work in her computer's temporary memory, so that the adaptation will vanish when she turns the computer off, or has she instead retained a copy of the do-it-yourself adaptation?[83]

These conditions should be cumulative. If the work is not 'free', or if the copyright owner has made the work available subject to the limitation that users shall not make even temporary adaptations of the work, then the 'time-shifting' should not suffice to exculpate the adaptation. Even if access to the work is 'free', the creation of multiple (across the universe of 'private' adapters) permanent adaptations interferes with the copyright owner's exercise of her 'exclusive' right to prepare derivative works (although the copyright owner may certainly disclaim that right when she makes copies available for free).

Thus, to return to the Game Genie, even if its producer was not a direct infringer, distribution of a device whose sole purpose was to alter the action of the Nintendo games should have made the producer a contributory infringer. Nintendo did not distribute its game cartridges for free, and for present purposes we may assume that if Nintendo distributed games online, it would not do so without placing payment and use restrictions on that distribution. Because access to the games is subject to charges and restrictions, 'time-shifting' should not be a defence.

One might object that if all the copyright owner need do to insulate itself from a fair use defence is to make clear that it is reserving all rights to make derivative works, then the fair use defence becomes meaningless. After all, the fair use defence trumps the copyright owner's claims to exclusive rights, when the balance between the copyright owner's interest in compensation and control and the public's interest in access to works of authorship tips in the public's favour. Nonetheless, in this instance, the making of even temporary adaptations could have a more severe economic impact in cyberspace than in the analog world. Indeed, the Game Genie example illustrates how 'time-shifting' may adversely affect the copyright owner's market for derivative works. In cyberspace it may be very easy

81. *Id.*

82. *See id.* at 451-55. By contrast, Justice Blackmun's dissenting opinion examined both 'time-shifting' and 'library-building,' and contended that neither was fair use. *Id.* at 483-84 (Blackmun, J., dissenting).

83. *Cf.* 17 U.S.C. § 117 (1988) (permitting owners of copies of computer programs to make copies or adaptations of the program, provided 'that such a new copy or adaptation is created as an essential step in the utilization of the computer program in conjunction with a machine and that it is used in no other manner').

for consumers to assemble derivative works from the elements available online. If so, there may be no need to keep a copy of the adaptation; rather, the user may simply recreate it each time she goes online. Indeed, for products like the Game Genie, the latter course may be preferable, because each time the user accesses the Game Genie or similar program, she may create a different alteration to the underlying game. In that case, there may be a third category of conduct – repeated time-shifting of the same material – whose economic impact may be the same as librarying.[84]

In sum, the derivative works rights of the author of a work created or posted in cyberspace should extend in principle to third parties' dissemination not only of fully realized adaptations, but also of work-specific components designed for users' incorporation with the underlying work. There are important corollaries to this principle. First, the third-party creator of a general purpose work, such as a translation program or a graphics program, should not be liable to the author of the underlying work if users employ these tools. A general purpose third-party work lends itself to too many 'substantial non-infringing uses'[85] to justify liability for contributory infringement. Thus, for example, the purveyor of the graphics program should incur no liability if a reader of our initiating author's collection of variously-ended stories downloaded the work and added images generated with the aid of the program.

Second, the end user's liability for direct infringement of the derivative works right would turn on fair use considerations. If the user has created an unauthorized derivative work, there is a prima facie violation of the author's exclusive rights. The fair use doctrine would excuse this violation if, most importantly, the creation of the derivative work threatened no significant economic consequences to the underlying work.[86] Evaluation of economic impact may turn on whether or not the user further disseminates the unauthorized derivative work. Thus, for example, if a user of our hypothetical story collection translated the work into Portuguese for his private enjoyment and edification, no infringement should be found. If, however, the user instead posted the translation to a generally accessible bulletin board, then infringement should be found.[87]

We have seen the contexts in which the reproduction, public performance and display, and derivative works rights can apply to cyberspace. But we have not yet explored how our initiating author will be able to enforce those rights. If indeed the

84. *Cf. Sony*, 464 U.S. at 485-86 (Blackmun, J., dissenting) (discussing the economic impact of 'time-shifting').

85. *See id.* at 442.

86. See *Harper & Row Publishers v. Nation Enters.*, 471 U.S. 539, 566 (1985) (fourth fair use factor, potential economic harm, is 'undoubtedly the single most important element').

87. If the user posts the translation to a few friends or to a small online Portuguese-language reading group, the fair use inquiry becomes more difficult. Arguably, the dissemination of the translation would remain sufficiently discrete to warrant application of the fair use exception. However, once the translation is posted in cyberspace, its proclivity to further dissemination may be too great to ignore its potential economic impact. *Cf.* text accompanying *supra* notes 52-59, on 'public' performances in cyberspace. For a discussion of whether the bulletin board or online service that carries the translation should also be liable, *see infra* text accompanying notes 104-113.

predominant exploitation of online works will be by the end users, how can a copyright owner police her rights?

4. Enforcement of Copyright in Cyberspace

Copyright owners have traditionally avoided targeting end users of copyrighted works. This is in part because pursuing the ultimate consumer is costly and unpopular. But the primary reason had been because end users did not copy works of authorship – or if they did copy, the reproduction was insignificant and rarely the subject of widespread further dissemination. Rather, the entities creating and disseminating copies (or public performances or displays) were intermediaries between the creators and the consumers: for example, publishers, motion picture producers, and producers of phonograms. Infringements, rather than being spread throughout the user population, were concentrated higher up the chain of distribution of works. Pursuing the intermediary therefore offered the most effective way to enforce copyright interests. By contrast, in cyberspace individuals will often commit the unauthorized acts, both for private consumption and for further dissemination to other individuals. Can there be meaningful, and palatable, copyright enforcement against individuals? Alternatively, will there still be intermediaries worth pursuing?

Some of the hypotheticals we have examined retained the presence of intermediaries – such as producers of components destined for consumer incorporation into derivative works – whom the copyright owner can locate and pursue in much the same way as copyright owners pursue unauthorized exploiters in the analog world. There are also other instances in which intermediaries persist, facilitating copyright enforcement. Most notably, authors and other copyright owners may be able to work with commercial online services to control the gate between author and public. The author, through the service, can impose contractual access and payment conditions on subscribers; the service may also implement technological impediments to unauthorized copying or redistribution.[88]

But if a work is disseminated without authorization on an unpoliced bulletin board or network, or if an online service declines to assume responsibility for monitoring what is placed on its network, the task of the copyright owner to discover and combat infringements seems overwhelming. Two complementary approaches may alleviate this problem. First, authors may form, or seek the assistance of already formed, collective licensing societies. Second, bulletin board operators and online services may be held directly or vicariously liable for the unauthorized dissemination of copyrighted works.

88. *See*, e.g., Karen Rodriguez, 'Vendors Rally to Secure Internet; Encryption-Based Systems Readied,' *InfoWorld*, Jan. 30, 1995, at 14; General Terms and Conditions for the Use of LEXIS-NEXIS Services (May 1, 1995); WESTLAW Subscriber Agreement (Aug. 1, 1995).

4.1 COLLECTIVE LICENSING

Two principal characteristics of the market for works in cyberspace make enforcement daunting: users are extremely numerous, and they are widely dispersed.[89] Nonetheless, this situation has low tech analogies. A similar problem has existed since the mid-nineteenth century with respect to the public performance of musical works. No one composer or publisher can find and license (or, failing a license, sue) every commercial music user, from restaurants, to retail establishments, to clubs, to concert halls, to broadcasters, etc. But the composers and publishers can pool their copyrights for collective licensing, and delegate the policing function to the collective licensing organization. Users get the right to perform all the music covered by the blanket license, and the authors and copyright owners create an organization with the resources needed to enforce the performance rights against uncooperative users.[90]

The music performance rights collectives are private law creations in the U.S. and, for the most part, abroad.[91] The rights holders have chosen to form the collectives; no composer or publisher is legally obligated to join them. But not all copyright sectors have formed collectives as pervasively or as willingly, despite the compelling economic incentives for doing so. In the U.S., the copyright owners of literary works, for example, have traditionally been reluctant to give up control over rights and permissions to copy in favour of collective licensing of photocopy rights.[92] Nonetheless, judicial and legislative activity in the U.S. and abroad point toward (or mandate) greater inclusion of literary works in the collective licensing repertory.[93]

For example, in a U.S. decision of primary importance both for its determination of copyright liability for photocopying and for its endorsement of collective licensing, the Second Circuit recently ruled that Texaco violated the

89. In addition, piratical users may be difficult to identify if they operate anonymously or under a pseudonym.

90. On collective licensing, particularly as practiced by the music performing rights organizations, *see* generally Stanley M. Besen & Sheila N. Kirby, *Compensating Creators of Intellectual Property: Collectives That Collect* (1989) (examining the role of performance and reproduction rights, organizations in the United States and other developed countries when 'decentralized use makes individual enforcement of (..) property rights uneconomic.'); *The Collective Administration of Copyright* (Canadian Conference on the Arts, et al., eds., 1995) (proceedings of a colloquium held October 31, 1994); Bernard Korman & I. Fred Koenigsberg, 'Performing Rights in Music and Performing Rights Societies,' 33 *J. Copyright Soc'y* 1986, 332, 348 (reviewing the 'development of the performing right in music and the operation of ASCAP, the oldest and largest performing rights society in the United States.').

91. *See* generally Besen & Kirby, *supra* note 90, at 15-44 (surveying domestic and foreign performance rights collectives).

92. *See* generally Besen & Kirby, *supra* note 90, at 45-63 (discussing reproductive rights organizations); Ferdinand Melichar, 'Collective Administration of Electronic Rights – A Realistic Option?,' elsewhere in this book, 147-152.

93. For an argument that collective licensing should become the predominant form of compensation for authors of works of visual art (and, by implication, for copyright owners in general) *see* Marci A. Hamilton, 'Appropriation Art and the Imminent Decline in Authorial Control Over Copyrighted Works,' 42 *J. Copyright Soc'y* 1994, 93, 115-25.

copyright in the *Journal of Catalysis* when one of its research scientists made and retained copies of articles from the journal.[94] The court rejected Texaco's fair use defence, holding (inter alia) that the copying diverted the market for the journal because the copyright owner could have licensed photocopying rights to Texaco. Acquiring a license would have been 'administratively tolerable'[95] for Texaco, because the plaintiff publisher had made its works available for licensing through the Copyright Clearance Center, a photocopy rights collective that represents scientific and technical journal publishers. The Second Circuit suggested that the fair use analysis might be different if the copyright owner were not making its works available for licensing.[96] In that event, indicated the court, it might even be appropriate for the court to impose a license that would compensate the copyright owner for the copying, but that would enable the defendant to make the copies without obtaining consent.[97]

As a result, *Texaco* makes user friendly licensing both a carrot and a stick for copyright owners. If the copyright owner can offer the user a collective or other administratively tolerable form of license,[98] then fair use claims whose primary justifications are burdensomeness or lack of economic impact on copyright exploitation may well be foreclosed.[99] On the other hand, if copyright owners do not facilitate licensing, then a court may step in and in effect grant the license anyway – on terms that the copyright owner will not have set. This result compromises copyright owners' rights to decide whether and to whom to license

94. See *American Geophysical Union v. Texaco Inc.*, 60 F.3d 913 (2d. Cir. 1994). The claim against Texaco involved systematic copying by hundreds of research scientists, but, for purposes of ruling on the fair use defense, the parties agreed to limit the record to one scientist's copying. *See id.* at 915.

95. *American Geophysical Union v. Texaco Inc.*, 802 F. Supp. 1, 25 (S.D.N.Y. 1993) (Leval, J.), aff'd, 37 F.3d 881 (2d Cir. 1994), order amended and superseded, 60 F.3d 913 (2d Cir. 1995).

96. *American Geophysical*, 60 F.3d at 931.

97. *Id.* at 932 n.19, citing *Campbell v. Acuff-Rose Music*, 114 S. Ct. 1164, 1171 n.10 (1994) (indicating that injunctive relief for copyright infringement may not always be appropriate, and that a continuing award of damages may in some circumstances best accommodate the rights of the copyright holder and the public's interest in access to unauthorized transformations of the plaintiff's work).

98. For example, the Copyright Office is currently enhancing its online database of copyright registrations to include information about obtaining licenses. The Copyright Office's project envisions an online clearance procedure that would make it possible for users to ascertain the status and ownership of a work, to obtain permission, and to pay for the use, all at the push of a few buttons. *See*, e.g., U.S. Copyright Office, Copyright Office Electronic Registration Recordation & Deposit System (1995); Guy Lamolinara, 'Copyright in the Digital Age: CORDS Project to Make Registration Verification Easier,' 54 *Library of Congress Information Bulletin* 1995, 267, 267; Eric Schwartz, The Herbert Tenzer Memorial Conference: 'Copyright in the Twenty-First Century: The Role of the Copyright Office in the Age of Information,' 13 *Cardozo Arts & Ent. L.J.* 1994, 64. *See also* NII White Paper, *supra* note 39, at 191-94, 235-36 (recommending measure to promote 'Copyright Management Information').

99. Market failure is not the only justification for fair use claims. In some cases, even if the copyright owner could license the use, copyright policy favors freeing the use from the copyright owner's control. Criticism and parody are leading examples of these kinds of uses: we would not want to limit the available commentary on works of authorship to authorized book reviews and licensed parodies. An authorized book review would be even more suspect than an authorized biography, and a licensed parody seems an oxymoron.

reproduction rights, but less so than would application of the fair use exception, which would deprive the copyright owner of both control and compensation.[100]

Some foreign jurisdictions have adopted stronger measures to promote collective licensing. In the Nordic countries, the 'extended collective license' provisions of the copyright laws force holdout publishers into the reproduction rights collective once a 'substantial portion' of national authors or publishers within a particular field have joined the collective licensing organization.[101] In France, a law promulgated in January 1995 provides that 'publication of a work entails the transfer of the right to reproduce by photocopying to [an approved collective licensing] society. Only approved societies may contract with users for the purpose of managing the right thus transferred (..).'[102] Thus, copyright holders covered by these laws have no choice but to cede photocopying rights to collectives that will grant blanket licenses covering the repertoire. In return, the copyright owners will be compensated according to the particular country's licensing fee formula.[103]

How would these models apply in cyberspace? A collective could assume (or at least assist in discharging) the burden of monitoring electronic bulletin boards and networks to discover unauthorized postings of its members' works. The burden would be substantial, however, since the content of cyberspace changes by the second, and new unlicensed postings will inevitably follow hard upon each perusal.

Even were monitoring feasible, whom would the collectives license? Despite the collectives' strength and resources, it could still be impractical to seek out and contract with individual users (or to pursue them, except perhaps on an occasional *in terrorem* basis). Rather, the likely targets of licensing and of infringement suits will be the persons or entities who make available and control the electronic fora for communication of unauthorized copies, displays, or derivative works: that is, the bulletin board services and the network operators.

---

100. The Copyright Clearance Center and the Folio Corporation have announced their intention to form an alliance to promote wide scale electronic clearance, billing, and distribution systems for local and wide-area digital networks (including Internet). See *Folio Corp. & Copyright Clearance Ctr.*, Press Release, Mar. 6, 1995 (on file with the Columbia Law Review).

101. See generally Gunnar Karnell, 'Extended Collective License Clauses and Agreements in Nordic Copyright Law,' 10 *Colum.-VLA J.L. & Arts* 1985, 73 (describing the extent and functioning of extended collective license systems in the Nordic countries).

102. Loi no. 95-4 du 3 janvier 1995 complétant le code de la propriété intellectuelle et relative à la gestion collective du droit de reproduction par reprographie, *Journal Officiel de la Republique Francaise*, 120 (Jan. 4, 1995) (Fr.) (adding a new art. L. 122-10 to the Code of Intellectual Property).

103. *See* generally Jane C. Ginsburg, 'Reproduction of Protected Works for University Research or Teaching,' 39 *J. Copyright Soc.* 1992, 181, 192-98 (discussing legal licensing regimes in foreign countries) and works cited therein. The fuller development of licensing collectives abroad may be due to a variety of additional factors as well. First, such collectives have existed for a longer time in other countries. Second, there may be fewer antitrust constraints on the price fixing that collective licensing often implies. Third, in many countries the government promotes or supervises collective licensing organizations. *See* generally, Besen & Kirby, *supra* note 90 (discussing copyright collectives throughout world).

4.2 LIABILITY OF ON-LINE SERVICES FOR COPYRIGHT INFRINGEMENT

The liability of online services for copyright infringements committed on 'their' networks or bulletin boards sparks much controversy – at least from the point of view of the service providers, who do not wish to bear the burden of monitoring the copyright compliance of their subscribers.[104] After all, in many cases, the services did not initiate the unauthorized copying or communication; they simply provided the means by which another party could disseminate the infringement to the public. However, the principle that parties who provide the fora of communication of infringement are also liable for copyright infringement is not new to copyright law. In fact, it is the cornerstone of many of the collective licensing and copyright enforcement activities of societies such as ASCAP and BMI (and their foreign analogues). ASCAP, the American Society of Composers Authors and Publishers, and BMI, Broadcast Music Inc., license their members' public performance rights, and initiate suits against users who decline to take the licenses. For example, the music performance rights societies license the venues in which live music is played (such as concert halls, jazz clubs, bars with live bands, etc.); they do not license the musicians.[105] The courts have confirmed the liability of the owners or managers of the restaurants and similar places that engage the performers of the music.[106]

Moreover, while restaurants that hire musicians to entertain the diners might be considered the employers of the performers, the doctrine of vicarious liability in copyright law extends beyond the master-servant relationship. As the Second Circuit held in 1963:

> 'When the right and ability to supervise coalesce with an obvious and direct financial interest in the exploitation of copyrighted materials – even in the absence of actual knowledge that the copyright monopoly is being impaired – the

104. On copyright liability for bulletin boards and online services, *see* generally NII White Paper, *supra* note 39, at 114-24 (reviewing current status of online service provider liability, and recommending against a diminution of the services' liability); Charles Cangialosi, 'The Electronic Underground: Computer Piracy and Electronic Bulletin Boards,' 15 *Rutgers Computer & Tech. L.J.* 1989, 265 (examining bulletin board services systems operator's liability for copyright infringement); Hardy, *supra* note 1; Loundy, *supra* note 1 (discussing legal issues related to copyright and computer information systems in cyberspace); Jonathan Gilber, Note, 'Computer Bulletin Board Operator Liability for User Misuse,' 54 *Fordham L. Rev.* 1985, 439 (proposing deterrent and mitigation measures against illegal bulletin board use). On the related topic of liability of online services for defamation committed by subscribers, compare *Cubby, Inc. v. CompuServe*, 776 F. Supp. 135 (S.D.N.Y. 1991) (declining to hold service liable for subscribers' online defamatory statements) with *Stratton Oakmont Inc. v. Prodigy Servs. Co.*, No. 31063/94, 1995 N.Y. Misc. LEXIS 229, at *6 (Sup. Ct. May 24, 1995) (holding service liable because Prodigy exercises some degree of control over the content of postings to its network).

105. *See*, e.g., Korman & Koenigsberg, *supra* note 90, at 358-59.

106. *See*, e.g., *Herbert v. Shanley Co.*, 242 U.S. 591 (1917) (Holmes, J.) (orchestra performing popular songs in restaurant); see also *Polygram Int'l Publishing v. Nevada/TIG, Inc.* 855 F. Supp. 1314, 1324 (D. Mass. 1994) (Keeton, J.) (distinguishing direct liability of performer from vicarious or contributory liability of party hiring the performer).

purposes of copyright law may be best effectuated by the imposition of liability upon the beneficiary of that exploitation.'[107]

Economic policy considerations supply the rationale for the doctrine of vicarious liability in copyright: the party having the 'right and ability to supervise' is best situated to pay for – or better, to prevent – infringement. Judge Keeton has recently elaborated the point:

> 'The enterprise and the person profiting from it are better able than either the innocent injured plaintiff or the person whose act caused the loss to distribute the costs and to shift them to others who have profited from the enterprise. In addition, placing responsibility for the loss on the enterprise has the added benefit of creating a greater incentive for the enterprise to police its operations carefully to avoid unnecessary losses.'[108]

Where a commercial online service is concerned, the 'direct financial interest' test should be satisfied. This is particularly clear if the service is set up as a forum for the communication and exchange of copyrighted material. But even where the transmission of copyrighted works is incidental to the service, the standard may continue to apply, especially if the availability of copyrighted works on the network enhances the service's appeal to potential subscribers.[109] On the other hand, under this standard, it is less likely that the operator of a non-profit bulletin board or network would face similar liability for its users' piracy. As for the 'right and ability to supervise' component, the nature of the digital communications forum may also be significant. While some fora appear to be rather anarchic,[110]

---

107. *Shapiro, Bernstein & Co. v. H.L. Green Co.*, 316 F.2d 304, 307 (2d Cir. 1963) (liability of a department store – that had not obtained a music performance right license – for violation of the public performance right when one of its concessioners played a phonograph record of the plaintiff's music).

108. *Polygram*, 855 F. Supp. at 1325 (liability of organizer of a computer software trade show – who had declined to take an ASCAP license, when exhibitors at the show were alleged to have performed copyrighted music at their booths). But see *Artists Music, Inc. v. Reed Publishing*, 31 U.S.P.Q.2d (BNA) 1623 (S.D.N.Y. 1994) (refusing to find trade show organizers liable for some exhibitors' unlicensed public performance of copyrighted music); *Fonovisa, Inc. v. Cherry Auction, Inc.*, 847 F. Supp. 1492 (E.D. Cal. 1994) (no liability for organizer of swap meet who rented booths to vendors at counterfeit audiotapes). In both cases, the courts found the defendants lacked the power to supervise and control the exhibitors' activities. The NII White Paper's analysis resembles Judge Keeton's: 'On-line service providers have a business relationship with their subscribers. They – and, perhaps, only they – are in the position to know the identity and activities of their subscribers and to stop unlawful activities (..). They are in a better position to prevent or stop infringement than the copyright owner. Between these two relatively innocent parties, the best policy is to hold the service provider liable.' NII White Paper, *supra* note 39, at 117.

109. For example, in *Polygram*, 855 F. Supp. 1314, the exhibitors were not performing the music in order to sell recordings (as was the case in *H.L. Green*), but in order to attract customers to their booths, where they sold computer software and related goods.

110. *See*, e.g., John P. Barlow, 'The Economy of Ideas: A Framework for Rethinking Patents & Copyrights in the Digital Age (Everything You Know About Intellectual Property is Wrong),' *Wired*, Mar. 1994, at 85-86 (describing present and future dilemma imposed by the "unbounded and perhaps permanently lawless waves of cyberspace"). Under this analysis, the universities and government agencies whose servers form the bulk of the Internet, a noncommercial, unmonitored

others are more closely controlled, at least with regard to some elements of their content, such as pornography and obscene, or even merely disrespectful, language.[111]

Finally, entrepreneurs may incur direct, as well as vicarious, liability. As a result of the technology of communication on digital networks (at least for now), the online service or bulletin board is itself engaging in acts of copyright exploitation. When a user posts a work on the bulletin board, a 'copy' of the work is made in the service's server.[112] When the work is communicated to subscribers, it is 'publicly displayed' on their screens.[113]

4.3 INTERNATIONAL CONSIDERATIONS

Finally, the ubiquitous nature of online delivery requires consideration of multinational enforcement. This raises international conflict of laws questions. In principle, there is no such thing as 'international copyright'; instead, there is a

series of networks, would not be vicariously liable for infringements transmitted on the Internet. On the other hand, commercial services offering connections to the Internet could be vicariously liable if an infringing communication to the Internet originated with a subscriber to the commercial service.

111. *See*, e.g., America Online, Terms of Service, §§ 1.3, 2.5, 4.2, 8.2, available in America Online, 'Member's Services' Area, 'Members' Online Support' Department (stating that members agree to a code of conduct and America Online can restrict their transmissions or expel them if code is violated); Geoffrey Moore, 'The First Amendment is Safe at Prodigy,' *N.Y. Times*, Dec. 16, 1990, 3, at 13 (explaining why Prodigy should and does edit the contents of its electronic bulletin board); Matthew L. Would, 'A Child's Internet Sins Visited on the Parent,' *N.Y. Times*, Feb. 26, 1995, 4, at 2 (describing instance in which adults were kicked off America Online after their children committed 'infractions'); cf. *Stratton Oakmont Inc. v. Prodigy Servs. Inc.*, No. 31063/94, 1995 N.Y. Misc. LEXIS 229, at 6 (Sup. Ct. May 24, 1995) (online provider's exercise of control over network justified liability for user's defamatory statements).

112. *See* discussion *supra* text accompanying notes 40-41.

113. *See* discussion *supra* text accompanying notes 54-59. In addition, were the Copyright Act amendments recommended by the NII White Paper to be enacted, communication to subscribers would also be a 'transmission of copies' subject to the § 106(3) distribution right. *See* NII White Paper, *supra* note 39, at 213-20, Appendix 1, at 2. Bills currently pending in both Houses of Congress adopt the White Paper's proposals. *See* S. 1284, 104th Cong. 1st Sess., 141 Cong. Rec. S 14550, Sept. 28, 1995; H.R. 2114, 104th Cong. 1st Sess., 141 Cong. Rec. H 9737, Sept. 29, 1995. There have been two decisions concerning bulletin board services' liability for copying and disseminating protected material. In both instances, the courts held the services directly liable for copyright infringement. In *Playboy Enters. v. Frena*, 839 F. Supp. 1552, 1555-59 (M.D. Fla. 1993), a federal district court sustained an infringement claim against a bulletin board service when one of its subscribers systematically scanned and uploaded Playboy centerfolds. In *Sega Enters. v. MAPHIA*, 30 U.S.P.Q.2d (BNA) 1921 (N.D. Cal. 1994), the service itself was directly encouraging its subscribers' unlicensed posting of copies of videogames. A pending action, *Frank Music v. CompuServe*, No. 93 Civ. 8153 (S.D.N.Y. Nov. 29, 1993), may afford greater guidance on the application of vicarious liability to a network operator who claims that its role in the communication of infringing materials on a bulletin board was too passive to give rise to liability for any kind of copyright infringement. The NII White Paper cites another claim pending against a Bulletin Board operator and an Internet access provider, *Religious Technology Center v. NETCOM*, No. C95-20091 (N.D. Cal.) (verified first amended complaint filed Mar. 3, 1995). NII White Paper, *supra* note 39, at 121-22 & n.391.

multiplicity of national copyright regimes.[114] However, the Berne and Universal Copyright Conventions and the TRIPs accord impose certain substantive minimum standards to which member countries must conform their domestic copyright laws (at least with respect to protection of foreign copyright owners).[115] These treaties also link the member countries through imposition of the non-discrimination rule of national treatment, which requires member countries to treat works from other member countries as if they were local works.[116]

The assimilation of foreigners to domestic copyright owners confirms the territorial character of international copyright. An author and international copyright owner possesses no extra-conventional supra-national rights; she is instead, and at once, the proprietor of a French copyright, a U.S. copyright, a Mexican copyright, a Japanese copyright, and so on. Thus, unauthorized copying of the author's work in each of these countries would give rise to an action for the violation of the local copyright law. Distribution of copies of an infringing work would be judged under the copyright laws of each country where copies were disseminated. Similarly, unauthorized public performance of a song on the radio would be analyzed under the laws of each country receiving the broadcast.

This approach may pose problems in cyberspace. Suppose, for example, that a hacker in Thailand had gained access to and copied the entirety of our initiating author's collection of variously-ended stories, and had posted it on 'Cyberworld', a (hypothetical) Canadian-headquartered commercial service. True to its name, Cyberworld can be accessed from anywhere in the world, and subscribers in France, Mexico, China and the United States do indeed download the collection. We will further assume that it is not worthwhile to pursue the individual international downloaders. If our author sues Cyberworld in the U.S., application of the principle of territoriality would mean that the forum would be obliged to apply scores of foreign laws, in addition to its own copyright law.[117] Such an exercise could prove daunting, particularly if the applicable laws differ significantly. Substantive differences between potentially applicable national laws

---

114. *See* Jon A. Baumgarten, 'Primer on the Principles of International Copyright,' in *Fourth Annual U.S. Copyright Office Speaks: Contemporary Copyright and Intellectual Property Issues* 470, 471 (1992) ('The term "international copyright" is something of a misnomer, for neither a single code governing copyright protection across national borders, nor a unitary multi-national property right, exists. What does exist is a complex of copyright *relations* among sovereign states, each having its own copyright law applicable to acts within its territory.').

115. *See* Berne Convention, *supra* note 46, arts. 5, 6*bis*, S. Treaty Doc. No. 99-27, at 41; Universal Copyright Convention, July 24, 1971, arts. 1-7, 25 U.S.T. 1341, 1344-63, 943 U.N.T.S. 177-78, 195-203; Agreement on Trade-Related Aspects of Intellectual Property Rights Including Trade in Counterfeit Goods, Dec. 15, 1993, arts. 9-14, 33 *I.L.M.* 1994, at 83.

116. *See* Berne Convention, *supra* note 46, art. 5(2), S. Treaty Doc. No. 99-27, at 40; Universal Copyright Convention, *supra* note 94, art. II; *see* also Sam Ricketson, *The Berne Convention for the Protection of Literary and Artistic Works: 1886-1986*, §§ 5.51-5.68 (1987) (demonstrating the scope and evolution of the principle of national treatment).

117. The NII White Paper confirms the application of U.S. law to the unauthorized dissemination of copies in the U.S. by recommending that the Copyright Act's importation provision be amended to specify that unauthorized transmission of copies into the U.S. violates the copyright owner's exclusive rights. *See* NII White Paper, *supra* note 39, at 107-109, 221. *See also* S. 1284, 104th Cong. 1st Sess., 141 Cong. Rec. S 14550, Sept. 28, 1995.

are likely to occur in many of the areas this Article has considered, including ownership of copyright interests in the work, existence and scope of exclusive rights in the work,[118] and existence and scope of liability of online services for either direct or indirect infringements.[119]

In the U.S., some courts have simplified the choice of law problem by applying U.S. law to the entirety of a multinational infringement claim when the root act of copying occurred in the U.S.[120] From this viewpoint, the extraterritorial infringements are all the direct consequences of a local U.S. infringement. Where, as in the hypothetical, however, the extraterritorial infringements cannot be rooted in a U.S. violation of copyright, U.S. law might not apply to allegedly infringing acts occurring beyond U.S. borders. Thus, the Ninth Circuit, having determined that a defendant's mere 'authorization' in the U.S. to reproduce copies without the copyright owner's permission was not itself a violation of U.S. copyright law, further held that the making of the reproductions abroad similarly did not infringe the U.S. copyright.[121]

As a middle ground, U.S. copyright law might apply to unauthorized reproductions occurring abroad if U.S. shores appear designed to be the ultimate destination of the foreign-made copies.[122] In practice, however, the middle ground may vastly expand: since cyberspace reaches every place, copyright infringements will almost inevitably come to U.S. shores, no matter what the point of origin of the communication, or whom the initial intended audience. The person or entity posting a work on a digital network in effect knows, or should know, that the U.S. will be a likely destination for the work. It may therefore be appropriate to distinguish between transmissions targeting U.S. recipients, and those for which the U.S. is an incidental stop in the stream of cyberspace.[123]

---

118. Moreover, in many foreign countries, authors' exclusive rights include not only economic rights, but the "moral rights" to preserve the integrity of the work and receive authorship credit for the work. *See*, e.g., Berne Convention, *supra* note 46, art. 6 *bis*, S. Treaty Doc. No. 99-27, at 41; Law No. 57-298 on Literary and Artistic Property, art. L. 121-1 (Fr.).

119. For a fuller discussion of these problems, *see* Jane C. Ginsburg, 'Global Use/Territorial Rights: Private International Law Questions of the Global Information Infrastructure,' 42 *J. Copyright Soc'y* 1995, at 318.

120. See *Update Art v. Modiin Publishing*, 843 F.2d 67, 72-73 (2d Cir. 1988).

121. See *Subafilms, Ltd. v. MGM-Pathe Communications Co.*, 24 F.3d 1088, 1091-94, 1096-98 (9th Cir.), cert. denied, 115 S. Ct. 512 (1994). Defendant from its California offices allegedly licensed the reproduction and distribution of videocassettes of *Yellow Submarine* around the world; the Court held the claim as to licenses for reproduction and distribution outside the U.S. was not cognisable under the Copyright Act. *Id.* at 1090.

122. *See*, e.g., *Metzke v. May Dep't Stores*, 878 F. Supp. 756, 761 (W.D. Pa. 1995) (offshore copying may violate U.S. copyright law if defendant commissioning the making of unauthorized copies abroad knew, or should have known, that the copies would be sold in the U.S.); see also *Nintendo of America v. Aeropower Co.*, 34 F.3d 246, 251 (4th Cir. 1994) (holding overbroad an injunction against sales by Taiwanese manufacturer of unauthorized copies of Nintendo videogames in Mexico and Canada, but suggesting the injunction should have been drawn to enjoin Mexican and Canadian sales of copies that were likely to reach the U.S.).

123. *Cf. World-Wide Volkswagen Corp. v. Woodson*, 444 U.S. 286, 296 (1980) (sending goods into the general stream of commerce, without further purposeful targeting or anticipation of the arrival of the goods in the forum, held not sufficient to satisfy due process requirements of assertion of personal jurisdiction over out of state car dealer).

The root act or master copy approach to choice of law resembles that of the European Union's Satellite Directive, which designates the law of the country of 'uplink' to govern liability for dissemination of programs by satellite.[124] Although the satellite signal can be received in many countries, the multinational communication can be traced to a single point of departure. In cyberspace terms, the place of the root act or uplink could be called the country of the 'upload'.

Designation of the law of the country of upload to judge alleged infringements occurring throughout the world would appear to enjoy the virtue of simplicity. However, it also shares the vice of manipulability.[125] The approach may work in the European Union because all member countries must adhere to a minimum standard of protection.[126] If the approach is extended to the whole world, however, cyberpirates will simply make sure they post the unauthorized copies from, or locate their services in, a country having an extremely lax intellectual property regime. Perhaps, just as certain nations have become the venue of choice for entrepreneurs seeking maximum banking secrecy and minimum taxes, some nations will endeavour to enhance the local economy by attracting professional infringers to their copyright-free shores.[127] Without a serious minimum standard applicable to all nations, or without a pirate nation exception from the application of the law of the upload, no choice of law approach will completely avoid the problem of the 'race to the bottom'.[128]

124. *See* Council Directive 93/83, pmbl. 14, art. 1.2(b), 1993 O.J. (L 248) 19.

125. Moreover, it may not always be simple to identify the country of upload; in some instances, the communication may emanate from more than one country. For example, our hypothetical initiating author may receive contributions to her collection of stories from participants in many different countries.

126. *See* Proposal for a Council Directive, Explanatory Memorandum, COM(91)276 final, at 4, 26-29 (establishment of a common level of protection for copyright and neighboring rights is necessary component of EC Satellite Directive).

127. *Cf.* Proposal for a Council Directive, *supra* note 126, at 4 (explaining that harmonization is necessary in order to avoid the creation of 'copyright havens').

128. *See* Lea Brilmayer, *Conflict of Laws* (1995) (explaining the 'race to the bottom' problem). Arguably, article 5.2 of the Berne Convention does not in fact mandate application of the law of each place of infringement. *See* A. Lucas & H. J. Lucas, *Traité de la Propriété Littéraire et Artistique* §§ 1066-1074 (1994) (raising, but rejecting, this interpretation). Rather, in designating the application of the law of the country 'where protection is sought,' the treaty is referring not to the places where the acts against which the copyright owner is seeking protection occurred, but rather to the forum country. After all, it is before the courts of that country that the copyright owner is seeking protection. Under this interpretation, a single law – that of the forum – would apply to the entirety of multinational infringements. This apparently would be the case even if no infringements were alleged to have occurred within the forum: there may be an independent basis, such as defendant's domicile, for a given country to be made the forum. For a fuller discussion of the conflicts of law problem, *see* Ginsburg, Global Use/Territorial Rights, *supra* note 119, at 330-35.

5. Conclusion

Cyberspace creators like our initiating author, and authors of previously created works subsequently posted in cyberspace, enjoy rights whose effective enforcement in cyberspace is today rather uncertain. Collective licensing could enhance the likelihood that authors would at least be compensated for copying (and public performance and display, or even derivative works). However, for many kinds of works of authorship, the collectives that would license electronic rights are only in the early stages of formation, at least in the U.S. Resistance to collective licensing has persisted, notably among publishers of traditional literary works, primarily because collective licensing implies the surrender of control over the selection and activities of its licensees. While some might think that in a networked environment any such control is illusory, others are extremely (not to say, unduly) optimistic that the online medium, combined with encryption technologies, will in fact afford copyright owners *more* control than they enjoyed in the analog world.[129]

Moreover, in many if not most instances, enforcement, whether by a collective or individually by our initiating author, will not be meaningful unless its target is a profitable intermediary, such as a bulletin board or commercial network operator. The effectiveness of pursuing the online provider will in turn depend on what national law (or laws) applies to determine liability for infringements created and/or carried online.

Finally, the 'information superhighway' will undoubtedly carry a great deal of 'information', but transmitting information is not the same as conveying authorship.[130] The viability of cyberspace as a medium for the consensual communication and creation of sustained works of authorship – real 'cars', not simply conversations, data of the day, or pirated postings – will depend on authors' and copyright owners' confidence that the kinds of questions raised in this Article will find solutions that will meet the needs of both authors and users.

129. *See*, e.g., Lance Rose, 'The Emperor's Clothes Still Fit Just Fine,' *Wired*, Feb. 1995, at 103, 104: 'Net cops can swiftly clean each new infringement out of the major online markets as soon as it appears. They will soon become better at it when copyright owners begin deploying software agents that can roam the entire Net, searching out anonymous infringements. Every time a pirated work is spread to the four corners of the Internet by an anonymous user, software agents will quickly sniff it out.'

130. See, e.g., *Feist Publications v. Rural Tel. Serv.*, 499 U.S. 340, 362 (1991) (useful and informative telephone white pages lacks sufficient originality to be considered a work of authorship).

Colloquium Discussions

*Madeleine de Cock Buning and Jaap Haeck**

1. Introduction

A major part of the Royal Academy Colloquium was reserved for discussion. Following a general introduction by Egbert Dommering, the two-day colloquium was divided into four sessions, each covering a separate theme. The first session, *Learning from old media experiences*, was moderated by Bernt Hugenholtz, and concentrated on drawing parallels with the analogue world. Ejan Mackaay spoke of the importance of 'fencing'. Paul Geller discussed the problems of international private law. Dirk Visser made a case for preserving certain copyright exemptions.

The second session, which was moderated by Jane Ginsburg, focused on *current network-related copyright problems*. Jaap Spoor traced the roots of the reproduction right in trying to determine whether or not the reproduction right is being overstretched in the digital environment. Bernt Hugenholtz examined the existing set of exploitation rights, notably the rights of reproduction and communication to the public, in the light of the information superhighway. Bruce Lehman offered a sneak preview of the White Paper of the National Information Infrastructure (NII) Task Force. Mihály Ficsor outlined the upcoming global solution in the framework of the Berne Protocol.

In the third session, moderated by Paul Geller, *practical and legislative solutions* were discussed. Charles Clark described various ongoing experiments with electronic copyright management systems, using either 'dumb' or intelligent identifiers. Ferdinand Melichar discussed the feasibility of collectively administrating electronic rights. Maria Martin-Prat, replacing Paul Vandoren of the European Commission (DG XV), presented a summary of the European Commission's Green Paper.

The fourth and final session, *Predicting the future of copyright*, was moderated by Egbert Dommering. First, Herman Pabbruwe spoke of the future of publishing and pricing. Next, John Perry Barlow offered a sweeping vision of cyberspace and the inability of the existing copyright system to cope with it. Finally, Paul Goldstein summarized two days of intense, highly interesting, often entertaining and sometimes provocative debate.

---

* Madeleine de Cock Buning and Jaap Haeck are research fellows at the Institute for Information Law of the University of Amsterdam.

2. Discussions

SESSION I: LEARNING FROM OLD MEDIA EXPERIENCES

Building fences

Barlow generally supports the views expressed in Mackaay's paper on 'fencing', but observes that the law as we know it now is about property. In contrast, the situation on the Internet is more similar to the situation that existed before Henry II; the notion of property is not known on the Internet. The order on the Internet has to do with friendship and relationships, not with law and physical property. The Internet is purely based on unmaterialized and unbounded matter. On the Internet ideas should not be made scarce, they should be shared. That's how they become valuable. The promise of the Internet is that everybody can express himself without being bound by any legal jurisdiction. We should not ruin this promise by building a global copyright regime.

Mackaay does not agree; friendship is not a commodity, therefore Barlow's reasoning is wrong. Property law deals with scarcity and value. At a certain point people want to get paid for their creativity, and that's where fencing comes in.

Goldstein believes that scarcity in relation to information is irrelevant. Scarcity is a troubled rationale when linked with information. In the new information infrastructure everyone is the 'owner' of information. Before Henry II the notion of property did not exist as we know it today. Those were the days of the hierarchical feudal system, a system which in a sense may be compared to the present situation in China. In China the Internet is totally controlled by the Communist Party. Nevertheless people will find their way in to it. Economics will eventually decide who controls of the system.

Dommering recalls that Mackaay distinguishes three kinds of property: property as an exclusive right, property on a contractual basis (with predefined relations), and property rights of clubs and associations. The latter kind of property does not seem possible on the Internet. Does Mackaay's analysis amount to the conclusion that contractual relationships will deal with the Internet? In response **Mackaay** observes that people tend to be very inventive, and will certainly find a way to fill the gap and protect their property. Club relationships are definitely possible on the Internet.

According to **Melichar** the concept of 'fencing' that was introduced by Mackaay is not correct for intellectual property rights. These rights exist even without fencing. **Mackaay** replies that the fences need not be of a physical nature.

Grosheide believes that Mackaay's fencing idea is illuminating, but wants to know what exactly the notion of property is that Mackaay uses in his paper. What is a property right? **Mackaay** responds by indicating that the notion of property is used as an analogy. Law emerges from people wanting to fence what is theirs; later on the legislator and the courts will implement these laws. Laws derive from practice, not from the legislator.

Lehman agrees with Mackaay. The analogy with real property is clear. If you own a big piece of land a lot of trespassing will be allowed, but if you own a jewellery shop you won't let anyone in unless you know it's safe. In the latter case you build a high fence. The law should provide the means to build fences with, but the people will have to decide for themselves whether they want to build a fence or not. This decision should be up to them; marketplace and culture will decide whether the tools will be used. The marketplace searches for solutions.

Working on the NII Task Force, two different business models can be seen emerging for the exploitation of works in cyberspace. First of all, the information on networks is made freely accessible. For example, most of the information on the on-line services is freely available, it is included in the basic subscription fee. Secondly, products can be seen which are now being promoted and given away for free, which later on will be charged for. For example, if you subscribe to America Online you can receive the New York Times every day. The New York Times could not possibly sustain itself from whatever small amount of revenue they receive from America Online, if this were their primary means of exploitation. The subscription fee would then have to be raised drastically.

How will advertising support these developments? It is much more difficult to include advertising when people can choose not to read the advertisements as they are clicking their way through the menu. There will be a lot of different models. One will just have to be patient seeing these models emerge. There will be a lot of free products and there will be some very expensive products. The marketplace will decide.

Barlow criticizes the NII Task Force. The Task Force had a lot of hearings. Only the publishers, rightholders and all the people who have a great deal to lose by a change of the old ways, have been heard. But the real Internet users (the 'net people') have not been heard at all. The net people are practically unified in their opposition to the Green Paper for the extension of copyright into cyberspace.

Lehman wants to know who the people of the net are. The NII has heard all the interested parties. Nobody seriously objected against applying copyright to the Internet. Besides, what will the market system look like if we don't have copyright? How will people get paid, how will they earn a living? Nowadays most people work with their minds, not with their muscles. Therefore we need an economic mechanism which permits people to get paid for working with their mind. Copyright is one of those mechanisms.

Goldstein observes that, historically speaking, the great virtue of copyright and free markets has been that it offers the most flexible and informed means for consumer welfare. A world without markets is a totalitarian regime. It is not a coincidence that political freedom and copyright have historically grown side by side. This is a strong argument to extend copyright into every corner where consumers place value on literary and artistic works. There are three classic arguments against extending copyright into certain corners that have been alluded to in today's discussion in some way or another. First of all: interest in privacy. Secondly: interest in freedom of expression. Neither of these interests has been contradicted by anything that has been said here in favour of property rights. The third argument against extending rights in a market system in any particular corner is the transaction costs; they must not get higher than the value of the work itself. The economic rationale of the U.S. fair use doctrine is essentially one of transaction costs. However, in the world that we are facing, transaction costs will largely disappear. Transactions will be electronically mediated virtually at the cost of electricity. Hence, a classic argument against extending copyright in most corners will disappear.

In this respect the role that libraries and educators have played in discussions over copyright reform leading to the 1976 Copyright Act in the U.S., is quite interesting. Their arguments originally were transaction cost arguments. The costs for a library to obtain permission from a rightowner every time it wishes to make a copy for inter-library loan purposes, and for a school teacher every time having to contact the publisher for every time he or she wishes to make copies of a poem to distribute in class, obviously are very high. These are cases of fair use; copyright exempts these uses.

What happens to the arguments of the librarians and educators once transaction costs are removed? Then they get to their real concern, that is expense. Their argument is now that their budgets are constantly cut. The budgets of libraries are small, so they say they cannot pay for the use of copyrighted works which they need to fulfil their purpose, i.e. distributing and sharing information. However, copyright exemptions will not resolve this problem. Libraries simply need more (tax) money to pay for copyrighted works.

For **Lehman** the real issue is not access. The essential question is whether access should be provided at the expense of the copyright owner. Lehman's answer is 'no'. If access were to be provided for at the expense of the rightholder, there would be nothing to access. No viable electronic publishing business would exist, works would not be made available in electronic form.

Ficsor agrees with both Goldstein and Lehman. If you start distributing wine without bottles, if you undertake to introduce products without a market, you will end up with something of a socialist situation. This, as we all know now, has not been a very successful thing. You simply need the bottles to protect the wine. Of course, (wine) producers can always choose to make available their products for free. In the field of copyright the way is to grant certain exclusive rights with certain appropriate exceptions. We can discuss what those rights should be, but we should not get rid of this paradigm.

Sakkers points out that the discussion of copyright in a digital environment is about opposing interests. The discussion is about whether we should start by building fences or by opening the field. This discussion is purely theoretical. It will be by-passed in practice by choices made by right owners for particular categories of content. Free flow of information does not imply free flow of commercially exploitable content. On the Internet free information will flow side-by-side with commercially exploited content. What will happen is that rightowners from particular segments of the industry will start building technical fences. Afterwards it will be determined who will have access to the field.

Ginsburg wants to know if Sakkers is really saying: 'It really doesn't matter what the copyright law says because we can apply technology to determine the terms of access, and we can also impose site licences or other contractual forms of protection. It is possible that a combination of a technological and contractual provisions could give a rightowner a better deal than copyright with its user exemptions'. Ginsburg indicates that this might be an exaggeration of what Sakkers said, but it is a source of concern amongst people who want access to information (e.g. librarians). **Sakkers** replies that the copyright regime is not irrelevant at this point in time. By virtue of the availability of technical means we find ourselves at a junction where many types of use that are currently occurring, may be brought back under the control of rights owners.

Conflicts of law

Seignette refers to Geller's paper. In respect of copyright contracts, he suggested as a principle of reference for solving conflicts of law that contracts should be construed restrictively. Geller also suggested to favour the solution that most enhances the variety of works made accessible in the marketplace. Seignette wonders which of these two principles should prevail if they would lead to different solutions. If a media company decides to make an interactive CD version of an animated film from the 1950's, the first principle of reference would mean that the artist would still own the right to make an interactive CD version, as his right was not specifically mentioned in the original transfer of rights to the company. The company would have to go back to the artist or his assignees to negotiate an additional transfer. As this may be hard to do, the media company may decide not to use the old cartoon at all.

Of course this would be different if the company were the first owner of the copyright in the cartoon, e.g. under the work made for hire rule of U.S. copyright law. However, a U.S. employer may not necessarily be the author and first copyright owner under all jurisdictions. The Berne Convention does not define the 'author', nor does it say which law should be applied to determine the 'author' in international situations. Moreover, the status of 'author' is not subject to freedom of contract. Distributors of copyright works therefore cannot fully rely on their domestic law or on contract in order to secure their title in all countries of exploitation. This may cause them to distribute those works only in such (new) formats for which they can easily secure new media rights.

Geller agrees that the conventions do not provide for solutions for all conflicts of laws. However, the principle of preference should be the basis. The creator (or contributor in the creative work) is, in principle, to be considered as the author, unless there is an argument for vesting the right in someone else. According to Geller one of the most important questions in respect of multimedia works is the use of prior works. For the use of large parts of the work the producers of multimedia works should hire lawyers to ask permission and make sound contracts. In this way litigation is avoided. If the producer of a multimedia work cannot find the rightholder of a specific work, he can always use a different piece or song. For the use of bits and pieces of prior works the courts should determine with great discretion whether this is fair use or not.

Geller also points out that the Berne Convention is originally a convention on the rights of individuals, it is about private international copyright law. However, in TRIPS we can see a shift towards public international copyright law. Nobody can predict how far this shift will go.

Exemptions

Hugenholtz argues that the crucial question is whether copyright owners will be able to control private use. According to **Visser** there should be no control of (secondary) private uses of otherwise legal copies of creative works. Control should be limited to the act of communicating the work to the public, or, as the Dutch call it, 'openbaarmaking'. A right of access would imply a reversal of the burden of proof; this is dangerous.

In **Geller's** opinion it is relatively easy to deal with secondary usage. The problem of sending articles to x, y and z is rather more difficult. To solve it we must fix a certain number of copies or retransmissions which people are allowed to make for private use (e.g. 'more than three retransmissions constitute public use').

Waaijers indicates that 'bodies of knowledge' (pictures, formula's and text) will emerge which the user may or may not use. The notion of an 'article' shall disappear from the user's perspective. The process of access will be ruled by what the parties agree upon.

Ginsburg points out that the distinction made by Visser in his paper between use *in* a library and use *outside* a library only works if there is a physical library. What happens to this distinction if the library is no longer a physical space but a cyberspace (e.g. an e-mail address)?

SESSION 2: CURRENT NETWORK-RELATED COPYRIGHT PROBLEMS

Exploitation rights

Quaedvlieg emphasises the basic principle of copyright. This is, and always will be, that the author has to receive a reasonable remuneration for his creation and for the exploitation of his work. The rights can be rights of reproduction, rights of communication to the public, or anything else. To these rights we might add new rights apt for the new digital environment. But we should not overstretch the reproduction right. Permanent storage is clearly a reproduction, but acts such as reception, transmission and screen display are different and should not be brought under the existing reproduction right.

The danger of overstretching the reproduction right is that copyright laws will no longer be understandable for normal people. The image used by Mackaay of changing the fences is appealing, but we should be careful not to change the field. We already see this tendency; new acts which were traditionally not subject to copyright now are (e.g. 'use' that is qualified as reproduction). This bears enormous risks.

Lehman wants to know in what way the reproduction right, which according to Hugenholtz is becoming overbroad, will hinder the use of the work or create problems in commerce in intellectual property. **Hugenholtz** replies that the central thesis of his paper was not that an overstretched reproduction right would in any way hinder commerce in copyright materials. However, an overstretched reproduction right may eventually back-fire and result in lobbying on a large scale for exemptions. The reproduction right should not be used to create a situation where every communication, every use, every reading or every screen display is a restricted act. It is not commerce, but privacy and the freedom of reception that we should worry about.

According to **Spoor** we have to remind ourselves that the existing reproduction right is what we have right now. To do away with it will lead to a lot of problems. The answer to the (Internet) machine might very well be in the machine, but it is certainly in the statute book. We are dealing with existing laws and rights.

Ginsburg observes there is some difference of opinion about whether the answer to the question of transient reproduction really is in the statute book. What do we mean by the words transient reproduction? We need agreement on that. **Spoor** adds that we are not even sure if we all agree on what is reproduction. Reproduction is a legal term, not a technical concept. It has to be interpreted time and again.

Ginsburg indicates that there seems to be a continuum. We seem to agree that the actual downloading to a fairly permanent storage medium (e.g. a disk or a hard copy) is a form of reproduction. Then we have various steps along the way, e.g. receipt in temporary memory of the computer. Then we have sending a file through the network. Here it may in fact be reproduced at various spots along the way. CONTU in the U.S. and the European Commission agree that the reception in the user's computer may well be reproduction, even if it does not result in a more permanent fixation. The reason for this point of view was pragmatic. For the lack of being able to track the temporary fixation when it is received in the user's computer, we call it a reproduction. Do those same pragmatic reasons apply to the transmission of a work as it passes through a network? Is there the same fear that if we don't call this a reproduction we will run the risk of having a lot of unauthorised copies floating around? Or is there something different about the work as it is in transience that makes it less vulnerable to copying?

A point of concern of **Grosheide** is that no one knows what effect newly created rights will have on the traditional copyright modes of exploitation. The idea of adding new rights, e.g. performance rights or broadcasting rights, to the existing catalogue of rights comes up in a digital environment. Adding these rights will most certainly have an effect on the exploitation of traditional objects. A non-unitary vision of copyright as a whole might be helpful here. New forms of exploitation are connected with new objects. A tailor-made copyright might be the solution for many of these problems now arising. Such a solution has been applied to computer software in many national laws. Copyright should be looked at from a pluriform perspective. Tailor-made legal instruments should be devised for various modes of exploitation that are required in different environments, all within a copyright framework.

Another question that has to be asked is whether adding new legal tools can endanger the existing tools used to regulate the 'old' media. One might consider applying these new instruments only to the new media. Again, tailor-made laws might be the solution. The same may be true in respect of collecting societies. We may want to can get rid of them in a digital environment, but that is not necessarily true for the analogue environment.

In reply **Lehman** notes that sui generis protection as proposed by Grosheide probably makes a lot of sense from an academic point of few: to tailor-make a perfect law, to deal with a new technology. However, in practice this cannot be realised. The statutes would look like preposterous monsters. The process of making laws for every type of work would be enormous. Making only general adaptations to laws and letting emerge from case law more detailed solutions is a much better option. **Grosheide** answers he is not in favour of creating new sui generis rights. What he advocates is making special arrangements within the copyright setting for different modes of exploitation.

For **Melichar** the discussion proves that it is very important that we preserve the very generally worded exploitation rights as we have them. We should not create tailor-made definitions for new exploitation forms. These would certainly become too detailed so that in future it would be even harder to apply them to new technologies.

Lehman explains why the NII Task Force advocates a high level of exclusivity. If you give the right owner the exclusive right to deny his product to the marketplace, he may be tempted initially to offer the product under terms and conditions which are unattractive to the consumer. This will turn out not to be a very viable business to him. So the marketplace will dictate the end result.

Lehman further observes that there exists a lot of anxiety amongst librarians and educators in the U.S. that somehow their access will be restricted through the exercise of copyright on the Internet. This is misplaced anxiety. Fair use was never an issue for librarians until twenty years ago. It was the advent of the photocopying machine that made fair use an item for librarians. In libraries one has to pay to make a photocopy. As we move into the digital environment, it will be entirely possible to licence the making of those copies and compensate the rightholders for the same or less. Right now nobody makes real money out of photocopies. Payment is used to pay for the photocopying machine. The Task Force believes that the marketplace will provide for comprehensive access through many means, also for libraries.

Geller wants to know whether the high level of exclusivity that Lehman speaks of is really a high level, or is it merely a clear profile? If the marketplace will decide how the system will work, then all you need is a benchmark for negotiation. As long as there is a four factor fair use test without any kind of weighing, any kind of ordering those four factors, all the attempts to clearly define the rights as benchmarks for negotiations are undercut.

Lehman indicates that the discussion gets to the point of the practicality of making the law in any democratic country, in particular in a large multi-cultural country as the U.S. There are a lot of people who would want a clear definition of fair use. Publishers want an extremely narrow definition of fair use, and some librarians and educators would like a very open definition. The fact is, however, that the four factor fair use test in Section 107 U.S.C. is the best the statutory process can produce. It is simply impossible for Congress to absorb these competing interests and produce a clear statutory fair use regime. Very little can be done in this respect.

The White Paper proposes to amend Section 108 (the library use provisions) to provide that the same copying which is currently permitted by means of photocopying for preservation or archival purposes, can take place in a digital context as well. This can be achieved because it does not raise any fundamental issue; it just deals with the same situation. It is extremely difficult to legislate fine points of copyright law in a country like the U.S. Fortunately we have a judicial system that does enable people to take fact-specific cases to court, so that over time enough of those cases make the law. In this way you get a pretty good idea of what fair use really is. It may be an imperfect system, but given the technology of legislation today it is the best we can do.

According to **Ginsburg** the lack of clarity in the fair use system of which Geller speaks so negatively, is actually very good. We have seen that in the old analogue world. The very lack of clarity of the fair use system is its salvation. Detailed exceptions as formulated in the laws of some civil law countries can cause tension when there are new forms of exploitation that would economically and politically justify new exemptions but just don't fit in the existing detailed rules.

Visser stresses that whether new legislation is politically realistic or not can never be a decisive factor. Why does Lehman advocate (small) changes to U.S. copyright law, while in fact the public performance right in the U.S. is already very broad? It covers video-on-demand as well as almost any other relevant activity on the network (except individual transmission). Why can't the rightholders be adequately protected by applying the public performance right, without having to resort to 'repro-thinking'?

Lehman replies that the U.S. public performance right has a big hole in it. With regard to sound recordings (which are protected under the U.S. copyright system) no right of public performance exists. If at present a sound recording would be marketed in the U.S. through the Internet, the only way the rightholder would have of securing his right would be through the reproduction right. The other factor is that the Berne Convention really only rests on the reproduction right. In the minimalist theory of wanting as few changes in the law as possible to evolve the system, one would like to be able to lock into the Berne Convention as much as possible through the use of the reproduction right. Continental Europe will tend to use the right of communication to the public as the legal foundation for licensing agreements in product-moving on the electronic highway. In the U.S. there will be a tendency to use the reproduction right, or better the right of distribution (a specific exclusive right to distribute copies). Most important is that the rights have to be exclusive and that you have to be able to transfer that exclusivity when you make transactions across the Atlantic Ocean.

Ginsburg indicates that the copyright systems of Europe and the U.S. are different, but that we have to remember that they have the same object: remuneration for the author. Whether you call it reproduction or communication to the public should ultimately not matter.

Brandt Jensen disagrees with Lehman's statement that in all comments on the U.S. Green Paper there was little or no opposition against applying copyright to the net. According to her that does not mean that there was no opposition to what the Green Paper proposed. There is not a single person in this colloquium that would argue that copyright should not protect against digital communication. But there are not two people that have the same definition of copyright or how it ought to apply to a digital environment. Where is this disagreement coming from? Some are talking about commercial exploitation, others want to protect works so that in the future the free flow of information is guaranteed. There is a tension between these two. As long as that tension exists we can sit here and define reproduction and public communication but we will never reach agreement. As Ginsburg says, it does not really matter what we call it if we can find some agreement on the basics.

Listening to the discussion, **Barlow** realizes that the philosophy, the consciousness and the political structure of the industrial era (a period of time in which large organisations tried to assemble material objects) are trying to extend themselves into the immaterial. If we would stick with copyrighting exactly what the law dictates that we should, that is fixation in tangible form, we would probably be doing all right. What in fact is happening in the discussion (e.g. on what is and what is not reproduction), is trying to extend into the intangible a form of tangibility, because what we do in our social and economic structures is 'stuff', not immateriality. But what is travelling through a fibre optic cable is not material 'stuff' as has been suggested. This industrial paradigm will not survive on the Internet. The markets for cyberspace are very different from the markets of the physical world. The worst thing we can do at this fragile initial stage, is to try to inject a lot of control based on principles of the physical world into this environment. This is not going to work, it will breed a lack of respect of the law, and it will create a great deal of chaos amongst the terrestrial governments of the physical world and it will solve nothing. In this respect we should also look at value in stead of simple money. On the Internet value is being exchanged in a demonetized condition. Information is directly exchanged for information. For this reason it would be helpful if the people that try to legislate the Internet would spend some time there.

Geller strongly feels that this topic cannot be discussed if we do not look at the goals of the definition of rights. The discussion on the applicability of existing rights has so far been medieval and scholastic reasoning. Why do we talk about definitions of this or that exclusive right, if in fact this is all scholastic wordplay? If Barlow believes that the free flow of information will be enhanced by no protection or ineffective protection, he should rejoice in the fact that these people are not talking about realities. If they talk about the definition of rights in a way that does not really correspond to the paradigm of the network, Barlow should be very glad, because that means that their law is not going to work. They have not looked at the way a true interactive network really operates. If Barlow wants cyberanarchy he should encourage these people to further redefine their definitions as fine as possible, and tell them to look for those angels on the heads of pins.

Hugenholtz responds that the existing set of exclusive rights will not work in a digital environment. It is very important that alternatives are looked at. These have to be kept in line with their original purpose, which is to protect against acts of exploitation. The way we are now stretching the reproduction right will undermine the copyright system. As a short term solution we should shift our focus from the reproduction right to the right of communication to the public. We should not try to devise Internet specific exploitation rights. That would make problems even worse.

According to **Spoor** copyright owners want control because they need a reward for their creativity and investments. If they do not get a reward their sources might dry up. At present we have a copyright system with certain tools. The reproduction right is one of those tools, which we will need to use and interpret. But of course new paradigms are welcome if they offer a good solution. These new paradigms might even be better than the old ones.

Ficsor wonders what Geller's alternative would be? Maybe Geller wants an international convention containing only three provisions: 1) all intellectual creations should be protected by copyright; 2) the protection should extend to any kind of exploitation; 3) some exemptions. According to Ficsor it is clear that this will not work in practice in a digital environment.

Dommering stresses that the discussion on reproduction and performance rights has not been scholastic at all. In the paper society we have established principles of privacy, copyright and freedom of communication. If you look at the electronic environment we have widened the scope of our communication, but we also had to give in on the rather stable notion of an exempted private circle because we have become part of a network. Keeping this in mind, this is not at all a scholastic discussion. As Spoor has made clear, the reproduction right gives the owner the strongest possible position on the network. He is able to control the whole chain of communication, from the point where information is entered into the network to the point it is received by the end user on his personal computer. Thus it will eventually be the right owners themselves that determine the terms of fair use by way of licensing. However, if we would choose for a more open concept such as a communication right or a performance right, all parties concerned will be able to negotiate the scope of fair use in the new environment.

Samuelson agrees; this is not a scholastic discussion as suggested by Geller. What the discussion is about is whether certain classes of behaviour of people on the network are already, or should be, within the scope of exclusive rights. That is in fact a very deep and important issue, especially because we do not all seem to agree. The reproduction right should not be stretched out to the point that it encompasses just about everything that happens on the network. Browsing, for instance, shouldn't be looked upon as reproduction. If that were the case, you would be an infringer if you looked in your e-mail box into which somebody put copyright material. The notion of looking at material in digital form being a form of reproduction is against common sense.

Samuelson further argues that we should be careful not to grant all control to one of the parties on the net, because this would endanger the balance between copyright and freedom of expression. The U.S. fair use doctrine is a helpful instrument in balancing the interests in the new environment.

SESSION 3: PRACTICAL AND LEGISLATIVE SOLUTIONS

Technical protection

Papapavlou observes that the discussion has been centred on acts made possible by physical technology. On the Internet we will have three kinds of information: information protected by copyright, information not protected by copyright, but which has to have some kind of protection, and information in the public domain. For the second category the European Union is creating an unfair extraction right in its proposal for a Database Directive. Papapavlou further notes that encryption may be a practical solution, but that it is politically still a very controversial subject.

Geller expresses his concern about the maintenance of rights in a digital environment. In his contribution Clark informed us that it will take five to ten years to get the fences up and running, and Melichar stated that the passage of time can erode legal rights. But what will happen in those five to ten years? Will the now existing rights indeed erode, and does that mean that we will not have any protection at all?

Mackaay stresses the importance of remuneration. How is payment going to work? There are several formulae currently being tested. If you want to collect money, the transaction costs associated with that have to be very low, and the rules have to be very simple, otherwise the people are not going to go for it. Some people don't want to sell information, they would rather share it. Waving your rights has to be a simple thing to do. What you want to share and at what point you want to be paid is something that people have to find out for themselves. When you give people rights, it does not necessarily mean that they end up with the money that the right will earn. The problem with rights is that the more detailed we will make them the more they will act as the tollgates in medieval commerce. The question is how we will know that there are too many tollgates about?

Quaedvlieg notes that we have been dealing with all kinds of information as if they were the same. In a digital world different kinds of information should be distinguished. We should distinguish between scientific and factual information on the one side, where it is not necessary to read the whole article or the whole book, and cultural information on the other side, where it is essential that you listen to or read the whole work.

Clark answers that one needs the same identifying system for both cultural and scientific information, otherwise the system will not work. **Quaedvlieg** wonders whether having access to cultural information is equally important as having access to scientific and factual information. For **Clark** information is information, no matter what the content is. To Clark a subject of greater concern is the authenticity of scientific information. How will a user be able to know that the work he has received is authentic?

Lehman comments that a main concern of the NII Task Force was to maintain copyright integrity. It is very important that information can be authenticated. Think of safe drug lists or financial information for which authenticity is vital. This has not only to do with copyright, but with privacy as well. Identifiers will have to be used for public domain information to make sure information is authentic.

Triaille notes that on the superhighway most information will be available in a digital format that is technically protected. It might no longer be the rightholder who decides what type of information will be protected. Originality may no longer be the standard for what is protected and what not. The information provider could become the one that will decide who will have access to what information. The selling of decoders will be made illegal. Technical protection might then replace copyright protection. Exemptions to copyright protection might be replaced by preferential terms and conditions. Public domain might be replaced by the notion of shareware. Triaille wonders if copyright law as a system for rewarding authors and ensuring the dissemination of information will be of any utility on the information superhighway. Will it not be replaced by legislation on unauthorized access to computerized systems?

According to **Clark** the identifiers will only identify copyright works and will not, and should not, identify public domain works. Technical devices are there for the enforcement of copyright. The publishers will seek to negotiate variable terms. Information prices will not be standard but diverse. For this the notion of 'dumb identifiers' is helpful. With a dumb identifier you are referred to a data bank. The data bank, held by a collecting society, actually tells you what the terms are. These are imposed by the author and the publisher, as they are now currently in the world of print on paper. In that respect there does not seem to be any difference in principle to what is happening now.

Triaille does not believe that only copyright material will benefit from technical protection schemes. If you would identify only copyright works, you will have to do some prior examination. What would you do with information that would turn out not to be copyrightable, but which might come under the new sui generis protection of the Database Directive?

Clark indicates that right now it is impossible to answer that question. The system has to develop, to be built; it will take some time. We are on the first lap of the track of a five year programme. We cannot get any identifier system actually working before five years from now.

Bing draws a parallel with the telecommunication sector, where almost every use (going in or out) can be registered. This might seriously conflict with the privacy rights of people. This should be considered although technology gives us the possibilities for all kinds of control.

Geller wonders how you could draft a law that would apply criminal sanctions to people that market unauthorized decoders. What do you do against the expected defence: 'I only use the decoder to decode messages that contain public domain material'?

Lehman replies that in the White Paper a criminal sanction is proposed against manufacturers and sellers of devices of which the primary purpose is to bypass the encryption for non-authorized uses. The provisions proposed will be part of the copyright law, but will not be a copyright cause of action. It will be similar to the provisions in the Federal Communications Act.

The electronic rental right

Ginsburg asks whether video-on-demand should be considered as a manifestation of the rental right when there is no exchange of a physical copy. This is important in view of the principle of national treatment. If it is considered as a reproduction or a public performance, the normal principles of national treatment apply. Therefore works from outside the European Community that were so communicated would be entitled to compensation. However, if it were characterised as a rental, what is the Commissions position on the national treatment of video-on-demand?

Martin-Prat answers that the position of the Commission is that the whole problem will be solved if we accept a rental right in the Berne Protocol. **Geller** questions if this means that rental does not fall under the national treatment rule of the Paris Act of the Berne Convention? According to **Martin-Prat** we can argue about that; some Member States seem to have their doubts. Therefore we need a rental right in the Berne Protocol. If we would decide that a rental right could be applied to video-on-demand, we will need some clarification, even in a short instrument, for the sake of legal certainty. We can not just assume that the Rental Directive applies here.

Lehman remarks that the main issue between the U.S. and Europe is national treatment. Some European countries interpret the national treatment rule in a very narrow sense, in a sense contrary to the Berne Convention. Intellectual property is used by these countries as a trade barrier to protect their national market. **Geller** agrees that the Berne Convention is based on the principle of national treatment with some odd exceptions. Does the Berne Convention have to shift its emphasis in a digital environment from national treatment to a stronger system of minimum rights?

Collective administration of rights

Ginsburg asks whether the answer to the collecting society is in the machine as well? In a situation outside the traditional music industry where the transaction costs are substantially diminished by the possibility of computerized permission systems, what kind of relationship will there be between publishers and collecting societies? **Clark** replies that if you use intelligent identifiers you do not need collecting societies any longer. But if you use dumb identifiers (which is most likely), there is a major role for collecting societies in the 'one stop shop'. They will serve as deposit houses and will function as intermediaries.

Melichar emphasizes that the relationship between publishers and author's societies is essential. Publishers and authors have the same interest; they should cooperate. At present CD-ROMs are being published with non-authorized copyright material, and no action is taken because of a lack of cooperation between authors and publishers.

Dommering points out that collecting societies were invented because of market failures, because of the difficulties of establishing direct relationships between users and authors. One of the utopian views about cyberspace is that we will be able to correct these market failures. In normal markets there are agencies playing an intermediate role between demand and supply. Agencies will play a role in the new environment as well, but why should these agencies be collecting societies with exclusive rights and exclusive monopoly positions? Why can't we have competition on that level as well?

Melichar responds that at present collecting societies are still collective by nature, but that they will become much more individualized. The reason why the collecting societies of most countries are monopolies, is that the user asks for that. Users want a one-stop-shop in stead of having to go to different agents not knowing who is the right one. According to **Dommering** this is the same argument telecommunication operators have used for many years to defend their monopoly position.

Geller offers an alternative: why not work with competing collecting societies by making a 'directory' of rightholders in different agencies? In two or three calls you could find the agency you need. Why would that not be adequate? **Melichar** argues that in the literature business one has to deal with thousands of rightholders. That is why it is very inefficient to have more than one collecting society.

Clark notes that in the U.K. rightholders do not grant exclusive licences to collecting societies; they grant licences on a non-exclusive basis. There are publishers who have refused to mandate the Copyright Licensing Agency because they prefer to deal with photocopying themselves.

According to **Beemsterboer** opening up the market and allowing competition would only work if you could get the same information from different agents. The problem is, however, that if you want specific information you can only get it at one address. Therefore it would be better to have a system of dumb identifiers and voluntary licenses with a compulsory central administration. But let us first see whether there is a role for collecting societies in the digital environment, whether users and rightholders are able to find each other in this environment.

Geller points out another problem: if you obtain a license from a large scale organisation with financial resources and that organisation warrants the authorization, you can proceed with a certain tranquillity in using the work. If you obtain the license from a small scale organisation that warrants you that they have the authority to license, but which would not be able to respond if they for some reason did not have the license, it would be worthless.

Hoeren wonders what DG IV of the European Commission will do from an anti-trust law perspective in respect of the one-stop shops that are being promoted in the Green Paper of DG XV. **Martin-Prat** replies that the management of collecting societies has been one of the most contentious issues in the Commission's consultation process. The Green Paper focuses on voluntary licensing. It is for rightholders to organize themselves and see what is best for them. This view was also strongly expressed in the public hearing that was held in July 1994.

Melichar indicates that in Germany collecting societies are compelled by law to apply standard tariffs. It is not allowed to set different prices for different works. If the future would bring us competing agents, we could end this situation; anti-trust law might be helpful here.

Goldstein points out that a 'one-stop shop' is not the same thing as 'one shop'. The existence of three collecting societies in the U.S. is a fine example of the merits of competition between collecting societies. There is no inefficiency in having two shops that both contain all the rights to all works. Rightholders could convey there non-exclusive rights to shop A and to shop B. There will be competition between these shops on price and service. If there is competition, the collecting societies will have to be efficient. Operating costs will be minimalized.

Geller is of the opinion that a lot of these questions could be resolved by the marketplace itself. The question that remains is whether we do need law. Do we need law to structure the organisation of the copyright societies? Do we need law in the field of anti-trust to control what happens in the market place?

Brandt Jensen believes that some kind of (anti-trust or copyright) law is necessary to make one-stop shopping work. The law must guarantee that the rightholders participate in the system. In the Copyright Clearance Centre mostly scientific publishers participate, while other publishers (e.g. legal publishers) do not.

Geller sees several possible responses to this problem, one of which is the Scandinavian solution: the extended collective license system. **Bing** wishes to make clear that the Nordic extended collective license for photocopying can not be understood properly without placing it in a certain social context. It is a solution for a situation where direct licensing is impossible. With the advent of electronic copyright management systems the extended collective license loses its justification. However, there may still be a role for collecting societies in facilitating one-stop shopping.

Tuomola explains that in 1994 the Finnish competition authorities conducted a study of copyright societies. They handed out a twofold decision. The reproduction rights organisation was not considered a cartel, but an organisation licensing a new kind of right on the market. It was allowed to continue its work provided it would not abuse its dominant position in the market. However, the composers' and conductors' organisations, as well as the performers', broadcasters' and phonogram producers' organisations were considered cartels under Finnish competition law.

Barlow wishes to make clear that in the U.S. there is no real competition between collecting societies. The overhead of ASCAP is outrageously high, and the organisation is inefficient. Real competition would be advantageous. However, the problem remains: what legal authority could competing societies invoke if both of them are trying to collect rightholders' royalties?

Lehman argues that the U.S. has a lot of experience with anti-trust law and collecting societies. In fact, the current structure of the U.S. collecting society system is the product of the application of anti-trust law. A really interesting development in the U.S. is the emergence of the newest collecting society, the Copyright Clearance Centre (CCC), that licenses photocopying rights for literary works. The CCC operates on an entirely different basis than ASCAP or BMI. It works as an agent, a clearance house; the terms and conditions of the licence are established by the author and publisher, rather than by the clearance centre itself. The CCC was set up that way specifically to deal with anti-trust law. The CCC model is more appropriate for the digital environment, because it will be possible to specifically identify the work involved. The reason why we have collecting societies in the music area is market failure. The technology of the 19th century simply did not permit contacting the author. In the digital environment this has changed. The agent model will eventually replace the collecting society model. This will create a crisis for the traditional music licensing societies.

SESSION 4: PREDICTING THE FUTURE OF COPYRIGHT

Pijnenborg notes that we have to remind ourselves that the exploitation of works has to do with both supply and demand. Until now the emphasis has been on the supply side. However, we need to look more at the demand side, the end user's perspective. According to Pijnenborg the real problem is that there is too much passive knowledge available for the user to cope with. The user needs means to make a selection of all the information he is offered. Thus the real problem is not in the storage, transmission or accessibility, but in mastering the information. This problem is not caused by technology, and therefore it is very unlikely that the solution will be found in technology. The solution lies in creating facilities that enable end users to cope with the complexity and quantity of information. We have spent a lot of time discussing the tension between intellectual property and technology. The key areas of attention are, however, the tension between property and added value, between authenticity and decision support, between integrity and internalization. The answer to the machine is in fact redefining the question: how to open up all the information so that we can actually use it?

Costers wants to know what will be the role of the end user in the future. There are two purposes of copyright: remuneration for the author and enabling access for the public, i.e. the interest of society. In the existing copyright system a balance is found between these competing factors. But where will the balance be in the future? We should take care not to shift the balance in the direction of the rightholders only.

Bing responds that end user situations are often analyzed in terms of the price of information. However, the price that the end user pays is not a major factor. The major cost for accessing information at the library would be the time the user spends in obtaining the information (going from the work place to the library at a time it is open). Through digitization information will be easily accessible for the end user at a low cost.

Barlow wishes to make clear that it is absolutely critical to maintain the rights as they exist in the physical world. One of his concerns is that by trying to make copyright fit for cyberspace, it will corrupt its application to the existing media. Trying to stretch it into the digital environment will decrease its usability in the analogue environment. Before we try to create a legal structure (e.g. minimum rights under the Berne Convention), we should wait to see how the situation in cyberspace develops. We do not even know the problems that will emerge.

Papapavlou asks whether privacy will still be relevant in the future; will the total concept change? Could it be that on the network remuneration will not be in money, but in glory? **Barlow** replies that you cannot eat praise. But a system is maturing on the network that allows you to pay directly for the information you use. This system is not based on copyright, but on ethics, relationships and social standards.

Triaille disagrees with Barlow; ethics will not replace the law on the Internet. This would only be possible in a small community. If the Internet keeps growing as it does, ethics will not be enough. This is even more true if in this community commercial operators will appear. Then you either have to accept anarchy or make good legislation. There is no good reason why the Internet should remain outside the law.

Oppenoorth points out that one very important problem has only been mentioned briefly, but not discussed in depth. How can we rely on the information that is provided, how do we know it is authentic? According to **Barlow** this problem can be solved by digital signatures and the like, but this is not allowed in the U.S.

Spoor refers to Barlow's statements that the copyright system will stifle the Internet and that it is not suitable for it. Spoor makes a comparison with the Dutch bicycle system. People steal a lot of bikes, but the notion of property is still valid. Even though there are a lot of infringers, the system does not break down. For the small part of information on the Internet which is copyright material, the copyright system might work very well.

In reply **Barlow** stresses that copyright law protects the fixation of information in tangible form. The information on the net is not fixed in a tangible form, it is all virtual. Information that is robust and that has good genetic material is a life form that selfreproduces in an open ecosystem like the net. It will be very difficult to stop that process or to trace the method by which it is being reproduced or even to trace the source it comes from.

According to **Ficsor** the majority of the material circulating on the Internet is not protected by copyright. We are only talking about the top of the pyramid of information. The participants of this colloquium are interested in that top. Barlow's paradigm might be applicable in this world, but in the world of entertainment it is not. In this world the answer may be, as Clark suggested, 'in the machine'. In the world of Barlow the interested parties may want to work out a system for themselves; we do not have to introduce standards. But in the world of entertainment, standards might in fact be needed.

Visser points out that Barlow and Lehman agree on a very fundamental issue: information that is produced at the cost of investment has to receive some form of protection, whether we call that copyright or something else. We do need copyright to protect creations that require large investments, and that can be easily reproduced. If the Internet will not allow copyright protection today, we have to rethink the system of copyright.

Quaedvlieg brings up the subject of moral rights. Moral rights and commercial rights are intertwined. What will remain of the moral aspect of the right of adaptation when (digital) manipulation will become easier? It will certainly become more important. Will the paternity right remain the same? In the digital world it seems relatively easy to have the name of the author appear on the screen automatically every time the work is used. Even authors who wish to be paid in praise and glory (as Papapavlou and Barlow suggest) need copyright protection. Here the commercial aspect of the paternity right comes into play. For you will only receive recognition if you have a paternity right. According to Quaedvlieg the existing distinction between moral rights and economic rights is not as clear as it seems; it will probably disappear altogether on the Internet.

Grosheide points out that the emphasis so far has been on the Anglo-American copyright system and not on the continental author's rights system. The emphasis has been on the market place, not on moral rights.

Lehman agrees that the discussion has been oriented towards the Anglo-American view. There is a fundamental philosophical difference between the continental European system and the U.S. system. This has to be addressed if you try to harmonize the rules. Copyright plays an important role in society; 4% of the U.S. economy consists of trade in copyright works. This area will only grow. These are not the products that Barlow refers to. These are commercial works, such as entertainment products and software. There has to be an economic mechanism for these to be traded world-wide. For this we need to face the relationship between the droit d'auteur concept and the copyright concept. The latter is largely a commercial concept. We need to find a standard for the relation between these concepts. It may be a good idea to try to incorporate some droit d'auteur concepts in U.S. copyright law. However, this may be a difficult, if not impossible exercise. In any case, the U.S. and Europe need a common standard for treating commercially exploitable works on the Internet. If Europe wants to be on the same level as the U.S., it will probably have to be without the author's rights paradigms. The U.S. most likely will not accept them.

According to **Ginsburg** there is considerable reason for optimism. Author's rights fit in well in the U.S. system. The Constitution secures the exclusive rights to authors. In the U.S. the right of attribution comes out quite well. The distinction between copyright and author's right is blurring. Both kinds of rights will be needed on the net.

End of discussion

The Future of Copyright in a Digital Environment

Summary of Discussion

*Paul Goldstein**

At the outset, I would like to express my gratitude to the Colloquium's academic organizers, Professor Egbert Dommering and Dr. Bernt Hugenholtz, not only for undertaking the onerous logistics of such an enterprise, but also for their insightful selection of topics and viewpoints. This has certainly made the task of summarizing the discussion of the past two days far more rewarding than it might otherwise have been.

In view of the necessary time constraints, I will not attempt to rehearse all of the topics presented, nor the interventions made, *seriatim.* Rather, I propose to extract three central and interrelated themes. I will also attempt toward the end of my remarks to locate these themes within a somewhat larger framework.

The first and overarching theme that emerged in this Colloquium concerns the nature and timing of the conditions that should govern the dissemination of content in the new digital environment. Is it better to have general *standards* or specific *rules* to mediate uses of literary and artistic works in the digital environment? What is the appropriate starting point for formulating standards or rules? A *tabula rasa*, with no legal guideposts at all? A precise and historically validated code of rules such as copyright and author's right? Or, some place in between?

The second theme concerns the interaction of property, privacy and freedom in a digital environment, and asks how the balance between these three interests – sometimes parallel, sometimes competing – should properly be struck.

Finally, what should be the respective roles of property law and contract law in organizing uses of literary and artistic works in the new digital environment?

1. Standards or Rules?

Much discussion of the conditions that should control dissemination of information in the new digital environment effectively centred on the choice between general standards and specific rules. Indeed, some thought was expressed that, as a starting point, the regulatory slate should be wiped entirely clean. Nonetheless, there was in fact substantial agreement on two analytical premises in the presentations and in the interventions.

---

* Lillick Professor of Law, Stanford University.

First, all participants appeared to agree that the ultimate purpose to be served by any allocative regime – copyright, contract or even self-help – is the enhancement of consumer welfare. The underlying, generally shared view of consumer welfare is that it implicates not only economic welfare, but also personal and political welfare, and requires that weight be given not only to the price and quality of goods, but also to interests in privacy and freedom of information.

Second, there was general agreement that, whatever allocative approach is taken, economic transactions in the digital environment should be shaped by free markets. Even those who would start from a clean slate adhered to this view. Specifically, although digital interaction between demand and supply will offer presently unparalleled opportunities to refine consumer signals, the point was not lost that today's free markets are themselves interactive in an important sense: producers, to survive, must respond – 'interact' in the current parlance – to signals of consumer demand generated by the price mechanism.

Consensus among participants began to break down on the question of what organizing methodology should be employed to secure consumer welfare within the framework of free markets. Even here, however, the differences were of degree, rather than kind, and lay along a temporal axis. At one end of this time line is John Barlow's notion that the slate should be kept clean until significant patterns of use emerge; once such patterns emerge, Barlow argued, legal rules can be shaped around them. At the other end of the time line is the belief, expressed by Commissioner Lehman, that emerging digital technologies could benefit from a slate already filled in with copyright principles.

It was clear that even a fully-etched copyright slate does not imply rigidity in principle. For example, as Dr. Hugenholtz observed in his paper, the doctrine of exhaustion is the servant not of physical law, but of economic principle: a publisher's economic control over a book ends with its first sale not because the book leaves the publisher's possession, but because certain economic realities, including the problem of transaction costs, make that a desirable stopping point for the publisher's and author's control. By contrast, in the new digital environment this same economic reasoning may dictate that copyright control extend well beyond the transfer of title in the material support.

Between these two poles of the continuum is the approach suggested by Professor Mackaay. This approach, which attracted substantial commentary from participants, is to sketch only the roughest outlines on an otherwise clean slate, giving content providers the opportunity to experiment with different methodologies for 'fencing out' unauthorized uses. Among the 'fences' alluded to were technical methodologies such as encryption, and legal methodologies such as contracts.

In retrospect, it appears that, at least in the case of large technological shifts, the approaches advocated by Mr. Barlow and Professor Mackaay have the weight of history on their side. For example, it took almost two centuries of experimentation after the introduction of movable type for copyright to be adopted as the organizing vehicle for rights in literary and artistic works. The 'fencing' experiment in the years before the Statute of Anne – principally the Licensing Acts as administered by the English Stationer's Company – is an example of fences with baleful effects, here the suppression of seditious publications at the instance of the Crown. The lag time between the introduction of a new technology and enactment of copyright amendments to bring the new technology under control shortened dramatically in subsequent years, and generally consumes about twenty years, as exemplified by the case of photography, cable retransmission and software protection.

While the approaches proposed by Mr. Barlow and Professor Mackaay may have some historical weight going for them, the approach proposed by Commissioner Lehman appears to have political reality on its side. As Dr. Ficsor noted in his paper, new information technologies confront lawmakers with a difficult choice between acting too early – passing a law that is inapt for the technology in issue – and acting too late – attempting, usually futilely, to pass a law that will govern already entrenched habits of use. The example of off-the-air copying through videocassette recorders, alluded to by Mr. Visser, is on point. By the time the United States Supreme Court decided in the *Betamax* case that certain instances of off-the-air videotaping constituted unrestricted fair use, the number of VCRs in American homes had grown to a point at which the widely-entrenched habit of free use doomed any prospect that the legislator would impose any form of copyright control on VCRs.

The discussion in these respects generally omitted one consideration that may become important to the proper framing of an allocative methodology: whether *all* electronic forms of dissemination of literary and artistic works should be subjected to the proposed methodology, or whether *only interactive* uses on digital networks should be subjected to the proposed methodology. Underlying this consideration is of course the question of the extent to which the latter will displace the former in the marketplace. My own view is that it seems likely that current patterns of mass dissemination of literary and artistic works will persist well into the next century, and that, whatever methodologies are chosen for networked, interactive uses, there is no reason to alter the current author's right and copyright regimes that are applied to the more traditional forms of uses.

2. Property, Privacy and Freedom of Information

There was some discussion among participants of the importance of freedom of information in the emerging digital environment. Nonetheless, discussion of this threesome focused principally on the interactions between property and privacy. The discussion divided along three specific themes: (a) property and privacy as mutually supportive; (b) property as defeating privacy; and (c) privacy as defeating property.

(a) Historically, in the case of literary and artistic works, the relationship between property principles and privacy principles has been a relationship of mutual support. The exclusive, and in some places close to sacred, right of first publication at once secures a central economic interest of copyright – the optimal timing of a work's dissemination – and the author's privacy interest in not having his work publicly disseminated at all. This relationship of mutual support seems likely to break down in at least two corners of the new digital environment.

(b) As amply demonstrated in the papers of Dr. Hugenholtz and Mr. Visser, the monitoring of individual uses of copyrighted works for purposes of assessing subscriber payments – effectively enabling information providers to develop 'dossiers' of information on user tastes – will enhance the economics of copyright ownership by enabling authors and publishers to market their works more effectively. At the same time, monitoring mechanisms may threaten the privacy interests of the individual user. As Mr. Visser observed, the question is not whether monitoring of individual uses is *possible*, but whether it is *desirable*. As he pointed out, although monitoring is desirable to perfect the economics of copyright beyond the degree possible even under compulsory licenses, it may be undesirable because of its threat to individual privacy.

(c) Professor Geller's apt metaphor, distinguishing between copyright 'leaks' and copyright 'haemorrhages,' highlights the fact that the continued, unregulated private uses of copyrighted works threatens to undermine traditional copyright economics which contemplate that copyright owners will reap their revenues – and incentives – primarily from public places, with the occasional private use only nibbling insignificantly at the margins of copyright. In the new digital environment, by contrast, the main economic locus of copyright will have migrated from public to private places. Movies will be watched individually, in the home, rather than simultaneously in theatres or over television. As a consequence, if copyright control is not extended into the private sphere, the main sources of copyright revenue will dry up and, with them, the incentive to create new literary and artistic works. Those who oppose copyright's extension into the private sphere commonly argue that this would invite the 'copyright police' into the privacy of the home, and so compromise interests in privacy generally. As elaborated in the discussion at the Colloquium, one great challenge for lawmakers will be to fashion copyright rules that ensure appropriate levels of compensation to copyright owners while not compromising individual privacy.

3. Property Law or Contract Law?

Much discussion at the Colloquium centred on where the reproduction right fits into the chain of uses of a copyrighted work over a digital network. Less, though still considerable, attention was paid to where in the chain a 'public communication' occurs. There was recognition that, in a digital environment, non-tangible uses such as performances and displays will assume increased economic importance and, indeed, may well transcend the reproduction right in terms of ultimate economic consequence. Also, as Professor Dommering pointed out, we can in the new digital environment expect boundaries between reproduction and communication to dissolve.

Over the intermediate and long term, an entirely non-copyright consideration seems likely to dwarf present legal determinations of 'reproduction' and 'public communication.' This new consideration is the role of contract law in mediating between producers and users of literary and artistic works. If technological developments follow their current trajectories, contractual arrangements may substantially displace copyright law.

Apart from Professor Mackaay's paper, there was little direct discussion of contracts as a solution to the appropriation of value over digital networks. Nonetheless, there was substantial *in*direct reference to contract regimes: discussion of technical measures such as encryption; Mr. Clark's notion that the answer to the machine is in the machine; Dr. Melichar's description of the emergent role of collecting societies. All these references point in a contractual direction, however implicitly.

To take one example, a content supplier will not seek encryption as an end in itself, but rather as the first step toward a contract with users that will, for a fee, entitle them to enjoy a disencrypted version of encrypted literary and artistic works. Similarly, in saying that the answer to the machine is in the machine, Mr. Clark is effectively saying that the answer to private, dispersed uses of literary and artistic works lies in the contractual relationships that will be created, monitored and executed by the machine that is within the machine.

Put simply, the technological prospect that a machine will monitor and execute individual uses implies thc legal prospect that a user will be charged for every use it makes, with the charge being made under an individualized, one-to-one contractual relationship. You rarely think twice about entering into a contract with the electric or telephone company under which you agree to pay a prescribed sum per kilowatt or per call, or about the fact that, if you fail to pay your bill at the end of the month, your service will be shut off. In the future, you will enter into contracts to pay for literary and artistic works to be delivered to your home and office, with payment commonly scaled to the value of the particular work; if you fail to pay your bill at the end of the month – or if the account to which the charge is automatically debited has insufficient funds – once again, your service will be shut off.

In light of this future, the most subtle legal task will be to coordinate contract and copyright principles. Structurally, there is no reason for copyright law to constrain contracts. When you contract to purchase electricity from a power company, the contract's validity does not depend upon whether the electricity supplied is the subject of copyright; indeed, to impose such a requirement upon contracts, would be an absurdity. But the example suggests that it would be equally competent for a publisher and user to contract to the effect that the user will pay not only for works that are presently in copyright, but also for works whose copyright term has expired. Similarly, under this analysis, a supplier and user could agree that the user will pay to use a copyrighted work even though, in the circumstances, under copyright law, the use would be excused as a fair use or fair dealing.

The fact that contract relations *can* be free of copyright constraints raises the difficult question whether, nonetheless, contracts respecting the use of literary and artistic works *should* be constrained by copyright rules. Mr. Clark has assured us that it would be unthinkable for his Electronic Management System to seek reimbursement for uses made of public domain works. But Mr. Clark's successors, or his counterparts in other countries, may listen to the beat of a different drummer and choose to override copyright constraints by contract, charging for public domain works and for uses that otherwise lie outside the range of restricted acts. The question will then be raised directly, whether contracts should be allowed to override an underlying copyright balance.

Even if contracts can run free of copyright constraints, they cannot run free of competition law. As some discussants at the Colloquium have pointed out, competition law will become particularly important in an environment in which property rights no longer serve their traditional function of promoting competition, and new contractual arrangements threaten competition and consumer welfare generally.

4. Configurations, Content and Context

The topics of this Colloquium belong to what I would characterize as the second generation of issues raised by the new digital environment. The first generation of issues occupied the decade of the 1980's, and the third generation will, in all likelihood, occupy the first decade of the next century.

Had our organizers convened this Colloquium five to ten years ago, I expect that its subject would have been the subject of so many other symposia at that time – the proper form of intellectual property protection for computer software. If our organizers choose to convene another colloquium ten to fifteen years from today, I expect its subject will be not 'The Future of Copyright in a Digital Environment' but, rather, something along the lines of the 'Economic, Social and Political Aspects of Law in a Digital Environment.'

I hope it will be helpful to take a brief moment to look backward to the first generation of digital issues, and forward to the next generation, for there are lessons to be learned from each generation that apply to the others.

The first generation of issues concerning copyright in a digital environment were questions of *configuration*. Computer software configures, and effectively drives, the digital network. Many of the concerns expressed at this Colloquium connect to first-generation concerns as well. For example, the question Professor Grosheide raised, whether the allocation of rights in digital networks should be left to copyright or made the subject of a tailor-made regime, directly echoes first-generation concerns over the proper form of intellectual property protection for computer software. Indeed, and in a larger frame, the Barlow-Mackaay-Lehman continuum of approaches effectively replays the questions that were addressed to software a decade or more ago: should we write on a blank slate and await the emergence of consumption and production patterns that will determine what legal regime is appropriate; should we experiment with 'fences,' as effectively was done in the early years of software when trade secrets were viewed as the appropriate vehicle for protection; or should we apply copyright directly to computer software?

Because copyright evolved as the ultimate regulator of rights in computer software – at least for the present, and before the patent dimensions are fully worked out – lessons about copyright's relative flexibility can be applied to both the present, second generation of issues and to third generation issues as well. For example, anyone who looks at the terms of the E.U. Software Directive, or at the evolution of rules in the United States, on scope of protection and decompilation of software will readily conclude that although copyright has been made the ultimate arbiter in both cases, it has effectively been allowed to serve this role only after the most rigorous reshaping to meet the specific needs of software; indeed, as applied to software, copyright has become something of a *sui generis* law.

Contract and competition principles also emerged in this first generation. The E.U. Software Directive effectively prohibits contractual overrides of the copyright rule respecting decompilation for purposes of achieving interoperability. And the recent *Magill* decision alluded to by Mr. Visser illustrates the importance of applying competition principles to ensure a level playing field in the information environment.

Passing over the second generation, the third generation of issues, which I would characterize as issues of *context*, also seem likely to benefit from the lessons of the past and the present. Issues of economics and politics – already alluded to in this Colloquium in the context of freedom of information – promise to be joined by social issues and a renewed interest in the role of authors.

From an economic perspective, it seems likely that an increased role for rigorous software protection will be needed if producers are to come up with software solutions to what Mr. Pabbruwe alluded to as the problem of masses of information and entertainment inundating the consumer. One very scarce resource will become increasingly vexed in the future information environment: the resource of human time. How, within the compass of a single day, will a consumer be able to navigate the cornucopia of information and entertainment flowing over these digital networks in order to pick out those that best suit his tastes? It seems likely that there will be an increased role for 'smart agents' – effectively computer programs that operate much as a human travel agent operates today, gathering information about an individual's preferences and selecting for that individual those opportunities that will be of most interest to him or her. Over time, as information and entertainment is accepted and paid for – or rejected and not paid for – by the consumer, this smart agent will iteratively refine the consumer's profile. For these agents to work, they will need to be powered by sophisticated software; in turn, that software will need to be empowered by rigorous legal protection.

Second, important questions of political freedom seem likely to emerge. As information is centralized in networks, and as use of information is decentralized throughout society, the temptation will arise, at least in totalitarian regimes, to control the network and consequently to control access to political information and the opportunity for dissent. But, I suspect that the 'hacker' mentality that presently exists on the Internet will endure and flourish, and I would consequently predict that no political regime will enjoy lasting success in suppressing dissent over digital networks.

The picture is less heartening from a social perspective. It will take education, leisure and some fair measure of wealth to take even close to full advantage of the new digital environment. Hardware and software prices will decline as their consumption increases over the coming years, but it seems likely that, even in the long run, society's 'have-nots' will continue to lack the price of admission to the future network facility. The possible – and great – tragedy here is that, as entertainment and information that is now available 'free' or heavily subsidized over commercial or public television and radio, and in newspapers and magazines, shifts to a digital environment where they will be available only on a pay per use basis, society's have-nots will be systematically excluded from the lifeblood of information. There may well be political implications to this as well.

Finally, it seems likely that the author, in the sense both of the author's rights and copyright traditions, will re-emerge in this third generation of legal issues. I can perhaps best express the reason for this by citing an observation I recently made in *Copyright's Highway: From Gutenberg to the Celestial Jukebox*[1] in connection with the shift to a digital information environment, for which I use the 'celestial jukebox' as a metaphor:

> 'The celestial jukebox can also be expected to reduce, or at least change, the role of today's book publishers and motion picture and record producers, giving authors a more central place in the creation and distribution of literary and artistic works. Economies of scale in production facilities, in risk finance, and in distribution networks have long placed these institutions at the centre of cultural life. But tomorrow's author, artist, or composer who has access to a networked computer – most will – can bypass not only these corporate entities – but also libraries and retail outlets, to communicate directly with his intended audience. Electronic bulletin boards that now vibrate with exchanges ranging from the hottest industry gossip to the most popular new restaurant will soon evolve into pathways for disseminating more extended and complete new works.'

To ignore the role of the individual author in this emerging environment would as a legal, social and economic matter be a great omission indeed.

1. Paul Goldstein, *Copyright's Highway: The Law and Lore of Copyright from Gutenberg to the Celestial Jukebox*, New York, 1994.